QUEST FOR THE LIVING GOD

QUEST FOR THE LIVING GOD

Mapping Frontiers
in the Theology of God

Elizabeth A. Johnson

continuum

NEW YORK • LONDON

2008

The Continuum International Publishing Group Inc
80 Maiden Lane, New York, New York 10038

The Continuum International Publishing Group Ltd
The Tower Building, 11 York Road, London SE1 7NX

Continuum is a member of Green Press Initiative, a nonprofit program dedicated to supporting publishers in their efforts to reduce their use of fiber obtained from endangered forests. For more information, go to www.greenpressinitiative.org.

Printed in the United States of America on 50% postconsumer waste recycled paper

Library of Congress Cataloging-in-Publication Data

Johnson, Elizabeth A., 1941-
    Quest for the living God : mapping frontiers in the theology of God / Elizabeth A. Johnson.
        p. cm.
    Includes bibliographical references and index.
    ISBN-13: 978-0-8264-1770-1 (hardcover : alk. paper)
    ISBN-10: 0-8264-1770-1 (hardcover : alk. paper)
    1. God (Christianity) I. Title.

BT103.J64 2007
231—dc22

2007026203

For Frank Oveis,

editor extraordinaire,
for a lifetime of service to publishing
carried out with sharp intelligence,
unflagging humor,
and quiet courage,
which have benefited the whole field of theology,
myself not least of all.

CONTENTS

ACKNOWLEDGMENTS

I offer warmest thanks to the following persons and institutions, whose support enabled and enriched this book:

❧ to my graduate and undergraduate students at Fordham University, whose searching questions and insights have kept this subject alive and growing in my mind over many years.

❧ to Fordham University for the gift of time provided by a research leave, and for the continued encouragement that administrative leaders endeavor to give to faculty research.

❧ to the communities of scholars who invited me to present this subject in public lectures where ensuing conversations opened up new vistas: the University of San Diego, University of Manitoba, University of Pennsylvania, Drew University, Canisius College, King's College, St. Joseph's College, Princeton Theological Seminary, St. Bernard's School of Theology in Rochester, New York; and especially the School of Theology at the University of the South, Sewanee, Tennessee, which published my 2004 DuBose Lectures in the *Sewanee Theological Review*.

❧ to colleagues who supplied me with hard-to-find research materials: Mary Callaway, Christophe Chalamet, Ann Michaud, Carmen Nanko-Fernández, Patrick Ryan, and Gloria Schaab.

❧ to colleagues who read different parts of this manuscript and offered critical suggestions: María Pilar Aquino, M. Shawn Copeland, Charles E. Curran, Miguel Díaz, Nancy Hawkins, Michael Lee, and especially Mary Catherine Hilkert, whose eagle eye called for greater clarification and caught several non sequiturs, some of them hilarious.

❧ to my religious community, the Sisters of St. Joseph of Brentwood, New York, whose 150th anniversary of arrival in Brooklyn provided the occasion for a festive consideration of this book's ideas; and to the National Federation of the Sisters of St. Joseph for the invitation to engage this book-in-the-making with a national audience of women religious.

❧ to my family and friends, whose ears were bent with more than they probably wanted to hear about God and whose support means the world.

This book's dedication to Frank Oveis pays tribute to his decades of unflagging work in nurturing writers and overseeing manuscripts into print. Early in his career he contributed to bringing translations of European theologians and biblical scholars to English-speaking audiences, working on books by Hans Urs von Balthasar, Bernard Häring, Hubert Jedin, Othmar Keel, Johannes Baptist Metz, Karl Rahner, and Edward Schillebeeckx, among others. In mid-career he tended the writings of influential North American thinkers such as Carol Christ, Lawrence Cunningham, Christine Downing, Joseph Fitzmyer, Langdon Gilkey, Bernard McGinn, Leo O'Donovan, Rosemary Radford Ruether, Elisabeth Schüssler Fiorenza, Francis Schüssler Fiorenza, and David Tracy. In recent years he has advanced the growth of original theological voices in the United States by editing new books by Katie Geneva Cannon, Martin Connell, Margaret Farley, Roger Haight, Jeannine Hill Fletcher, Bradford Hinze, James Keenan, Judith Kubicki, Paul Lakeland, Vincent Miller, Kevin Seasoltz, and Terrence Tilley, among others. Frank Oveis is perhaps the only editor to have nominated two winning books for the prestigious Grawemeyer Award in Religion. One recent coup was the posthumous publication, after a decade of negotiation and supervision, of the English translation of Abraham Heschel's classic 850-page work *Heavenly Torah: As Refracted through the Generations*, which is being received with enthusiasm both by scholars in the field and by the Jewish community.

It has been my good fortune to have worked with Frank Oveis as editor on most of my books. Largely unsung, he like other editors of theological works makes an indispensable contribution to the whole field. With this dedication, I offer a heartfelt and simple "thank you."

Grateful acknowledgment is given to editors for permission to use material previously published in these journals:

Theology Today 54 (October 1997): "Trinity: To Let the Symbol Sing Again," pp. 299–311.

Sewanee Theological Review 48, no. 3 (Pentecost 2005):

"Frontiers of the Quest for the Living God," pp. 273–86.

"The Living God in Women's Voices," pp. 287–300.

"The Living God in Cosmic Perspective," pp. 301–15.

INTRODUCTION

S ince the middle of the twentieth century, a burgeoning renaissance of insights into God has been taking place. Around the world different groups of Christian people, stressed by particular historical circumstances, have been gaining glimpses of the living God in fresh and unexpected ways. So compelling are these insights that rather than being hoarded by the local communities that first realized them, they are offered as a gift and a challenge to the worldwide church. We are living in a golden age of discovery, to the point where it has become customary for theologians to say that we are witnessing nothing less than a "revolution" in the theology of God.

It is not the case that a wholly different God is being discovered from the One believed in by previous generations. Christian faith today does not believe in a novel God but, finding itself in strange situations, seeks the active presence of divine Spirit precisely there, in their midst. Aspects long forgotten are brought into new relationship with current events, with the result that the depths of divine compassion are appreciated in ways not previously imagined. "O Beauty, ever ancient, ever new, late have I loved you," cried the North African bishop Augustine in the fifth century. Since the middle of the twentieth century, people of faith actively engaged in different situations have been questing for, finding, and expressing this ancient Beauty in ever-new terms. The emerging ideas of who God is, how God acts in the world, and what it means to say "We believe in one God . . ." have opened up what amounts to genuine frontiers for faith and action.

1

This book sets out the fruit of some of these discoveries. Written with a broad audience in view, its aim is to enlighten the minds of those who seek understanding about spiritual matters; to encourage those who doubt to keep faith with their questions; to give energetic support to those who work for the good of others; and to provide those who teach or preach in the church with food for thought that they can use to nourish others. There is such a hunger for a mature faith in many people today. Women and men yearn for a relationship with the living God commensurate with their aspirations, competencies, and struggles in our perilous times. Stale, naive, worn-out concepts of God no longer satisfy. Insights emerging in various contexts around the world and articulated in theology, however, are setting out rich fare.

It is important to underscore that the theology this book traces does not usually begin as an academic or intellectual exercise but arises from practical commitments. On different continents groups of Christian believers become actively engrossed in issues that affect the welfare of people and the natural world. They aren't necessarily thinking directly about God, but in the thick of their worldly engagement—out of the corner of their eye, so to speak—they glimpse something of the truth of the living God that surprises and sustains them. Over time they reflect on their experience, articulating what they have come to realize. Theologians who are part of these communities then frame these insights into new patterns of thought that seek to understand something of the divine Mystery being encountered in these ways. Each of these verbal interpretations of faith, in turn, opens up a concrete path of discipleship which broadens out to invite and challenge the whole church beyond the originating group.

The process unfolds from religious experience among an active community in a particular context, to popular and critically trained theological reflection, to continuing practical action arising from spiritual and moral commitment. Insight develops, in a word, from heart to head to hands.

Reading between the lines, one can see that in mapping new glimpses of God this book is also about the work of theology. Through thick and thin, through blessing and scandal, through politics inside and outside the church, through silencing and persecution and suffering, even the murder of colleagues, theologians have continued energetically to practice their craft, which, by definition, is to speak about God (from the Greek *theos*, which means God, and *logos,* which means word or reasonable speech). They ply their craft by marshaling reasons, laying out arguments, making a case the way a trial lawyer might do, seeking to present an intelligible and convincing scenario. By listening to peoples' experience in specific situations, reading scripture, consulting tradition, and drawing on the humanities, the sciences, and the social sciences, theologians have been working creatively to prepare such briefs in our day. This is not to say that merely keeping up with the times is the goal. The world being sinful as well as graced, society as indeed the church itself is in need of criticism and transformation. There have been times in the past when theology sealed itself off from pressing questions, failing to trust that the substance of Christian faith was up to a confrontation with new ideas. Such a failure of nerve does not plague theology today, which seeks understanding of God at once contemporaneous with culture and resistant to its wrongs.

This book shares the fruit of many such theological labors carried out in different places amid the unspeakable brutality, bewilderment, and blessed achievements of recent history. The first chapter provides brief background and lays out the rules of engagement for the journey. Each succeeding chapter then presents a discrete idea of God. To clarify the meaning of this insight, each chapter describes the context in which it has arisen, the reasoning that explores and explains it, and the challenge to spiritual and practical life that it entails. Featured are transcendental, political, liberation, feminist, black, hispanic, interreligious, and ecological theologies, ending with the particular Christian belief in the one God as triune. At times the focus is on the work of particular theologians; at other times a whole school of thought carries the banner. At the end of each chapter, recommendations for further reading will point the interested reader to broader and deeper sources.

This is not a comprehensive canvas. Reams of books have been written about the subject of each chapter, including fundamental analysis of method, connections with other teachings on Jesus, sin and grace, the church, and critical assessments from within and without that refine a particular theology's central approach. The choice made here, however, is to keep a laser beam trained simply on the idea of God, distilling this idea from discussions that surround it in order to present this core concept as it undergoes development in today's living tradition.

A word about the phrase "the living God" used in the title. This way of speaking runs through the Bible from beginning to end to identify the Source of life as dynamic, bounteous, and full of surprises. When they entered into covenant, the people of Israel "*heard the voice of the living God*" speaking out of the fire at Sinai (Deut 5:26) and knew "*the living God is among you*" as they crossed into the promised land (Josh 3:10). When Daniel was saved from the lion's den, a foreign king recognized that the God of Israel is "*the living God enduring forever*" (Dan 6:26). Christians, too, now included in the ancient promise, understand that they are "*children of the living God*" (Rom 9:26) thanks to the marginal Jew Jesus Christ, "*the Son of the living God*" (Matt 16:16).

Living means the opposite of dead. A well that is living never dries up but has water that is always springing up and running; its living water is fresh, alive, flowing. "*My soul thirsts for God, the living God*" (Ps 42:2), prays the psalm writer, making this connection. As used in this book, this appellation summons up a sense of the God who is full of energy and spirit, alive with designs for liberation and healing, always approaching from the future to do something new. In addition, the term "the living God" evokes the realization that there is always more to divine Mystery than human beings can nail down. It prepares those who use it for astonishment.

One day when the apostles Paul and Barnabas were preaching in Lystra, they saw a man who had been crippled from birth and healed him. The crowds, knowing that the man had never walked before, thought these two newcomers were gods from heaven. Full of enthusiasm, they and their priest brought oxen and garlands to sacrifice before them. Distraught, the apostles waded into the crowd and shouted:

> *Friends, why are you doing this? We are mortals just like you, and we bring you good news, that you should turn from these worthless things to the living God, who made the heaven and the earth and the sea and all that is in them.* (Acts 14:15)

Signifying the Creator, Savior, and Lover of all the world, the whole cosmos as well as all human beings, the phrase "the living God" elicits a sense of ineffable divine mystery on the move in history, calling forth our own efforts in partnership while nourishing a loving relationship at the center of our being: "*my heart and my flesh sing for joy to the living God*" (Ps 84:2).

When medieval map makers came to the limit of their knowledge of the known world, they ofttimes wrote in the empty space, "Here be dragons." There is something frightening about moving into the unknown, which might harm or devour us. Readers are invited to test where the limits of their own ideas about God might be and, guided by the different theologies presented here, to risk a journey through dragon territory to new places already discovered to be life-giving and true by others in the church. The result can be a richness of faith that cleaves to the living God even in darkness and shows itself in passionate, responsible care for this good but terribly fractured world.

1

ANCIENT STORY, NEW CHAPTER

FROM THE BEGINNING

The proliferation of insights into God in our day is a new chapter in an immense story whose beginning is lost in the mists of time. From the dawn of human history when self-consciousness first flickered into being on this planet, members of the species *homo* seem to have lived with a sense of being surrounded by numinous power. They felt that the pattern of their lives was shaped by unseen forces that pervaded the world with purposes they could not control but with which they could be in tune. This they did by means of stories, symbols, and rituals subsequently called by the umbrella term "religion." The way some prehistoric societies buried their dead with such care is one indication of this outlook. They smeared the dead body with ochre to represent blood, the pulse of life. In preparation for new birth, they flexed the body into a fetal position and enclosed artifacts in the grave for future use. Such evidence of belief in powers that could make death a gateway to further life leads scholars to suggest that a sense of the sacred was a widespread part of early human societies. Speaking of beliefs and rituals that enabled groups to make life meaningful in the light of divine presence, John Esposito suggests that "the record of human life indicates that in every society over the last 100,000 years, a progressive complexity in the mastery of tools was accompanied by the development of language ability and the unmistakable presence of religion." In a word, religion emerged with tools and fire.

With the transition from simple subsistence, hunter-gatherer societies to settled villages and then to great urban city-states that started about 3000 BCE, basic awareness of the presence of the sacred became organized into all manner of structured religious activity. Particular configurations of stories and songs, symbols and rituals, dedicated sacred times and sacred spaces, ethical practices, and priestly hierarchies and charismatic seers orchestrated peoples' relationship with divine presence in different cultural milieus. In our day the scholarly study of this colorful and complex history of religions traces the changes rung over millennia in religions great and small, highly organized and indigenous, currently practiced and extinct.

Even a cursory look at this history reveals it to be a vigorously dynamic phenomenon with emotional, intellectual, and institutional elements. In trying to understand it and pinpoint what distinguishes religion from other human activities, scholars note that a group's deity or deities, however named or pictured, generally symbolize a reality greater than the fragments of everyday mundane life, a totality greater than people themselves, a wholeness beyond what the senses can grasp, a horizon that encompasses everything. The presence of this great powerful wholeness has the character of something numinous, that is, intangible but real, like light shining from a cloud. People have perceived this sacred presence disclosing itself in the most diverse ways: in nature; in historical events; in art, music, and dance; in interior peacefulness and exterior healing; in the whole range of human experiences both good and bad, particularly love and loss. They have sensed it when they meet limits, the uncanny, the surprising, an unusual fullness or emptiness of life, and have sought union through a vast variety of practices.

In the early twentieth century, Rudolf Otto launched a classic study of how human beings experience this numinous presence at the core of religion. Calling this presence "the Holy," he teased out three overlapping elements that characterize human encounter with it. We experience the Holy, he wrote, as a *mysterium tremendum et fascinans*, that is, a *mystery* at once *awesome* and *attractive*.

> ❧ *Mysterium* refers to the hidden character of the Holy, beyond imagination not just because of our own intellectual limits but because of

the very nature of the subject. Far from being a pessimistic experience, however, encounter with the Holy as mystery is laced with the promise of plenitude: more fullness exists than we can grasp.

- ☙ *Tremendum* denotes the awesome character of this mystery insofar as it is beyond our control. We cannot domesticate the power of the Holy. This gives rise to a feeling of reverence akin to fear, an earth-shaking dread: we are so small in the face of this majesty.

- ☙ *Fascinans* expresses the attractive character of this mystery insofar as it is overwhelmingly gracious. Experienced as love, mercy, and comfort, the Holy makes us blissful. People hunger with an immense longing for this goodness, which gives the Holy the power to entrance, entice, and lure our hearts.

People who belong to a religion are initiated into a particular living tradition of encounter with the Holy. Countless ancestors over the centuries, having experienced this awesome and attractive mystery in their own lives, translated their experience into particular texts, rituals, and practices that captured what they felt and knew to be true. By engaging in the life of the community, believers discover the sense of the Holy handed on by their forebears. In turn, their own seeking, finding, and "practicing" this earth-shaking and fascinating mystery in the stresses of their own era keep the process going for generations still to come.

Taken as a whole, the changing phenomenon of the world's religions displays the character of an enormous quest, an ongoing search for what is ultimate and whole. The critiques leveled against religion by modern atheism starting in the nineteenth century and continuing today gave rise to the idea that this quest for the living God was finished, that the march of technical progress would soon make religion wither in those naive outposts where it continued to cling to life. But ongoing history indicates that the death of God was greatly exaggerated.

Religion is not an unalloyed good. All too often groups have yielded to the temptation to make their deity into a god of their tribe, hostile to outsiders. This has instigated horrific bouts of violence. The religious philosopher Martin Buber wrote scathingly that the word "God" has blood all over it and should be retired from our vocabulary, at least until it recovers from such misuse. This ambiguous heritage needs to be constantly kept in mind as a critical corrective to any smug, triumphal tooting of the religious horn. At the same time, the unexpected vitality of religion into the twenty-first century, for better and for worse, along with the emergence of new forms of spirituality outside organized religion, show that connection with the sacred still matters to a goodly number of people. The quest for the living God has been and continues to be a perennial activity of the human spirit.

PEOPLE OF THE BOOK

One might think that this ongoing quest would end in the religions that trace their origins explicitly to divine revelation, namely, Judaism, Christianity, and Islam. Such faith traditions are built on the idea that God's self-disclosure occurred in historical events and words and is preserved in their holy books: the Hebrew Bible, the New Testament, and the Qur'an. But even in these monotheistic faiths, which could conceivably settle down with the certainty that they possess definitive knowledge of the Holy, there persists an active seeking for deeper understanding, closer union, greater fruitfulness. Consider these key texts.

In the Hebrew Bible the theme of searching for God with all your heart pervades the sacred books from Moses through the prophets and psalmists to Job and the wisdom writers. Despite God's covenant with the people, or rather, because of it, the seeking never lets up:

> O God, you are my God; early will I seek you;
>   my soul thirsts for you,
> my flesh longs for you,
>   like a dry and thirsty land without water. (Ps 63:1)

The search for God goes on in response to what people sense is a divine call to do so:

> Thou hast said, "Seek ye my face."
>   My heart says to thee, "Thy face Lord do I seek."
> Hide not thy face from me. (Ps 27:8–9)

Happily, the mandate to seek is accompanied by the promise of joyful finding. Seeing trouble ahead, Moses tells the people they will go astray:

*From there you will seek the L*ORD *your God, and you will find him if you*
search after him with all your heart and soul. (Deut 4:29)

Later on, with the disaster of the exile in Babylon in view, the prophet Jeremiah proclaims hope in God's name:

Then when you call upon me and come and pray to me, I will hear you.
When you search for me, you will find me; if you seek me with all your heart,
I will let you find me. (Jer 29:12–13)

Typical of the Jewish relationship with the divine, there is intense
mutuality in the quest, each side seeking the other. While promising that
"those who seek me diligently find me" (Prov 8:17), Wisdom, a female per-
sonification of the God of Israel, herself walks through the marketplace
seeking those who will listen to her loud cries of instruction; she sends her
maidservants out to invite everyone to feast at her table and to walk in the
way of insight (Prov 9:3–6). As for those who don't listen and go astray, the
God of Israel seeks them out like a shepherd going after lost sheep (Ezek
34:11–16). Far from a static condition that bores the spirit, this pattern of
religious belief offers a gift of adventure. The covenant relationship with
God opens up to ever-new discoveries in pace with the changing circumstances of life.

This same dynamism of Jewish faith flows into the Christian scriptures,
where themes of seeking and finding—or, terribly, not finding—pervade
the gospels. In explicit terms Jesus teaches his disciples to seek God, phrased
in the circumlocution to *"seek first the kingdom of God"* even amid anxiety
about food or clothing (Matt 6:33). With this counsel comes a promise of
discovery:

Ask, and it will be given you; seeek, and you will find; knock, and the door
will be opened for you. For everyone who asks receives, and everyone who
seeks finds, and to everyone who knocks, the door will be opened. (Matt
7:7–8)

This human seeking for God is matched by the divine hunt for the ones
who are lost. Jesus' parables depict God the Redeemer searching like a
woman for her precious coin or like a shepherd going after his straying sheep
(Luke 15:3–10). One of the great summary texts on this subject appears at

the end of Jesus' encounter with short, rich, cheating Zacchaeus. This tax collector's heart is so changed that he is moved to give half his wealth to the poor and repay those he had defrauded fourfold. Rejoicing that salvation had come to this house Jesus declares, *"For the Son of Man came to seek out and to save the lost"* (Luke 19:10).

The theme of seeking and finding appears again in the Qur'an, where it is most often associated with the desire to behold the Face of Allah, the face being a symbol of God's presence and self-disclosure. "Wherever you turn, there is the Face of Allah" (Sūra 2:115). Devout Muslims may find a glimpse of this face in every human face as well as throughout the workings of the natural world. It is especially through daily prayer that every sincere Muslim seeks to encounter divine presence. This becomes evident in the story about God's reprimand to Muhammad. It seems that the Prophet issued a directive to his followers, mostly pious slaves and poor people, that they should disappear when wealthy and powerful men approached. His obvious purpose was to make contact with him easy and pleasant for these elite persons, for if they were converted they would influence many others. But this was not the way of Allah, who rebuked Muhammad and affirmed the religious seeking of the poor: "Be thyself patient with those who call upon their Lord at morning and evening, desiring His Face" (Sūra 18:28–29). The aspiration to reach the realm of divine presence characterizes in a particular way adherents of Sufism, the generally accepted name for Islamic mysticism. But all true Muslims engage in a lifelong quest as did Muhammad, "only seeking the Face of his Lord the Most High" (Sūra 92:20).

The monotheistic religions do not extinguish the human spirit's history-long quest for the living God. Rather, they encourage it. As Augustine described the dynamic, "God is sought in order to be found more sweetly, and found in order to be sought more eagerly" (*De Trinitate* 15.2).

WHY THE SEARCH?

The open-endedness of this age-old search for the living God is rooted in three factors.

¶ First, the very nature of what is being sought is incomprehensible, unfathomable, limitless, ineffable, beyond description. The living God literally cannot be compared with anything in the world. To do so is to reduce divine reality to an idol. This divine magnitude means that no matter how much we know, the human mind can never capture the whole of the living God in a net of concepts, images, or definitions, or preside over the reality of God in even the most exalted doctrines. A Zen-like riddle preached by Augustine preserves this wisdom succinctly: "If you have understood, it is not God" (*Sermon* 117.5). If you have fully figured out who God is, then you are dealing with something else, some lesser reality. It is a matter of the livingness of God, who is not just a bigger and better object in the world but unspeakably Other.

℀ Second, the search goes on because the human heart is insatiable. A universal experience of immense longing propels the human adventure in all fields. When it comes to matters of religion, as God-seekers of every age have testified, the human spirit cannot rest in any one encounter but, intrigued by the glimpse already gained, continues to hunger for more. People keep on journeying through beauty and joy, through duty and commitment, through agonizing silence and pain, toward greater meaning and deeper union with the ineffable God, to their last breath.

℀ The third factor in the ongoing quest is the changing history of human cultures. The experience of God is always mediated, that is, made concretely available through specific channels in history. When circumstances change, the experience of the divine undergoes a shift. Images, intellectual constructs, and rituals that mediated a sense of God in one age often do not make sense in the next with its change of perceptions, values, and lifestyles. The search must be undertaken anew if religious traditions are to remain vibrant and alive. *Right now.*

Putting all three factors together leads to an interesting realization: the profound incomprehensibility of God coupled with the hunger of the human heart in changing historical cultures actually *requires* that there be an ongoing history of the quest for the living God that can never be concluded. Historically new attempts at articulation are to be expected and even welcomed. An era without such frontiers begins to turn dry, dusty, and static.

The thesis of this book is that Christianity today is living through a vibrant new chapter of this quest. People are discovering God again not in the sense of deducing abstract notions but in the sense of encountering divine presence and absence in their everyday experiences of struggle and hope, both ordinary and extraordinary. New ideas about God have emerged, for example, from the effort to wrestle with the darkness of the Holocaust; from the struggle of poor and persecuted people for social justice; from women's striving for equal human dignity; from Christianity's encounter with goodness and truth in the world's religious traditions; and from the efforts of biophilic people to protect, restore, and nurture the ecological life of planet Earth. No era is without divine presence, but this blossoming of insight appears to be a strong grace for our time.

POINT OF DEPARTURE: MODERN THEISM

There is a settled country from which the quest for the living God sets out in our day. Inherited from recent centuries, this view envisions God on the model of a monarch at the very peak of the pyramid of being. Without regard for Christ or the Spirit, it focuses on what trinitarian theology would call the "first person," a single powerful individual who dwells on high, ruling the cosmos and judging human conduct. Even when this Supreme Being is portrayed with a benevolent attitude, which the best of theology does, "He," for it is always the ruling male who stands for this idea, is essentially remote. At times he intervenes to affect the laws of nature and work miracles, at times not. Although he loves the world, he is uncontaminated by its messiness. And always this distant lordly lawgiver stands at the summit of hierarchical power, reinforcing structures of authority in society, church, and family.

Without undue stereotyping, it is fair to say that this is the picture that prevails in common public discourse and in the media in Western culture. It provides the foil for modern atheism, which denies that such a Supreme Being exists. In a review of Richard Dawkins's book *The God Delusion* (2006), which sets out the case for atheism based on scientific materialism, the critic Terry Eagleton perceptively noted that one of the main problems with Dawkins's thesis is that he envisions God "if not exactly with a white beard, then at least as some kind of *chap*, however supersized." In truth, Dawkins did not spin this view out of thin air. Such a superficial idea is taken for granted also by many believers, who see God as one particular individual in the whole of reality, even if the highest and most powerful. That this invisible, greatly powerful, grand old man in the sky might not really be God at all is never seriously considered.

The history of theology makes clear that this construct as we know it today came into being at the time of the seventeenth- and eighteenth-century European movement known as the Enlightenment. This movement rejected the dogmatic authority of religion and tradition in favor of "enlightened" investigations of human reason to figure out how the world works. In response, Christian theologians of the era also used rational arguments to defend the existence of God. Before this time, theologians drew the idea of God from scripture, sacramental worship, and theological tradition, using philosophy to interpret and clarify certain points. This kept them focused on divine incarnation in Jesus Christ and on the Spirit's gift of indwelling grace as essential components of the Christian idea of God, which is trinitarian. Now, however, to counter the Enlightenment's criticisms, they switched to the same playing field as their opponent. Leaving behind Christian sources and adopting philosophical methods of thinking that sought objective knowledge about the universe on a rational basis, they set out to shape "clear and distinct ideas" about the divine. Starting with the natural world, they reasoned to the existence of God using a process of inference, thereby constructing a theology where God appears as the highest component in an intellectual system. This all but assured that while God is a powerful individual above other powers in the world, he remains a member of the larger household of reality. His attributes are deduced by a reasoning process that contrasts what is infinite with the limitations of the finite. Thus, God is immutable (only creatures change), incorporeal (bodies are the site of change), impassible (only creatures suffer), omnipotent, omniscient, omnipresent, in contrast to creatures who are limited in power, knowledge, and presence.

The resulting construct is known today by the shorthand term "modern theism." In a fascinating way it compromises both the transcendence and immanence of God as honed in classical Christian theology. Transcendence, or the otherness of God beyond all imagination, is cut short by bringing the divine within the system of coordinates of the world as we know it; making all claims about the divine answerable to rational argument assures that in the end there is no lasting surprise or mystery. Immanence, or the nearness

of God beyond all imagination, gets lost in the univocal stress on divine difference; emphasizing the high position of the divine in the hierarchy of the
world allows little room for indwelling presence. The Enlightenment goal
of a clear and distinct idea of God, although worked for with good apolo-
getic intent, led theology to miss the mark.

As it trickled into preaching and personal piety, this construct became
ever more simplistic, leading to contemporary Western society's characteris-
tically trivial image of God. In the 1960s a small ecumenical book entitled
Your God Is Too Small laid out some of the popular images that carried modern theism into churches and into hearts. People viewed God as a grand old
man; or a resident policeman; or a tape of parental hang-ups; or a consum-
mate churchman; or a managing director; or a dictator; or a disappointing
protector; or a spoilsport. Clearing the ground of these unworthy notions,
the author J. B. Phillips writes that if people "could see beyond their little
inadequate god, and glimpse the reality of God, they might even laugh a little and perhaps weep a little." The result would be a liberation from the worship of what in effect amounts to an idol, something less than the living God
masquerading as ultimate. Flinging wide the doors of their minds and
hearts, people could set out to discover a God truly worthy of their lives.

The theologies traced out in this book, in contrast to modern theism,
are deeply concerned with God's relationship to the world: whether and to
what extent God is so related, how and to what effect, and what this means
for people's lives and actions. It is a given in their thought that divine transcendence is beyond the beyond, being not different in degree but in kind
from the whole world. Thus God cannot be classified among other things or
agents or located closer or farther away. Because of this transcendence, God
can also be most immanently present everywhere, within the world but not
contained or confined by it, nearer to us than we are to ourselves. Reclaim-
ing radical transcendence and radical immanence in equal measure rather
than opposing them in a zero-sum game, contemporary theologies view the
unknowable God as the very Ground not only of the world's existence but
of its fragmentary flourishing and hope against brokenness. They shift
attention to the liminal places, the margins of dominating power where God
appears in the gestalt of compassion and liberating love, closer to the history
and mess of the world. They greatly expand divine graciousness beyond the
boundaries of Christianity to include all peoples, and beyond the human

race to include the whole natural world. If it were possible to sum up their rediscoveries in one metaphor, it would be the classic Christian belief that "*God is Love*" (1 John 4:16).

GROUND RULES FOR THE JOURNEY

To equip the reader for the exploration that lies ahead, it is vital to dwell on three ground rules for talking about God. Drawn from early Christian and medieval theology, these rules of engagement are emphasized by contemporary theology as an antidote to the overrationalizing pattern of thinking that threw Enlightenment theism off the track.

1. The first and most basic prescript is this: the reality of the living God is an ineffable mystery beyond all telling. The infinitely creating, redeeming, and indwelling Holy One is so far beyond the world and so deeply within the world as to be literally incomprehensible. The history of theology is replete with this truth, teaching in its finer moments that the human mind can never classify the divine in word or image no matter how true, beautiful, or exalted. Christians believe that God has drawn near in Jesus Christ, but even there the living God remains unutterable mystery and cannot be encompassed. As Paul eloquently put it, we see only dimly, as if looking in a dark, cracked mirror (1 Cor 13:12).

The great old story of Augustine on the beach provides a graphic illustration. It seems that one day the bishop was walking along the Mediterranean shore, puzzling over some point about the Trinity for the treatise he was writing. Deep in thought, he half-watched a small child going back and forth from the water's edge, repeatedly filling a pail and pouring the water into a hole dug in the sand. Intrigued, Augustine finally asked the child what he was doing. "Trying to put the sea into my hole," was the reply. "You can't do that; it won't fit," said the adult with common sense. The child, who turned out to be an angel in disguise, replied, "Neither can you put the mystery of the Trinity into your mind; it won't fit." Thus was passed on the wisdom of the ages to one of the keenest minds in the Christian tradition. Like the sea which cannot be drunk dry, God surpasses whatever we can understand and account for in terms of our human categories. To use another water metaphor developed by Karl Rahner, we are like a little island surrounded by a great ocean; we make forays into the sea, but the depths of the ocean forever exceed our grasp. It is a matter of the livingness of God.

2. Consequently, there is a second ground rule: no expression for God can be taken literally. None. Our language is like a finger pointing to the moon, not the moon itself. To equate the finger with the moon or to look at the finger and not perceive the moon is to fall into error. Never to be taken literally, human words about God proceed by way of indirection. They set off from the spare, original, strange perfections of this world and turn our face toward the source and future of it all without capturing the essence of the mystery.

Catholic theology has traditionally explained the indirect play of God-language by the theory of analogy. Based on a belief that the created world is fundamentally good, analogy holds that all creatures participate in some way in the overflowing goodness, truth, and beauty of the One who made them. Therefore, something of the creature's excellence can direct us back to God. In the process, however, as the Fourth Lateran Council (1215) taught, there is no similarity between creatures and God but the dissimilarity is "always ever greater." Analogy operates with this realization, putting words about God through a threefold wringer: it affirms, negates, and then negates that negation itself. This third step brings the mind through to a new affirmation of God, who transcends both assertion and negation "in the brilliant darkness of a hidden silence" (Pseudo-Dionysius, *Mystical Theology, PG* 3:998).

Take, for example, the term "good." Inevitably, our understanding of what "good" means arises from our experience of goodness in the world. We experience good persons, good satisfactions, good weather, and so on. From these we derive a concept of goodness that we then *affirm* of God who created all these good things. But God is infinite, so we need to remove anything that smacks of restriction. Thus we *negate* the finite way goodness exists in the world, shot through with limitation. But still we think God is good, so we *negate that particular negation* and judge that God is good in a supremely excellent way that surpasses all understanding. According to analogy, when we attribute goodness to God the theological meaning is this: God is good; but God is not good the way creatures are good; but God is good in a supereminent way as Source of all that is good.

At this point our concept of goodness cracks open. We literally do not understand what we are saying. Human comprehension of the meaning of "good" is lost, for we have no direct earthly experience of anything that is the Source of all goodness. Yet the very saying of it ushers our spirit toward the presence of God who is good, a reality so bright that it is darkness to our mind. In the end the play of analogy brings us to our knees in adoration.

Realizing that the word "person" goes through the same wringer provides a helpful counterweight to the individual "chap" of modern theism. From our experience of our own self and our interactions with other human beings, we develop an idea of what it means to be a person. Then we attribute this excellence to God. Analogy escorts this idea through its three-fold paces. We affirm: yes, God is a person. We negate: no, God is not a person in the finite way we know ourselves to be persons. We counternegate in order to affirm: still, God is a person in a supereminent way as Source of all who are persons. In other words, God is not less than personal but is super-personal, personal in a way that wonderfully transcends the human way of being a person. At this point we've lost the literal concept. We don't really understand what it means to attribute personhood to God. But in the very saying, our spirits are guided into a relationship of personal communion with the Holy.

Theology done with the dialectical imagination of Protestantism more typically explains God-language by the working of metaphor. Familiar from poetry but actually pervasive in daily language, metaphor is a word, image, or assertion that links two disparate realities in a kind of strange association: "the lion is king of the beasts." As light is shed from the better known reality onto the lesser known, new meaning is created. Crucial to metaphor's working is the active tension between similarity and dissimilarity, between the "is" and the "is not" of the two terms. "A mighty fortress is our God": the play of metaphor starts with a literal base, places it in a new context, subverts and extends its literal meaning until it is logically quite absurd, but nonetheless leads to a kind of insight. It is true without being literally a fact. The listener is startled into a new and paradoxical awareness.

All fruitful metaphors have sufficiently complex grids of meaning at the literal level to allow for extension of thought beyond immediate linkages. That is why God can be seen as a king, rock, mother, savior, gardener, lover, father, liberator, midwife, judge, helper, friend, mother bear, fresh water, fire, thunder, and so on. In every instance the permanent tension between the "is and is not" dynamic of metaphor has to be maintained in order for its intellectual and affective power to work. Religious tradition with its habitual repetition in ritual and teaching is liable to forget this pivotal point. But without the tension of "is and is not," metaphors get taken literally and become trite, losing their power to shock and surprise. In such instances, the distance between the better known thing and the unknown God is collapsed. As history shows, dead metaphors make good idols.

In addition to analogy and metaphor, a number of theologians today also explain God-language with the theory of symbol. As Paul Tillich helpfully laid out, symbols are images, gestures, concepts, things, or persons that point beyond themselves to something else. Unlike signs—and this is a crucial point—they participate in the reality they point to, being one way that reality comes to expression in the world. Symbols open up levels of reality that would otherwise be closed to us, and simultaneously open up depths of our own being that would remain otherwise untouched. We cannot create symbols at will: they emerge from a deep level of consciousness. Finally, symbols can grow old and die, losing their affective power in changing cultural situations. Tillich considered "God" the symbol of our ultimate concern and labored mightily to refresh its significance in our era of estrangement.

Whatever theory is used, whether analogy, metaphor, symbol, or some combination thereof, the wisdom of this second ground rule is that we are always naming *toward* God, using good, true, and beautiful fragments experienced in the world to point to the infinite mystery who dwells within and embraces the world but always exceeds our grasp. "As two movements, affirmation of the names of God and the counteraffirmation that God cannot finally be named work together," writes Jeannine Hill Fletcher; this delivers us from the temptation to control God, and opens us to divine overabundance that fills our humanity to its depths and then overflows: "there is no end to the being, fullness, and mystery of God." Sallie McFague, who has worked extensively on metaphorical theology, suggests that only the practice of religious contemplation or prayer is sufficient to keep toxic literalism at bay. Only when discourse about God is rooted in discourse *with* God, only when the presence of God encounters us at our very deepest point are we freed from the desire to grasp and define. To this the example of mystics in every tradition can testify.

3. "From this," Thomas Aquinas argues, articulating the third ground rule, "we see the necessity of giving to God many names" (*Summa Contra Gentiles* I, 31:4). If human beings were capable of expressing the fullness of God in one straight-as-an-arrow name, the proliferation of names, images, and concepts observable throughout the history of religions would make no sense at all. But there is no one such name. Rather, in jubilation and praise, lamentation and mourning, thanksgiving and petition, crying out and the final falling into silence, human beings name God with a symphony of notes.

The Bible itself witnesses to multiple expressions for God. At the center is the name revealed to Moses at the burning bush, YHWH, "I AM WHO I AM," the unpronounceable tetragrammaton interpreted by scholars of Hebrew as "*I will be there; as who I am will I be there with you*" (see Exod 3:14). Christian belief sees this name becoming flesh and dwelling among us, being "there" with us in life and death in the person of Jesus Christ. In both Testaments an abundance of images spells out the One who is there. In addition to terms taken from personal relationships such as father, mother, husband, female beloved, companion, and friend, and images taken from political life such as advocate, liberator, king, warrior, and judge, the Bible pictures God on the model of a wide array of human crafts and professions: shepherd, midwife, farmer, laundress, construction worker, potter, artist, merchant, physician, bakerwoman, vinedresser, teacher, artist, metal worker, and homemaker, to name a few. Despite the predominance of imagery taken from the experience of men, the Bible also carries evocative images of God taken from the experience of women, including the female figure of cosmic power and might known as Wisdom/Sophia, and the domestic images of God as a woman giving birth, nursing her young, and dedicated to child care for the little ones. Pointers to the divine are drawn also from the animal kingdom, with God depicted as a roaring lion, hovering mother bird, angry mother bear, and protective mother hen, and from cosmic reality such as light, cloud, rock, wind, fire, refreshing water and life itself. Since no one term alone is absolute or adequate, a positive revelry of symbols pours forth to express divine being.

In the face of all this richness, however, what Aquinas calls the "poverty of our vocabulary" continues (*Summa Theologiae* I, q.37, a.1). Even taking a thousand names, images, and perfections and adding them together will not deliver a completely adequate understanding: "If you have understood, it is not God."

These rules of engagement for speaking about the divine, illustrated above with story and example, do not float arbitrarily in the air but are deeply rooted in the truth of the living God. From the Hebrew prophets' warning against idols:

> *To whom will you liken me and make me equal,*
>   *and compare me, as though we were alike?*
>
> . . . .
>
> *for I am God, and there is no other;*
>   *I am God and there is no one like me.* (Isa 46:5, 9)

to the Christian epistle writer's exclamation that God "*dwells in unapproachable light, whom no one has seen or can see*" (1 Tim 6:16); and from the wisdom of the saints and mystics to the reflections of church councils and major theologians, the incomprehensibility of God runs like a deep river through every affirmation. Simultaneously, monotheistic faith holds at its center the belief that, rather than remaining aloof, God engages the world with merciful love, bringing the mystery ineffably near.

It would be an understatement to say that these rules of engagement are simply ignored in the contemporary world. Tidal waves of words about the deity pour forth in church and society with no accompanying awareness that the subject of all this talk exceeds our grasp. By contrast, these ground rules work to free our imagination from the standard cultural model of the divine, the paltry heritage of modern theism, while assuring that a certain modesty characterizes talk about what is glimpsed on new frontiers. There is no absolutism possible, but powerful claims about where the living God is to be found may convince the reasoning mind and the seeking heart if they are offered with clarity and humility.

HIGH STAKES

Like millions of plant and animal species, many religions have gone extinct in the course of time. Studying this phenomenon of obsolescence, German theologian Wolfhart Pannenberg made a poignant observation: "Religions die when their lights fail," that is, when their teachings no longer illuminate life as it is actually lived by their adherents. In such cases, the way the Holy is encountered stalls out and does not keep pace with changing human experience. History's dynamism is inexorable. Some people will cling to the old views, but eventually most will move on, seeking ultimate meaning in a way that is coherent with their current experience of life. Then the lights of the old religion dim out; the deity becomes irrelevant. This phenomenon is not a case of human beings dictating to God what they want in a deity, as some fear. Rather, Pannenberg argues, it is a test of the true God. Only the living God who spans all times can relate to historically new circumstances as the future continuously arrives. A tradition that cannot change cannot be preserved. Where people experience God as still having something to say, the lights stay on.

As this book aims to show, the fact that in our day multiple, rich Christian theologies have been seeking and finding the living God in ways coherent with our changing times testifies that this particular Way remains a vital, viable option. It is true that none of these theologies speaks the last word. They enact but the latest chapter in a long-running quest that has no foreseeable end as long as human beings continue to exist. Nevertheless, their insights open up fresh ways of relating to the living God in prayer and praxis that deeply satisfy the desire for a meaningful life in our day, both for individuals and for the community of disciples that is the church.

FOR FURTHER READING

The origin of religion among early human beings is carefully traced in D. Bruce Dickson, *The Dawn of Belief: Religion in the Upper Paleolithic of Southwestern Europe* (Tucson: University of Arizona Press, 1990); Timothy Insoll, *Archaeology, Ritual, Religion* (London: Routledge, 2004); and John Esposito, Darrell Fasching, and Todd Lewis, *World Religions Today* (New York: Oxford University Press, 2006), from which the citation is taken.

Certain works that analyze religion from the existential point of view have become classics. These include Rudolf Otto's treatment of the rational/irrational experience of God as numinous found in *The Idea of the Holy*

(London: Oxford University Press, 1926; originally 1917); Paul Tillich's engaging discussion of God as the symbol of one's ultimate concern in *The Dynamics of Faith* (New York: Harper & Row, 1957); and in a most readable way, John Haught's work *What Is God? How to Think about the Divine* (New York: Paulist, 1986), which probes the human experiences of depth, future, freedom, beauty, and truth for clues about what we mean by this three-letter word *God*.

The subject of how Enlightenment theologians constructed a concept of God that omitted most of what Christians held dear is thoroughly studied by Michael Buckley, *At the Origins of Modern Atheism* (New Haven: Yale University Press, 1987). His book *Denying and Disclosing God: The Ambiguous Progress of Modern Atheism* (New Haven: Yale University Press, 2004) explores the subsequent internal contradictions of modern theism that have given rise to various forms of atheism. A critical but sympathetic and more accessible presentation of modern theism and its forgetfulness of mystery is laid out in William Placher, *The Domestication of Transcendence: How Modern Thinking about God Went Wrong* (Louisville: Westminster John Knox, 1996). For the popular result, see J. B. Phillips, *Your God Is Too Small* (New York: Macmillan, 1961).

An excellent treatment of metaphor is provided by Sallie McFague, *Metaphorical Theology: Models of God in Religious Language* (Philadelphia: Fortress, 1985). For discussion of analogy and symbol, see Battista Mondin, *The Principle of Analogy in Protestant and Catholic Theology* (The Hague: M. Nijhoff, 1963). The God as "chap" citation is from Terry Eagleton, "Lunging, Flailing, Mispunching," *London Review of Books,* vol. 28, no. 20 (Oct. 19, 2006). Wolfhart Pannenberg's thesis is found in "Toward a Theology of the History of Religions," in his *Basic Questions in Theology,* vol. 2 (Philadelphia: Fortress, 1971), 65–118.

For almost every chapter that lies ahead, the excellent work by Gregory Baum, ed., *The Twentieth Century: A Theological Overview* (Maryknoll, N.Y.: Orbis Books, 1999) provides thick historical background. Robert Schreiter, *Constructing Local Theologies* (Maryknoll, N.Y.: Orbis Books, 1985), lays out the theoretical underpinnings for the fact that wisdom can arise from local churches.

2

GRACIOUS MYSTERY,
EVER GREATER, EVER NEARER

CONTEXT: A SECULAR WORLD

Consider the insight into God that emerged in western Europe in the middle of the twentieth century. Rebuilding from the devastation of two world wars, society was being shaped by profound changes whose origin reached back centuries before the wars to the Reformation, the Renaissance, and the Enlightenment. Seeds stemming from these movements had taken deep root and flowered into a culture that was recognizably modern and secular. Three salient components of this culture had a particular influence on the spiritual climate.

Scientifically, rapid advances in discoveries about the natural world provided empirical explanations for events, leading to a pragmatic mentality rather than one oriented to supernatural causes. This knowledge also opened the door to technological inventions that provided a measure of control over nature. A rising standard of living, including new organized enjoyments, ease of travel, and comforts in everyday life, went hand in hand with the specter of mass extermination raised by nuclear weapons.

❧ *Politically*, after violent bouts with fascism and communism, democracy became established as the preferred form of government, giving average persons a greater measure of freedom and authority in the running of their lives. Coupled with this as a condition for democracy's success, the spread of universal education produced a level of literacy in the mass of average citizens, both men and women, that allowed for greater critical questioning and independent judgment. New media of mass communication via radio and television vastly increased the amount of information available to the ordinary person.

❧ *Intellectually,* a series of astute thinkers in philosophy, literature, and psychology had measured the adequacy of the idea of God against whatever benefit it might bestow on human beings, and had found it wanting. In the nineteenth century Ludwig Feuerbach judged God to be a projection, formed when human beings extrapolate their own strengths and imagine them writ large in a superior being: human beings create God in their own image rather than vice versa. Karl Marx famously excoriated religion as "the opiate of the people," providing a narcotic for life's unjust suffering with its promise of divine reward in heaven, rather than providing a basis for the struggle for justice on earth. In his novels Fyodor Dostoevsky protested the existence of God in the face of innocent suffering, especially that of children; his character Ivan returns his ticket of admission to the religious universe, passionately rejecting any part in a setup that allowed such outrages to happen. Sigmund Freud pronounced God to be an illusion, generated to fulfill the human wish for a strong, protective father figure to guard us amidst life's buffeting; the mature personality would grow up and take responsibility without this fiction. Coming from multiple directions, the formidable challenge of atheism had enormous cultural growth in modern Europe.

More poetically, on the brink of the twentieth century Friedrich Nietzsche crafted a parable that pointed to the winds of disbelief that would blow over modern society. A madman lit a lantern at noon and went into the public market looking for God: "Where is God?" Mocked by the townspeople in an escalating series of exchanges, he finally threw the lantern to the ground. It shattered, and its light went out. "God is dead," cried the madman, "and we have killed him." Let the churches begin the funeral. While everyone laughed, he predicted that his generation was not yet ready for the news. But it would reach the ears of a future generation. Then the horizon would vanish, there would be no more up and down, and people would get dizzy with the fall into freedom.

By the mid-twentieth century in Europe the madman's news had arrived. The prominent scientific, political, and intellectual features of modern culture combined to present a new challenge to faith. The challenge can best be appreciated against the foil of the premodern era when, in Hans Küng's deft description, Christianity had been a big church in a little world. Before modern times in Europe for the most part, a relatively unified worldview had prevailed whereby not only the individual but society as whole took Christianity for granted. Yes, there were others in the world, but they were peripheral to daily life, either enemies or those quietly explained by some theological theory. The majority of persons with their families and neighbors were Christian by birth and social custom. Conviction was not put to the test.

In modern society, however, Christianity became a little church in a much bigger world. Believing Christians found themselves a cognitive minority scattered in a wider culture that bore the stamp of other influences, both secular and religious. Consequently, a variety of viewpoints pressed themselves on the average person, along with a wide array of values according to which one could live one's life. Science's ability to find inner-worldly, empirical explanations for all phenomena made the world seem ultimately more godless, while the human ability to plan and rationally master nature made the everyday world seem more profane. Participation in the secular political process along with high levels of education removed the average person from the direct influence of church authority. The coruscating wind of atheism, which outrightly refutes the reality of God, along with its sibling, agnosticism, which maintains a studied neutrality on the issue, blew down complacency in religious belief. At the very least, the modern atmosphere of skepticism made all truth claims sound relative.

As a result, Christian faith was thrown into crisis. Thinking people questioned what it all meant, this old, rather creaky tradition of luxuriant doctrines and rituals and hierarchy and pious customs, and whether any of it was true. Large numbers of people simply drifted away from the church under the pressure of modern social patterns, giving rise to the phenomenon of bourgeois indifference to religion. The realities of civil life and the reality of Christian faith diverged, seemingly unable to be integrated.

In this situation philosophers and theologians with an ear for people's questions and an eye for pastoral needs labored vigorously to interpret Christian belief in ways that could be newly meaningful. Truth be told, the European situation at mid-century is now writ large around the world wherever modern culture takes root. But hammered by modern atheistic criticism and agnostic indifference, European theologians were the first to contend for the soul of the modern person in secular society. From a wealth of fine efforts, including the Catholic *nouvelle théologie* pioneered by Henri de Lubac and Jean Daniélou and the Protestant reemphasis on the God of revelation spearheaded by Karl Barth, this chapter tracks the insight of the German theologian Karl Rahner, whose work began in the 1930s and continued through the second half of the twentieth century until his death in 1984. Committed to critical dialogue with the Enlightenment and its legacy, his project profoundly renewed thinking about the living God in the face of the challenge of atheism. A close look at his line of reasoning will make clear Rahner's breakthrough idea of God, as well as its spiritual and practical import.

WINTER

A wintry season: such is Rahner's metaphor for the situation of faith in the modern world. Keeping his eye on middle-class, educated European persons who are trying to live a Christian life, he sees that this is a world that no longer easily communicates the faith. First off, a person can no longer be a Christian out of social convention or inherited custom. To be a Christian now requires a personal decision, the kind of decision that brings about a change of heart and sustains long-term commitment. Not cultural Christianity but a diaspora church, scattered among unbelievers and believers of various stripes, becomes the setting for this free act of faith. Furthermore, when a person does come to engage belief in a personal way, society makes this difficult to do. For modern society is marked not only by atheism and agnosticism but also by positivism, which restricts what we can know to data accessible from the natural sciences; secularism, which gets on with the business at hand, impatient of ultimate questions, with a wealth of humanistic values that allow a life of ethical integrity without faith; and religious pluralism, which demonstrates that there is more than one path to holy and ethical living. All of these call into question the very validity of Christian belief.

When, nevertheless, persons do make a free act of faith, the factors characteristic of the modern world impart a distinctive stamp to their spiritual experience. This is not surprising, since the path to God always winds through the historical circumstances of peoples' times and places. Inhabiting a secular, pluralistic culture, breathing its atmosphere and conducting their daily lives according to its pragmatic tenets, Christians today have absorbed the concrete pattern of modernity into their very soul. It runs right through their own heart, shaping their mind-set and psychology. As Rahner observed, "agnosticism which knows it doesn't know . . . is the way God is experienced today." Certainly this is not true of all believers. For psychological and historical reasons, some still dwell with an unperturbed God-filled heart in the framework of a previous era. But as Rahner once famously noted, not all who live at the same time are contemporaries. His concern is focused on Christians who are people of their own modern times, surrounded by spiritual ambiguity. When such people "come to church," they do not leave their complex inner and outer worlds at the door but bring the ambiguities right up to the altar. Since mature spirituality requires integrating the basic experiences of one's life into a wholeness before God, modernity forms a crucial element in the act of faith.

Thus the metaphor of winter. The luxuriant growth of devotions and secondary beliefs, all these leaves and fruits that unfurled in the season when Christianity was dominant in the culture, have fallen away. The trees are left bare and the cold wind blows. In such a season, belief must get back to basics. It will not do to spend energy on what is peripheral and unessential, as if it were high summer. To survive, people of faith need to return to the center, to the inmost core that alone can nourish and warm the heart in winter. In this situation there is only one big issue, and that is the question of God.

It is a source of never-ending concern to Rahner that much of what people hear in the preaching and teaching of the church draws on a primitive idea of God unworthy of belief, rather than communicating the reality, the beauty, the wonder, and the strange generosity of the mystery of God. The average sermon, along with the popular piety it encourages, has a basically retarded notion of God, he judged, acknowledging neither the absolute difference of God from the world nor the marvelous truth that God's own self has drawn near as the inmost dynamism and goal offered to the world. All too often sermons work with the tired ideas of modern theism, reflecting a precritical mentality that sees God as a particular element of the whole, even if the highest. They refer to God as someone whom we can calculate into our formula of how things work, thus replacing the incomprehensible God with an idol. They fashion the Holy in the image of our own concerns, our neurotic fears, our puny hearts, rather than honoring the improbable outpouring of love by which God not only sets up the world in its own integrity but, while remaining radically distinct, gives the divine self away to this world. They neglect to inform us of the most tremendous truth, that we are called into loving immediacy with the mystery of God who self-communicates to us in unspeakable nearness. After listening to such dismal sermons, can we really say that the word "God" brightens up our lives? Unfortunately, Rahner wrote, it is more often the case that the words of the preacher fall powerlessly from the pulpit, "like birds frozen to death and falling from a winter sky."

In this wintry season, church statements about God are ordinarily too naive and too superficial to help believers, let alone convince unbelievers. In a sense the onslaught of atheism might perform a service, prodding faith to purify notions of God that, while they may be traditional, are woefully deficient to the point of being idolatrous. Is God dead? If we mean the God imagined as a part of the cosmos, one existence among others though infinitely bigger, the great individual who defines himself over against others and functions as a competitor with human beings, then yes, the God of modern theism is dead. But as Rahner appreciated, atheism sets a condition for faith that in response must reach far deeper for its truth: "the struggle against atheism is foremost and of necessity a struggle against the inadequacy of our own theism."

Through a lifetime of writing, teaching, and preaching, Rahner set out to uncover truth about the living God that would provide warmth and sustenance in winter. Holding himself accountable to everyday believers, he focused particularly on those beset by doubts engendered by the precarious existence of Christian faith in the secularized, scientific-industrial societies of modern Europe. He made their doubts his own and responded to them with the full force of his penetrating grasp of the resources of the Christian tradition. His method engaged people not by pouring solutions from above into bewildered souls but by inviting them to take a journey of discovery into the virtually uncharted territory of their own lives. Johann Baptist Metz, whom we will read in the next chapter, argues that this is the deepest source of Rahner's greatness as a theologian: he invites the ordinary, average person on a personal journey that ends up being a journey of mind and heart into God. In the end Rahner's method of proceeding and its resulting insights have profoundly renewed thinking about the Christian doctrine of God. Tracing out the logic of his project will disclose both its spiritual fruitfulness and its influence on much else that follows.

MYSTERY EVER GREATER

Starting with the Human

For centuries the usual way of arriving at an idea of God was to start with the natural world and then, pondering its existence and organization, to conclude something about its Maker. Aquinas provides a stellar example. Noting that the world does not cause itself but is contingent, that is, essentially unnecessary, he reasons that to explain the existence of the world there must be a cause uncaused by another, a Being that exists necessarily and causes all other causes. "And this is what people call God" (*Summa Theologiae* I, q.2, a.3). In the modern era philosophy shifted the starting point of reflection from the cosmos to the human being, from what seems simply external to our lives to our internal human experience, from nature to human nature. Fascinated with what it means to be human, thinkers probed ultimate questions through the lens of human struggle, human consciousness, human freedom. Convinced that this philosophical approach can provide fertile ground for explaining Christian faith, Rahner begins his approach to the idea of God by executing this "turn to the subject," that is, by focusing on the person not as a mere object but as a human subject with interiority, a thinking mind, and freedom to choose.

Of all the aspects of human life that reveal our subjectivity, the early

Rahner opted to focus on our curiosity. His doctoral dissertation opens with the words, *Man fragt*, which translated means *One asks*, or *A person asks a question*. This is a typical human act, one that can be found at all times in all cultures. From the child's "why is the sky blue?" to the young adult's "what should I do with my life?" to the mid-lifer's "do you still love me?" to the dying elder's "is there any hope?"—from asking directions when lost, to starting a business, to exploring the rain forest, to holding a press confer-ence, to checking on the latest news, to figuring out how to deal with your cancer, to wondering about the meaning of life, questions both existential and practical pour forth in an unending torrent. One asks.

Ponder what this ordinary experience reveals about human nature. A question presumes that we do not know something. In an interesting way it also implies that we already do know a little something or it would be impos-sible to ask about it to begin with. Most tellingly, asking a question shows that we have a desire to know something. It brings to light a certain dyna-mism in the human spirit that drives us toward wanting to know something more, thereby expanding our connection with our own depths and with the wider world. In asking, we anticipate that there is a reality to be found. When an answer crystallizes, the mind grasps it and judges whether it fits or does not satisfy the question that was asked. Even a perfectly good answer does not allow our mind to rest for long, because the answer nestles against a background of related things that trigger our curiosity anew. And so the answer becomes the basis for a new question.

How long can this go on? Is there a limit to the number of questions we are allowed to ask before we have to stop? The very idea makes people smile. There is no set quota that, once we have reached it, would prevent us from asking further questions. Imagine how that would cramp our spirit. It would be like hitting a brick wall, becoming brain dead. Instead of a meager ration of preassigned questions, however, human beings are capable of pursuing new questions as long as they live. While analyzing, weighing, judging, and defining concrete objects in the world, our reasoning power keeps on slip-ping beyond standard definitions to seek new horizons. The number of questions we can ask is limitless.

What makes this basic human phenomenon possible? By analyzing the process of inquiry so that it leads up to this question, Rahner reveals that he is employing the method of thinking known as transcendental philosophy.

Pioneered by Immanuel Kant, this philosophy explores the human subject in our typical behaviors and asks: what is the condition for the possibility of human beings acting this way? Invited into a science lab, for example, where a white-coated scientist is peering intently into a microscope, a transcendental philosopher would not ask to have a peek to see the discovery being made. Rather, the philosopher would focus on the scientist and wonder what basic condition of human nature makes it possible for her to pursue evidence and make this discovery in the first place.

Following Rahner's train of thought, we started with the subject who asks a question. What is the condition for the possibility of this lifelong, universal behavior? It can only be that the human spirit is characterized by an unrestricted drive toward the truth, which is ultimately boundless. In every question we ask, we transcend the immediate point and reach dynamically for something more. Even in the most mundane inquiry we go beyond the matter at hand toward the next thing, and the next, and ultimately toward . . . what is infinite. In an unthematic and ever-present way, human beings are oriented toward boundless truth. If this were not the case, then even a person's first question would never be asked, let alone the questions of the human race as a whole, for having to halt at some regrettable limit would alter the nature of our mind. But our questions, driven by profound yearning to know, are made possible by the very structure of human nature, which is dynamically oriented toward all the reality there is to be known. As this analysis shows, human persons don't just ask questions: we are a question in search of the fullness of truth.

This same pattern can be traced again if we start not with the human mind and its desire to know but with the human will and its experience of freedom. As Anne Carr explains, for transcendental philosophy freedom is not something one has, like a motor in a car. Rather, it is the situation of being persons present to ourselves, "given over to ourselves and ultimately responsible for ourselves," able to some degree to transcend forces and objects that might predetermine who we are. Freedom is actualized over time in everyday decisions and relationships. "It includes what one is in the worlds of family, community, business, politics, work of all kinds, and who one ultimately is in acceptance or refusal of the infinite and mysterious horizon of one's very existence." Here, too, we experience a never-ending dynamism of desire to seek and receive that propels the spirit forward. Every act by which a person loves another, for example, deepens the ability to give and receive yet more love in a widening circle of relationship that defines who we are. In every aspect, human freedom, like reason, is a dynamism that keeps on transcending beyond everything it grasps. What is the condition for the possibility of freely summing oneself up in the declaration "I love you"? It is the open structure of human nature that is oriented toward a boundless fullness of love. *Grace*

Once one grasps this pattern of human self-transcendence, one sees that this single basic experience is present in a thousand forms. Not only do we curiously question and freely love, but we desire happiness, we know loneliness, we doubt, we resist injustice, we plan projects to benefit others, we act responsibly, we remain faithful to conscience under pressure, we are amazed at beauty, we feel guilt, we rejoice, we grieve death, we hope in the future. Undergirding all these personal existential moments is an immense and driving longing. At root we experience that we are oriented to something more. Let us not, for the moment, say what this more is. It is something like a horizon that opens up the landscape and beckons us onward, encircling our lives though we can never reach it.

This orientation to the horizon is part of the life of every person whether they pay attention to it or not. It is not one particular experience among others, but the ultimate depths of every other distinctively personal experience, the very condition that makes them all possible. Because where would we be if there were only a limited number of questions we could ask, a set number of free decisions we could make, a restricted amount of beauty we could enjoy, or a quota on tears? We would not be recognizably human. As it is, however, we experience ourselves as beings who constantly reach out beyond ourselves toward something ineffable. This orientation is what constitutes us as spiritual subjects, or *persons*, properly so called. In fact in a paradoxical way, the moment we become aware of our radical limitations, we have already overstepped these boundaries.

In mid-century Europe an interesting debate broke out about what this might mean. Existential philosophers with a fierce commitment to atheism, thinkers such as Jean Paul Sartre, concluded that life is absurd. The universe with its empty heaven endlessly frustrates human questing. Since there is no ultimate fulfillment to our self-transcending, all our desires come to naught. Held for a few brief moments over the void, human beings with all our

strivings are the butt of a great cosmic joke. Religious thinkers, to the contrary, contended that life is meaningful because an infinite holy God who is
the surrounding horizon of human questing intends to be our fulfillment.
Whether it is nothing or everything that awaits, however, both sides agreed
on the dynamic structure of human experience, which is oriented always to
the "more."

The Whither of Our Self-transcendence

Having established this point about human self-transcendence in his own
way, Rahner's argument now becomes explicitly theological. Note that he is
not trying to "prove" the existence of God in some objective manner. Such
proof is not possible. Rather, working within the context of modern culture,
he is trying to relocate the question of God. He is moving it from a question
about a Supreme Being "out there" to a question about what supports the
dynamic orientation of human nature. If God exists, he argues, it is no accident that we find ourselves so open and so yearning. The Creator would
have made us this way in order to be, as infinite Truth and holy Love, the fulfillment of our questioning, loving, thirsty-for-life selves. To appreciate this,
we must get away from the conventional picture that the very word "God"
conjures up, which too easily leads to inadequate misunderstanding. What
would be an appropriate way to refer to this boundless plenitude that is the
vis-à-vis of the human spirit? Strange as it may sound, it would be helpful to
use for a time the archaic term *Whither*. This term refers to a point of arrival,
a destination, as in the question "Whither goest thou?" The Whither of our
self-transcendence is that toward which we are journeying, the goal toward
which our self-transcending minds and hearts are forever reaching.

What must this Whither be like? Here we reach the heart of the argument as we fathom something characteristic of the divine, given the transcending dynamism of the human spirit. The only satisfactory vis-à-vis to
such a dynamic human spirit would be something itself forever unbounded,
so that reaching the goal would not shut the human being down. The term
of our self-transcending spirit must be itself infinite, indefinable, forever
beyond our grasp, not at our disposal. To this ineffable plenitude Rahner
gives the name "holy mystery." Every epoch, he observes, has different catchwords for God, specific terms that evoke the whole. In this wintry season,
"holy mystery" will do for us.

Mystery here is not meant in the spooky sense of something weird or ghostly. Nor does it have the mundane meaning of a puzzle that has yet to be solved, as in a literary murder mystery. Rather, mystery here signifies the idea that the Holy is so radically different from the world, so wholly other, that human beings can never form an adequate idea nor arrive at total possession.

The Whither of human self-transcendence is and must remain incomprehensible in depth and breadth, forever. We will never reach the end of exploring, having figured it all out. It is something like parallel train tracks that appear to meet at a point in the distance, but when you get to that point the tracks have opened up to another distant point. It is something like the horizon one sees when flying in an airplane; no matter how fast the jet goes, it never catches the horizon, which remains still farther beyond the window. It is something like being in love and finding your beloved endlessly interesting and beautiful. There is always more. Rahner describes the idea of God as holy mystery in poetic, geographical terms:

> The horizon itself cannot be present within the horizon. The ultimate measure cannot be measured; the boundary which delimits all things cannot itself be bounded by a still more distant limit. The infinite and immense which comprises all things: such an all-embracing immensity cannot itself be encompassed.

This is why it is a mistake to think we can prove the existence of God the same way we prove the existence of a new planet or any other particular object of our experience in the world. We cannot discover God directly or indirectly as we might find a subatomic particle in the trailings of a cloud chamber. God is not one being who appears alongside other beings that exist, not even if we envision God as the greatest one, or the first, or the last. It is a mistake to think of God as an element within a larger world, as a part of the whole of reality. Holy mystery cannot be situated within our system of coordinates but escapes all categories. Hence, to think rightly of God we must give up the drive to intellectual mastery and open up to the Whither of our spirit's hungry orientation. "The concept 'God' is not a grasp of God by which a person masters the mystery; but it is the means by which one lets oneself be grasped by the mystery which is present yet ever distant."

Stressing the incomprehensibility of holy mystery as Rahner does is not a novelty. It runs like a deep river through the whole Jewish and Christian tradition from scripture to the wisdom of saints, mystics, and theologians across the ages. Aquinas, to whom Rahner is indebted, underscores this point with his famously blunt statement:

> Since our mind is not proportionate to the divine substance, God remains beyond our intellect and so is unknown to us. Hence the supreme knowledge which we have of God is to know that we do not know God, insofar as we know that what God is surpasses all that we can understand.(*De Potentia,* q.7, a.5)

Rahner's contribution is to arrive at this insight through the dynamism of human experience, making God's incomprehensible holy mystery the very condition that makes possible the functioning of our human spirit. The experience of transcendence carries every act of knowledge and love beyond itself into the presence of mystery. Whether we are consciously aware of it or not, whether we are open to this truth or suppresses it, our whole spiritual, intellectual, and affectionate existence is oriented toward a holy mystery that is the basis of our being:

> This mystery is the inexplicit and unexpressed horizon which always encircles and upholds the small area of our everyday experience of knowing and acting, our knowledge of reality and our free action. It is our most fundamental and natural condition, but for that very reason it is also the most hidden and least regarded reality, speaking to us by its silence, and even while appearing to be absent, revealing its presence by making us take cognisance of our own limitations.

And this is what people call God.

Understood in this way, the Whither of our self-transcendence exercises strong implications for human well-being, for such ineffable incomprehensibility bears up and assures the human spirit's continued operation. Even if we were eventually to know every blessed truth there is to know in the entire universe; even if we were to have our fill of loving pressed down and running over; even if we were to experience all dimensions of life in abundance—there would still be more, the Whither, calling forth and sustaining our spirit. When we become aware of this and lucidly allow ourselves to be encompassed by God so understood, then our *not* knowing God who is boundless mystery "is not a pure negation, not simply an empty absence, but a positive characteristic of a relationship between one subject and another." Such incomprehensible mystery creates the condition for the possibility of the religious relationship being at once a true home and an unending adventure of exploration for yearning, seeking, weeping, laughing, knowing, loving, and hoping human beings.

Holy mystery perdures forever. In Rahner's day the dominant form of Roman Catholic theology was neo-scholasticism, a strongly rationalistic form of thinking centered on an idea of God that we would recognize today as theism. Neo-scholastic theology had assumed that in the beatific vision when the blessed in heaven would see God face to face, all would become clear. In an interesting twist, Rahner does not deny fuller knowledge to the blessed but characterizes it as knowledge of divine plenitude precisely as mystery. Far from being a regrettable limitation of our happiness, God's abiding incomprehensibility even in heaven

> must rather be thought of as the very substance of our vision and the very object of our blissful love. Vision means grasping and being grasped by the mystery, and the supreme act of knowledge is not the abolition or diminution of the mystery but its final assertion, its eternal and total immediacy. . . . Mystery is not merely a way of saying that reason has not yet completed its victory. It is the goal where reason arrives when it attains its perfection by becoming love.

The incomprehensibility of holy mystery, then, does not belong accidentally to God like a qualification that could just as well belong to something or someone else. It characterizes the Whither of our transcendence by definition, solely and primordially and forever. Without this, God would not be God. With this, we encounter the fulfillment of our lives.

For some people struggling with faith amid modern culture, the idea of God as incomprehensible mystery comes as an enormous relief. It liberates them from cramped, confined notions of theism and places their spirit into a relationship where they can soar. As Jeannine Hill Fletcher explains, "Incomprehensibility is not so much a sad reflection on human limitedness, but rather the exuberant celebration of God's limitlessness. . . . [It] means that the human person glimpses the mystery of God not as absence, but as overabundance." This glimpse makes other people dizzy and disoriented; they experience such boundlessness as a loss of connection to the domesticated, even if authoritarian, God of theism they were used to. Still others become fearful because the nameless, ineffable Whither seems so distant and aloof. All need to recognize, however, that at this point in the argument the idea of God as holy mystery is only half-finished.

MYSTERY EVER NEARER

At the heart of Christian faith is the almost unbelievable idea that the infinitely incomprehensible holy mystery of God does not remain forever remote but draws near in radical proximity to the world. This is accomplished in a single act of self-bestowal that shows itself in two mutually conditioning elements. In doctrinal terms these are incarnation and grace; in personal terms, they are Jesus Christ and the Holy Spirit. Together they form the self-communicating gift pulsing outward from the very depths of divine being whereby this holy mystery draws near to the world in unspeakable nearness.

Rahner set the stage for appreciating this in a very personal way when he crafted a prayer to the incomprehensible God. Trying to take the measure of this ineffable greatness reduces him to a state of high uneasiness. The prayer begins: "Whenever I think of Your Infinity, I am racked with anxiety, wondering how You are disposed to me." The prayer goes on to plead that God speak a word of consolation:

> You must adapt Your word to my smallness, so that it can enter into this tiny dwelling of my finiteness—the only dwelling in which I can live—without destroying it. If you should speak such an "abbreviated" word, which would not say everything but only something simple which I could grasp, then I could breathe freely again. You must make your own some human word, for that is the only kind I can comprehend. Don't tell me everything that You are; don't tell me of Your Infinity —just say that You love me, just tell me of Your Goodness to me.

Only then will this theologian be able to get on with his life with a modicum of peace.

Incarnation

Christian faith holds that in Jesus Christ the incomprehensible God actually does speak such an abbreviated word in the language of our common humanity: "*the Word became flesh and dwelt among us*" (John 1:14). Living a genuinely historical Jewish life in first-century Galilee, conditioned by the physical and psychological limits of our species, Jesus preached the reign of God, healed suffering people, sought out the lost, and offered hospitality to all comers. In this he expressed what God is and always is: prodigal love. Drinking the bitter dregs of violent death on a cross outside Jerusalem, he placed the infinite mystery of God in solidarity with all vulnerable creatures who end in the dust. The presence of the Source of life in the depths of death awakens hope, seen first in the resurrection of Jesus, that there will be a future for all the defeated and the dead. Here the self-communication of God to the world in the person of Jesus Christ as a child of Earth is the linchpin that holds together the whole adventure of Christian faith.

Rahner placed his interpretation of the incarnation within the framework of God as love, thereby taking sides in an old debate. Since medieval times theology has argued over the motive for the incarnation. The Dominicans, led by Aquinas, took their clue from a straight reading of the opening chapters of the book of Genesis, where, after Adam and Eve ate the forbidden fruit, God promised a redeemer who would crush the serpent's head. The coming of the Messiah is the fulfillment of this promise. Therefore, the motive of the incarnation is redemption; the Word became flesh to save the human race from sin. The Franciscans, led by Duns Scotus, thought otherwise. Guided by the principle that love seeks union with the beloved, this school of thought held that the motive of the incarnation is love. The Word became flesh so that God who is love could enter into deep personal union with the world, the beloved. This would have happened even if human beings had not sinned. The fact that the world is sinful entailed that the suffering and death of the cross become part of Jesus' story. But the primary purpose was union in love.

The strength of Rahner's view of the loving self-gift of God in Jesus Christ can be seen in his option for the Scotist position, which had fallen under the radar of the prevailing Roman theology of the day. "The incarnation is first in the divine intention," he mused, meaning that God who is love eternally desires to communicate the divine self to the "other" who is not divine, and so creates a world to allow this to happen. In this view the narrative of sin and redemption is embraced by a primordial love that creates and seeks union regardless of the circumstances. The Whither of our self-transcendence has endlessly sought to be our fulfillment from the beginning.

Grace

Anchored in history by Jesus Christ, the holy mystery of God takes the initiative to surround the lives of all human beings from beginning to end with redemptive love. In Christian language, this is expressed in the idea that the Spirit of God is present at the center of every life. Rahner's explanation ties this very closely to his transcendental analysis of human nature. Since our concrete acts of transcending ourselves, even when normally ignored amid the press of business, disclose that human persons are dynamically structured toward the infinite, faith interprets that persons are always referred beyond themselves toward an ineffable Whither. The good news treasured by Christian faith proclaims that this ineffable horizon graciously approaches us and bids us approach, enfolding us in an ultimate and radical love. This love, experienced at the ground of our being, is nothing other than the gift of God's own self. It is offered freely to everyone without exception as light and the promise of life, and becomes visible in history wherever love of neighbor, faithfulness to conscience, courage for resistance to evil, and any other human witness to what is "more" takes place.

It is true that the dynamic presence of this love in human history is often marred by sin, human beings shutting themselves off in refusal. But in spite of this wretched inward-turning and its tragic results in murder and all manner of harm, the divine offer of love is always and everywhere present, being more powerful than the mystery of human guilt.

Such loving presence is what theology calls grace. Neo-scholastic theology dealt with the concept of grace primarily as *created* grace, seeing it as a finite gift that removes sin and restores our relationship with God. The standard language of created grace led to the unfortunate impression that grace was a kind of objective "third thing" between God and human beings, something almost quantifiable that could be lost by sin and gained again by penance, and thus could be governed by individual human actions. Drawing from biblical, patristic, and medieval theology, Rahner shifted the focus to the more primordial, subjective form of grace called *uncreated* grace. This refers to God's own Spirit imparted freely and immediately to all human beings. It is God's own self-communication, which permeates the world at its inmost roots. Not a separate thing or a special gift that shows up now and again, grace is the animating force of all of human history, present even before Jesus Christ. Coextensive but not identical with our race, it comes to expression wherever people express their love in care for others, creative art, literature, technology, all the good critical dimensions of responsibility, and trust, even in darkness.

Uncreated grace is the Spirit of God dwelling at the heart of our existence. Thanks to this gift, Rahner argues, the transcending reach of the human person in knowing and loving is actually oriented to the immediacy of God. One can accept or refuse this offer of closeness, but the offer is not thereby revoked. The language of grace, then, does not signify a lovely gift distinct from God. Rather, in what Rahner characterizes as the most tremendous statement that can be made about God, "the Giver himself is the Gift."

Through incarnation and grace, therefore, the silent, indefinable, and inviolable Whither of human self-transcendence, God the absolute holy mystery, offers to every person the gift of personal, saving presence:

> We can therefore affirm at once with certainty that the two mysteries of incarnation and grace are simply the radical form of the mystery which we have shown to be the primordial one: God as the holy and abiding mystery for the creature, and not in the guise of distant aloofness but in that of radical proximity.

Jesus and the Spirit articulate the one single mystery drawing intimately near to the world in loving self-communication. Herein lies the specific character of the Christian concept of God. Rather than being the most distant being, transcendent holy mystery is engaged in all the realities of the world around us, being concerned especially with the desperate and the damned.

HOLY MYSTERY

In the neo-scholastic theology dominant at mid-twentieth century, "mystery" stood for matters that ordinary reason found difficult to understand. As used in preaching and teaching, it was thought to have three characteristics. It is plural, for there are many mysteries. It is propositional, for these mysteries reside in verbal statements of doctrine or creed, such as that there are three persons in one God. And it is provisional, lasting for this lifetime only; after death all will be made clear, as when a theater curtain rises to reveal scenery and actors on a stage. Can't understand a Christian teaching? It is a mystery. But all will be revealed in the world to come.

Rahner finds this an astonishingly limited notion of mystery. Transcendental analysis of the human subject allows the term to be rehabilitated to serve as the central idea of God in the wintry season of modernity. Rather than a plurality, there is only one mystery in Christian faith. Rather than being propositional, it does not reside in doctrinal statements but in the reality of God's own being as self-giving love. And rather than being provisional, it is not temporary but endures for all eternity. This one holy mystery is the ineffable God who while remaining eternally a plenitude—infinite, incomprehensible, inexpressible—wishes to self-communicate to the world, and does so in the historically tangible person of Jesus Christ and in the grace of the Spirit so as to become the blessedness of every person and of the universe itself.

Note the twin ingredients in this idea of God that Rahner thinks can nourish and warm the spirit in winter. First, the idea of transcendence, God's fathomless otherness, is taken as absolute and articulated as mystery always ever greater. Second, and of equal weight, the idea of immanence, God's intimate and faithful nearness, is also taken absolutely and articulated as mystery always ever nearer. In one fell swoop, this insight moves beyond the conventional view delineated in modern theism, which for all its good intentions does justice to neither divine otherness nor divine nearness. In the same fell swoop, this notion of holy mystery also moves beyond the narrow notion of God as the deity of the Christian tribe alone by affirming the universality of God's gracious presence to each and every human being. Christian faith, of course, has always held that what God has done in Jesus has benefitted the whole human race and that the Spirit of God dwells among all people. This had been covered over in practice, however, by a long history of polemic against nonbelievers coupled with their social marginalization. The modern world's contact with multiple cultures in addition to its own internal pluralism makes this exclusivist view of God's salvific purpose, meant only for certain right-thinking and observant people, increasingly untenable. It is not the case that divine nearness is checkered, close to some, far from others. Rather, with loving generosity holy mystery graciously offers the gift of divine life to everyone, everywhere, and at all times. A person may reject this offer, human freedom being held in respect by the Creator of freedom. Nevertheless, all are included in God's universal saving will and offer of redeeming grace.

Let God be God!—that is, the incomprehensible holy mystery full of surprising love.

Throughout a lifetime of writing that numbers over three thousand entries, Rahner worked with modernity's challenge to lay out this core of belief for a wintry season. In the end, he insists, all Christian doctrine really says only one thing, something quite simple and radical: the living mystery of absolute fullness, who is nameless and beyond imagination, has drawn near to us amid the tangle of our lives through Jesus and the gift of grace, even when we do not realize it, in order to be our salvation, splendor, and support over the abyss. Consequently, while the outcome of our own life and that of the world is not yet known, we can have confidence that it is an adventure held safe in God's mercy. Faith then becomes an act of courage. We can dare to hope.

LOVE OF GOD AND NEIGHBOR

This glimpse into the mystery of God ever greater, ever nearer, logically flows into a path of discipleship comprised of love of God and love of neighbor, or in Rahner's terms, mysticism and responsibility, which are inseparable. The mysticism envisioned here is not an esoteric spirituality. Rather, it is a basic way to God in our time when faith is stripped down to its bare essentials. Because faith is no longer supported by the manifest religious customs and general commitment of society, Rahner is adamant that "the devout Christian of the future will either be a 'mystic,' one who has 'experienced' something, or he [she] will cease to be anything at all."

What is to be experienced? Nothing less than God, under the rubric of the specific Christian way of apprehending God, namely, as infinite holy mystery who draws near in self-bestowal through incarnation and grace. Christianity at heart proclaims a simple message: we are called into the immediacy of God's own self. If we accept the silent immensity that surrounds us as something infinitely distant and yet ineffably near; if we receive it as a sheltering nearness and tender love that does not make any reservations; and if in this embrace we have the courage to accept our own life in all its concreteness and yearning, which is possible only by grace, then we have the mystical experience of faith. Accepting our life means letting ourselves fall into this unfathomable mystery at the heart of our existence in an act of loving self-surrender. Such an act does not make everything clear; God does not spare us bewilderment. And our turning toward God is always under threat from sin. But God is present where life is lived bravely, eagerly, responsibly, even without any explicit reference to religion.

The point is this: people who courageously accept themselves, who accept their own life with all its quirks and beauty and agony, in point of fact accept holy mystery, who abides within them addressing them as self-offering love. This entails no loss of individuality but rather a growth in personhood that is liberated and fortified. For far from being a rival to human authenticity, holy mystery positively wills the world and ourselves in our finite worldliness. Rahner captures the noncompetitive nature of this relationship in his famous axiom, "nearness to God and genuine human autonomy increase in direct and not inverse proportion."

Jesus Christ is at the center of this form of mysticism. In Jesus, crucified and risen, the self-promise of God to the world has won through to victory. As a definitive event with its roots in history, this victory can no longer disappear. It is eschatological, irrevocable, assuring us that the incomprehensible mystery will bring us, too, to a blessed end in God's presence forever. Those who hear this word and bear witness to this truth in history form the community of believers. In this theology, the church is not primarily an institution for the promotion of individual piety and moral living. First and last the church is the sacramental presence of the promise of God to the world, a community that despite its sinfulness signals to the whole world that God's self-gift is continuously offered to all.

The bounden duty to take responsibility for the world is integral to the practice of this mysticism. In truth, the basic relationship to the living God of our life can be expressed and given credible form only in an unconditional love of our neighbor. Self-centered as we are, love of others can become corrupted into an expression of hidden egotism. Surrendering to the incomprehensible mystery at the core of our life, however, allows the liberating grace of God to be at work. This is the case even if we do not explicitly acknowledge it, as the parable of the sheep and goats makes clear: "*I was hungry and you gave me to eat. . . whatever you did for one of these least brothers or sisters of mine, you did for me*" (Matt 25:35, 40).

Rahner observes that the tendency today to talk not so much about God but about one's neighbor, to preach more about love of one's neighbor and to avoid the term God in favor of the world and responsibility for the world—this tendency has a solid foundation. Not that we should go to the extreme of banishing God-talk, which would be false to faith. But since both transcendental anthropology and Christian revelation show holy mystery to be profoundly present and committed to the world and every person in it, then loving God means loving the world. In this theology, an a-cosmic, unworldly relationship to God is not possible. Encompassed by incomprehensible holy mystery, we allow our hearts to be conformed to God's own heart, which pours out loving-kindness on the world in unrepentant faithfulness.

In our day, an older Rahner noted, love of neighbor needs to take a form that goes beyond the realm of private, individual relationships. Given our knowledge of how systems affect the individual, love today must be expressed also in Christian responsibility for the social sphere. Acting in this way is more than a humanitarian undertaking, noble as that would be. In a time of growing solidarity on a global scale, work for justice is stimulated by the Spirit of Jesus, for whom the neighbors' good has an incomprehensible value, commensurate with the love of God poured out upon them.

It may be winter when luxurious foliage no longer clothes the trees of piety. But the bare branches enable us to see deeper into the woods. There we glimpse the gracious mystery of God, whom we cannot manipulate either conceptually or practically, but who abides as the very Whither of our questing being. The question facing us, Rahner urges, is which do we love better: the little island of our own certitude or the ocean of incomprehensible mystery? The challenge facing us is whether we will suffocate in the tiny hut of our own shrewdness, or advance through the door of our knowing and acting into the uncharted, unending adventure of exploration into God, whose silent immensity we can trust absolutely and love through care for this world.

As the theology discussed in this chapter has shown, human understanding of God never exhausts the richness of the incomprehensible holy mystery. Consequently, Rahner reasons, this "actually postulates thereby a history of our own concept of God that can never be concluded." Historically new attempts at envisioning and articulating this mystery should be expected and even welcomed. The following chapters distill highlights of yet further attempts to speak about God resulting from the seeking-and-finding dynamism of the living Christian tradition in our day. The rules of engagement governing religious language are in play on every continent as new voices contribute to the whole church's understanding of the holy mystery at the heart of faith.

FOR FURTHER READING

The most readable explanation of atheism from a Christian point of view along with a point for point refutation is Hans Küng, *Does God Exist? An Answer for Today* (Garden City, N.Y.: Doubleday, 1980). Walter Kasper proposes the Trinity as the antidote for atheism in the section entitled "The Denial of God in Modern Atheism," in his *The God of Jesus Christ* (New York: Crossroad, 1984), pp. 16–46. A selection of primary texts of major atheistic thinkers is presented in Julia Mitchell Corbett, ed., *Through a Glass Darkly: Readings on the Concept of God* (Nashville: Abingdon, 1989). On the problems that atheism poses for faith in general, see J. J. C. Smart, *Atheism and Theism* (Malden, Mass.: Blackwell, 2003). The work of Julian Baggini, *Atheism: A Very Short Introduction* (New York: Oxford University Press, 2003) gives a positive reading of atheism and shows its attraction for many thoughtful people.

Twenty-three volumes of *Theological Investigations* carry a myriad of Rahner's essays. Especially pertinent to the subject of this chapter are: "The Concept of Mystery in Catholic Theology," vol. 4, pp. 36–73 (one of Rahner's most significant essays showing that all Catholic doctrines reflect aspects of the one incomprehensible mystery of God); "Thoughts on the Possibility of Belief Today," vol. 5, pp. 3–22 (a rich and deeply felt introduction to the wintry situation of faith); "Being Open to God as Always Ever Greater," vol. 7, pp. 25–46 (a devotional reflection on human dynamism toward God as the horizon of all our activity); "Theology and Anthropology," vol. 9, pp. 28–45 (a key essay that illuminates transcendental method); and "The Church and Atheism," vol. 21, pp. 137–50.

For a technical treatment of transcendental analysis of the human person in a world of sin and grace, see Rahner's *Foundations of Christian Faith*, trans. William Dych (New York: Seabury, 1978), chapters 1–4. This same book goes on to join God's incomprehensibility with incarnation and grace in a clarifying way.

A collection of Rahner's prayers that express his theology of God appears in *Prayers for a Lifetime*, ed. Albert Raffelt (New York: Crossroad, 1984); the prayer cited is from "God of My Lord Jesus Christ," pp. 38–39. Valuable and accessible insights into spirituality appear in Rahner's *Encounters with Silence* (South Bend, Ind.: St. Augustine's Press, 1999); and *The Great Church Year: The Best of Karl Rahner's Homilies, Sermons, and Meditations*, ed. Albert Raffelt and Harvey Egan (New York: Crossroad, 2001).

For informative discussion of Rahner's method and insights, consult Mary Hines and Declan Marmion, eds., *The Cambridge Companion to Karl Rahner* (Cambridge: Cambridge University Press, 2005); and Leo O'Donovan, ed., *A World of Grace* (New York: Seabury, 1980), especially Anne Carr, "Starting with the Human," pp. 17–30.

3

THE CRUCIFIED GOD OF COMPASSION

CONTEXT: UNSPEAKABLE SUFFERING

Consider the insight into God that emerged on the European continent blasted to shreds by the Second World War. Millions dead, cities in ruins, farming and food distribution disrupted, the economy devastated: the suffering did not end with the armistice but radiated into the subsequent years like shock waves. At the center of the horror, shouted in cries and in whispers, loomed the Nazi Holocaust of the Jews. While there were stunning examples of Christian resisters and rescuers, for the most part those who ran the death camps were baptized. Standing in the ruins, theologians not only had to face the failure of Christianity to motivate people of faith to resist such evil. In the face of the enormity of what had happened, they also had to take the measure of traditional arguments used to explain the ways of God in the face of suffering. Six million people, men, women, and children, uprooted from their homes and neighborhoods, transported like cattle on precision-run trains, separated into those marked for immediate slaughter and those healthy enough to provide slave labor, and all ultimately headed for death by gassing, gunshot, disease, or starvation, their bodies disposed of in the burning crematoria. Hitler's goal was to wipe this people and their heritage off the face of the earth. The suffering, undeserved and inhumane, beggars the imagination.

The enormity of the crime left thinkers stunned. They began to speak of the Holocaust as an "interruption" that invaded Christian theology's view of a rationally ordered world. It was an "earthquake" that cracked open the ground of faith's confidence in God; an unbridgeable "chasm" that split history and its supposed progress into an incommensurable before and after; a "tremendum" that shattered belief not only in God but also in humanity and its secular projects. Taking the measure of the Shoah, one simply could not go on as before crafting interpretations that would allow this magnitude of suffering to make some kind of sense in God's plan for the world.

I remember the day I took a train from Munich to the concentration camp at Dachau. The town of Dachau itself dates from the Middle Ages and lies only a few stops on the suburban line out from the big city. Having read extensively on the Holocaust I felt quasi-prepared for what I would encounter, although the impact of actually being in the presence of the bunkers and ovens was viscerally almost too powerful to bear. There was one unexpected moment, though, that stunned my thought. In the camp museum, amid the tools of torture and other paraphernalia, there hung a striped outfit worn by one inmate named Albert Mainslinger. Next to it were displayed two pieces of paper, documents filled out when he entered and left the camp. In 1939 his admission form listed his weight as 114 kg (250 lbs) and, further down, his religion as Roman Catholic. In 1945 his discharge form, signed by the American administrator of the camp, contained different information. His weight was 41 kg (90 lbs). On the line for religion was written *Das Nichts*, nothing. I stared, struck silent. Who can fathom the suffering—unjust imprisonment; years of slow starvation; morning, noon, and night trying to evade the terror meted out by the guards; unremitting hard labor in the cold and heat; people in agony all around; having no idea when this would ever end or if the next minute would bring his death. As his body withered so too did his soul, any trust in a good and gracious God evaporating away.

Herr Mainslinger was one of the lucky ones, insofar as he survived. Multiply his experience by three million other Gentiles who died in such places. And then focus specifically on the six million Jewish people who were systematically rounded up and barbarically killed in the camps simply because they were Jews. The force of this event's interruption to the religious project of speaking about God becomes clear. Theologians reflected that such evil is a surd, an irrational force that cannot be made to fit meaningfully into a divine plan for the world. Even to try to make it fit would be to tame the evil, to dilute its terror, to give it, albeit unintentionally, a right to exist. Such attempts at rationalization drown out the voices of the victims. And to allow that this event is part of an overall divine plan for the world would be to make God into a monster, no matter how much one talks about divine goodness and power. The "fissure" in the classical pattern of thought is so great that in questing for the living God some theologians began to change the question about suffering itself. The proper question is not *why* did God permit this to happen, or *how* can this be reconciled with divine governance of the world. Rather, thinking on the far side of the break brought about by this experience, the proper question becomes the anguished query: *where* is God, where is God now?

For good reason, Jewish religious thinkers have taken the lead in pursuing this question amid the shattering of faith's confidence. Taking different avenues of thought, various Jewish scholars have envisioned different answers. We do not know where God was. God was hidden, or silent, or absent, or dead. God's face was turned away. God was there, suffering with the victims, weeping with their pain. Or most radically, the only rational way to think about God after Auschwitz is to admit that God does not exist. Whatever the theology, it leads to an ethical mandate: Never Again.

THE FAILURE OF THEODICY

Both Jewish and Christian thinkers who grappled with this issue did so against the background of a long tradition reaching back to the Bible itself. Why is there so much moral evil and suffering in the world if God is all-powerful and all-good? Could God not stop it? If not, then God must not be all-powerful. Does God not want to stop it? If not, then God must not be all-loving. But if God could stop it and wants to, why does suffering continue?

Traditional theology is virtually unanimous in maintaining that God does not will suffering directly. Rather, having created a world with its own natural laws, a world, moreover, where human beings have free will, God allows or permits disaster to happen. Different schools of thought adduce a variety of reasons to explain why this is the case. God permits suffering to punish sin, or to test character, or to educate persons in mature virtue, or to refine and purify souls for heaven. Even when suffering is unjustly inflicted on the innocent, God allows it out of respect for human freedom. No matter what happens, God will bring good out of evil in the end. All of these arguments endeavored to reconcile human suffering with divine love and power, making the case that the travail somehow served divine purpose.

At the time of the Enlightenment these attempts to justify God's ways in a painful world were given the name "theodicy." The term was coined as the title of a book by the philosopher Gottfried Leibniz in 1710, who sought to make sense of suffering as part of his argument that this is the best of all possible worlds. By then the God of modern theism was in the ascendancy, and it was theism's construal of an omnipotent, omniscient Supreme Being that needed to be defended in the face of terrible things that happened in the world which "he" created. After the Second World War, theologians began to think that measured against the Holocaust, both traditional theology's explanations and the Enlightenment theodicy project had failed. To say that the Jewish people deserved this as a punishment for sin flies in the face of the fact that, apart from sharing in common human sinfulness, most of those murdered were innocent of egregious evildoing; one million were children. To say that such suffering formed souls in virtue belies the fact that it literally destroyed persons and left survivors with a lifetime of physical, psychological, and spiritual struggle. The free will defense raised more questions than it answered, just pushing the question back to human beings and creating the need for an "anthropodicy." Indeed, the Holocaust of the Jews is an incomprehensible scandal that defies rational justification. Trying to reconcile it with a loving, powerful God ends up trivializing the evil.

There have been other genocides since this event. The Khmer Rouge regime under Pol Pot brought almost one-third of the Cambodian people to the killing fields. In Rwanda the Hutu people with fire and machete wiped out 800,000 of their Tutsi neighbors in several weeks before international intervention made the killing stop. Even as I write, the agony of Darfur, incredibly, continues. It was in mid-century Europe, however, where the issue first rose up sharply in contemporary Christian thought. It was European theologians who had to deal with the question of God in the dark of the Shoah, which shredded to bits every rational argument that tried to justify divine ways. Their work has affected theology's dealing with massive public suffering ever since.

Three Young Germans

It is no small grace that among the cohort of theologians who began to deal with this issue were three young Germans. All of them grew up under the dark shadow of National Socialism and experienced firsthand the devastation of war during their teenage years. All studied theology at universities just getting reestablished in ravaged postwar Germany. Now it was no longer the atheism of the secular world that challenged faith, but the issue of horrific suffering. When they became theologians, all subsequently refused to look away from the Holocaust but rather took the event with utmost seriousness as a challenge and guide to thinking about God.

Jürgen Moltmann tells of how he witnessed the Allied fire-bombing of Hamburg, which left whole swaths of the city in ashes. Held as a prisoner of war by the British, he looked through the barbed wire of the camp and wondered how to think about God in the midst of such utter breakdown; the ideas of the Reformed Protestant tradition in which he had been schooled seemed so inadequate. Early in his studies he rediscovered the cross of Christ, which became the firm ground beneath the feet of his theology. "Shattered and broken, the survivors of my generation were then returning from camps and hospitals to the lecture room. A theology which did not speak of God in the sight of the one who was abandoned and crucified would have had nothing to say to us then." The theology of the cross became ever more significant as he began to take the measure of the genocide of the Jews. It became imperative for the integrity of theology to connect the cross with Auschwitz.

Dorothee Soelle tells of her young years being "defined by hunger, bombing, coldness, and need. Spiritually, it was a ruined landscape as well." During the war her family hid the Jewish mother of one of her classmates in their attic. One of her older brothers was killed on the Eastern front. As a young theologian she traveled to the death camp in Auschwitz, Poland, an unusual move at the time. There, where so many were brutally murdered, she felt the theological ground silently shift beneath her feet. Her classical

Lutheran training and piety had been founded on the God of classical theism with all the "omni" attributes: omnipotence, omniscience, omnipres-
ence. After her trip she could no longer understand how theology could talk
like that. "In the light of Auschwitz, the assumption of the omnipotence of
God seemed a heresy," ethically offensive and impossible to believe. Often
citing the poetry, last letters (farewell discourses), and memoirs of Jewish
people who were in the camps or of German resisters in Nazi prisons, she
considers this crime against humanity the most important event her generation has had to deal with.

❧ Johann Baptist Metz tells of how as a religious youth sixteen years of
age he was taken out of school, forced into the German army, and sent to the
front. His company numbered well over one hundred teenagers, all young
like himself. One evening he was sent to deliver a message to headquarters.
During his absence his company was wiped out by Allied tank and bomber
assaults. Upon returning, "I found only the dead . . . I could see only dead
and empty faces where the day before I had shared fears and youthful laugh-
ter. I remember nothing but a wordless cry. Thus I see myself to this very day,
and behind this memory all my childhood dreams crumbled away." A fissure
had opened in his Catholic imagination with its impregnable confidence
that God is good and the world is orderly. The fissure became unbridgeable
when, as a graduate student of Rahner's and then as a young professor, he
gradually took into account the boundless horror of the Holocaust. Instead
of drowning out the cries, he began to wonder what would happen if one
remembered the victims and with them tried to speak about God. Thus the
God-question forced itself on him "in its strangest, most ancient, and most
controversial form," namely, from the depths of suffering. Theology simply
can no longer do its job, he concluded, that is, talk about God, with its back
turned to Auschwitz.

As their lives developed in different venues and each rose to international prominence, these three became friendly acquaintances and gave each
other collegial and moral support. The impetus to think in new ways about
the living God amid suffering broadened out in their thought to include not
only the Holocaust but also the barbarous glut of evil in human history as a
whole. Their concern was not first of all the suffering of individuals that
comes in the ordinary course of earthly life as bodies age, sicken, and die, nor

yet the suffering that results from setbacks and losses in relationships or work. While presenting religious questions of their own, these events are part of the warp and woof of every human life on this earth, which is not paradise. But beyond this personal, existential, relatively private suffering there is a wretched excess of affliction that occurs from injury that people inflict unjustly on each other en masse: grinding poverty and hunger, slavery, domestic abuse, rape, murder, war, genocide. This is harm that destroys persons and their ability to love; it assaults their identity and violently extinguishes their life. Looking back over the history of the human race, such suffering is a red thread that runs through the whole bloody tapestry.

The solution, each of these theologians wrote, does not lie either in ignoring suffering intellectually or in trying to avoid it in practical terms. The latter tendency, characteristic of materialistic culture in first world countries, began to creep into German society as postwar rebuilding started to succeed economically. Middle-class life seems to run on an expectation that life will be comfortable. Attending to material satisfactions in a consumer society, people tend to think that anything painful needs to be expelled. When suffering does arrive at their doorstep, they do not know how to achieve meaning. To forestall this pain and panic, they insulate themselves with banal activities instead of risking a life rich in engagement with its mourning and consolation. As for those who suffer beyond their immediate circle, people wrap themselves in their own world and look right through, around, beyond the torment of others, showing an inability to suffer even in the cause of aiding those being afflicted. The result of this avoidance, especially clear in young people, is boredom, stagnation, inability to experience intense joy—in a word, apathy.

In crafting an approach to theology that would deal with massive public suffering and the middle-class attempt to ignore it, the young Germans began to use the term "political theology," from the Greek word *polis*, meaning city. This is not theology done in direct connection with political parties or movements, lobbies or governments, as the name might suggest. Rather, it is theology that seeks to connect speech about God with the *polis*, the city, the public good of massive numbers of people, living and dead. Political theology as they developed it is wary of a privatized type of religion that focuses on an individual's religious experience and morality alone. Such a narrow view contributed to the failure of the churches to vigorously oppose Hitler, allowing a complacency that enabled faith to be bound up with an unjust social order. Expressing the intent to give religion a public face, political theology crafts a broader view, attempting to hold belief in God accountable in the public arena. Deeply spiritual in its approach, it also turns practical in making compassion in solidarity with victims an essential part of faith. As Metz described it, this theology emphasizes "the mystical-political element that challenges the privatization of bourgeois religion and locates the experience of God not in peaceful tranquility but in protest to God about evil in the world, a questioning of God, and a suffering unto God."

The God of Pathos

Post-Holocaust political theology rediscovered a God deeply involved with the pain of the world. Moltmann and Soelle, among others such as Eberhard Jüngel, heeded the famous insight of Dietrich Bonhoeffer, a Christian theologian hanged by the Nazis, who wrote from prison that in the midst of this disaster: "Only a suffering God can help." They developed the powerful symbol of the suffering God who endures and is defeated with those who suffer. This symbol opens up the idea that God takes the pain of the world into the divine being in order there to redeem it. Taking a different tack, Metz, among others such as Edward Schillebeeckx, envisioned a God of deep compassion who stands in solidarity with those who suffer, although suffering does not enter the divine being as such. Whichever symbol they chose, these political theologians glimpsed a God of overwhelming *pathos* whose presence enables hope even in the midst of brutal death.

In exploring this idea, political theologians found the work of Jewish religious scholar Abraham Heschel to be highly valuable. Heschel, who dedicated his book *The Prophets* "To the martyrs of 1940–45," saw that the biblical prophets such as Isaiah, Jeremiah, and Amos were riveted by a glimpse of God's heart, which burned with care. It was this view that gave them the strength to proclaim, in God's name, their biting critique of social evil and hopeful consolation for the afflicted. Heschel characterizes this divine care for the world as "pathos." As a term, pathos signifies a kind of suffering feeling; it is the root of the word "a-pathetic," meaning without feeling, as well as its opposite, "sym-pathetic," meaning with feeling for others in their troubles. In the prophetic texts of the Bible, God is a God of pathos who feels intensely: loves, cares, is glad, gets angry over injustice, urges, prods, forgives, is disappointed, gets frustrated, suffers righteous indignation, weeps, grieves, promises, pours out mercy, rejoices, consoles, wipes away tears, and loves some more. Pathos, then, is a central symbol of the prophets' understanding of God. It serves as a theological category of God's living care in dynamic relation to Israel, a code for the covenanting God's participation in the life story of the world.

Knowing that this view of God stands in profound contrast to modern theism, Heschel employs a traditional scholarly template to explore the difference. According to this template, Christian thought about God follows one of two routes: Greek or Hebrew. The Greek way is steeped in reason and philosophy, while the Hebrew way traces the historical revelation at the core of biblical religion. There are many nuances that fudge this division, making it less clean than it first appears. Greek Hellenism, for instance, seeped into Jewish consciousness and can be found in the later writings of the Hebrew Bible. Still, to get a broad picture, the template serves to clarify two genuinely different methods that come up with different results. One key difference lies in how they evaluate feeling, especially the emotion that results from being affected by another.

⚜ The Greek philosophical pattern has a strong tendency toward dualism, driving a wedge between spirit and matter. What pertains to spirit is higher in value and closer to the divine, while what pertains to matter drags the spirit down to the messiness of earth. Applied to human beings, this pattern of thought privileges the immortal soul and its reasoning power, while the body and its emotions are devalued as closer to the realm of change and, ultimately, to death. In this view, God, being pure Spirit, is totally above the fray, beyond all emotion. Possessing all perfections in an unimaginable way, the divine nature has no possibility for change, cannot be affected by the world, and, of course, cannot suffer. Divine dignity depends on this. The ideal for human beings is likewise a self-conquest that will enable people to control their passions and dwell in the untroubled realm of spirit.

⚜ The Hebrew historical pattern, by contrast, entails a nondualistic view of creation. Thus, emotion, although perhaps embarrassing to the stoic temperament, is every bit as spiritually valuable as thought. In this view the overwhelmingly transcendent God freely becomes active in history, covenants with a people, and through word and deed is encountered as the One who is passionately related to what goes on. Thereby it is revealed that God's own self is caring, loving, involved. The ideal for human beings who are made in this divine image is to be conformed to God's heart by a sympathetic involvement in the joys and turmoil of history. The real opposite to being God-like in this model lies not in being passionate but in being indifferent. To be moved by suffering and to relate to those in need with compassion is to be theomorphic, conformed to God's image.

Far from fitting into the philosophical model, the God of the Bible is a God of pathos. To protect divine freedom, Heschel reflects that pathos is not a *necessary* divine attribute, one that belongs to the eternal God as infinite. But in view of Israel's history it is *in fact* how God freely chooses to respond to the human dilemma, namely, with sympathetic engagement. Pathos has the quality of an ethical category, a stance of living care. To say that God is compassionate, feelingly and concretely concerned, is to say that God cares passionately about human well-being for all, which includes especially those ground down as victims of historic injustice. Hence, to call God a God of pathos is not a psychological claim but a theological one. Like all theological language it is inadequate. But it is not false as a way to illuminate God's compassion.

This Jewish theology of divine pathos provided an inviting way for Christian theology to approach the idea of God in relation to suffering. For at the heart of Christian faith is the belief that in the advent of Jesus Christ God's compassion became ever more intimate, sharing the pain of the world in the flesh. Political theology ventures this interpretation. Focusing intensely on the cross and resurrection of Christ, it finds there the revelation of God's compassion poured out.

Central Vision

Christians remember that Jesus suffered under Pontius Pilate, was crucified, died, and was buried. In the midst of the physical torment of this Roman form of execution, he also endured spiritual agony, conveyed in that unforgettable, anguished cry from the cross, "*My God, My God, why have you forsaken me?*" (Mark 15:34). In the midst of this hell, where was God?

Christian tradition is constant in insisting that the mystery of God is profoundly connected to this event. The cross signifies that God, who is love, whose will stands in contrast to such misery, nevertheless freely plunges into the midst of the pain and tastes its bitterness to the bitter end in order to save.

Faith pivots on the belief that by the power of the Spirit Jesus died not into nothingness, into annihilation, but into the embrace of the living God. In solidarity with this victim, God encompassed him with loving power that ultimately transformed him into new life. We cannot imagine this, but the heart of faith breaks forth in the exclamation, "Christ is risen. Alleluia!" This is not a new chapter that erases what went before. As Metz declares, "Whoever hears the message of the resurrection of Christ in such a way that the cry of the crucified has become inaudible in it, hears not the Gospel but rather a myth." The resurrection opens up a future for the crucified one. Far from being good news about his personal destiny alone, this event pledges a future of life for all who go down into the darkness of death.

Political theology interprets this event in the framework of hope for the whole world at the end of time, referred to in theology as the "eschaton" and reflected upon in a field called "eschatology." Here it draws on the wisdom of ancient Israel's history with God, which cannot be underestimated as a vital source of wisdom for Christian faith and theology. In trying to annihilate the Jewish people, the Nazis were also destroying their religion, which would have taken the indispensable ground out from under the feet of Christian believers. For not only did the Jewish people encounter the God of pathos in the midst of their turbulent history, always under threat. They also understood God to be the One who will wrap history up, establishing justice and bringing all to fulfillment at the end of time.

This victorious vision flows from the Hebrew scriptures through the New Testament, which ends with the expectant cry *Maranatha*, "Come, Lord," full of desire for the moment when the new dwelling of God among people will wipe away all tears, and death and mourning shall cease, and all things will be made new (Rev 22:20 and 21:1–5). In the face of the mystery of suffering, political theology affirms: time will end. God, to whom time belongs, has set boundaries to it. The future, as with the whole universe, is in God's hands, and those hands are caring, sustaining, consoling, wiping away tears. We can, then, dare to hope for salvation, not only for ourselves but also for all the defeated and the dead with their unspeakable suffering.

Israel's history with God has given birth to this great promise. But all the evidence is not yet in; the divine response to suffering has not yet fully appeared. It has made a down payment in the resurrection of Jesus, but the fulfillment is up ahead, at the end. Thus, an eschatological proviso must qualify all our assertions, lest triumphalism lead to forgetfulness of the cross. Even in the light of biblical revelation, we walk by faith, not by sight. This faith risks the hope that YHWH is a God of both the living and the dead who does not abandon anyone in their defeat. Without this hope the whole Christian project falls flat. "For discourse about God is either about a vision and promise of universal justice, touching even the sufferings of the past," Metz writes, "or it is empty and void of promise, even for those alive today."

The presence of the living God in the cross and resurrection of Jesus interpreted in this global-historical perspective awakens a daring kind of hope. This in turn has a wholly social significance, stimulating solidarity with all who suffer now in this world and inspiring participation in the divine work of bringing life where degradation and suffering grind people down. Against weariness, discouragement, and the desire to forget, those who follow Jesus are moved to act continuously and responsibly with practical and critical intent. Resisting what damages people, they set about working without violence or hatred for a world of goodness and grace even in the teeth of contrary forces.

Furthering this theological approach, each of the aforementioned trio of Germans contributed a distinctive idea that fleshes out the idea of the God of pathos surfacing in post-Holocaust political theology.

THE CRUCIFIED GOD

Christian reflection has always held that there is a real sense in which the cross reveals a crucified God. Insofar as Jesus who is crucified is the Word incarnate, his suffering is the suffering of God with us. But this same theology also traditionally holds that the Word of God suffered only in his human nature, the divine nature being infinitely beyond such passion. Moltmann pushes beyond this limitation to locate suffering in the very being of

God. Pressing Luther's bold phrase newly into service, he proposes the idea of "the crucified God," which entails that God really suffers with all who suffer in this world. To explain this he composes a midrash, an imaginative gloss, on the event of the crucifixion.

To begin with, he proposes, we need to understand that the being of God is self-giving love. The event where this love most profoundly showed itself is the death and resurrection of Jesus Christ. The kernel of theological significance in this event lies in the riveting, appalling, unforgettable cry of Jesus on the cross, *"My God, My God, why have you forsaken me?"* (Matt 27:46). How should we think about God from the godforsakenness of the cross? Rather than explaining this away, we should hear it literally. This terrible cry reveals that on the cross something is going on between God and God. Handed over by his Father for the sake of sinners, the Son is rejected and actually abandoned by God. He suffers violence and dies a godforsaken death.

Moltmann dares a further step. While his Son is dying on the cross, God the Father suffers too, but not in the same way. The Father suffers the loss of his Son, experiencing infinite grief. There is total separation between them; they are lost to each other. At the same time, however, they have never been so close. They are united in a deep community of will, each willing to do this for love of the world. As a result, the Holy Spirit who is love, the Spirit of their mutual love, flows out into the broken, sinful world. Their Spirit justifies the godless, rescues the abandoned, befriends the lonely, fills the forsaken with love, brings the dead alive, and guarantees that no one will ever again die godforsaken because Christ is already there in the depths of abandonment.

The cross opens up a great fissure in God's own being, the Father abandoning, the Son being abandoned. In so doing, the cross not only plunges God deep into the suffering of the world. It also opens a reverse pathway on which suffering travels back into God, there to be redeemed. "Only if all disaster, forsakenness by God, absolute death, the infinite curse of damnation and sinking into nothingness is in God's own self, is community with this God eternal salvation," Moltmann writes. The whole uproar of history with all of its dilemmas and its despairs continues to enter into divine being through the pathway of the cross, there to be redeemed into the joyful future which God alone can open up.

A few caveats are needed to make this midrash work. God truly suffers, but this is not the same kind of suffering that humans experience. In our case suffering comes upon us as a result of our finite deficiencies. We are overtaken by suffering as though by an alien force; it descends unasked, and we bear it under constraint. By contrast, suffering does not come upon God by necessity or by chance. The crucified God freely chooses to suffer with us, and does so actively out of the fullness of love. It is this suffering love in the midst of history that bears the world toward the fullness of resurrected life. The cross reveals God's inner nature to be the trinitarian event of self-giving love capable of suffering, thereby releasing the Spirit who fills all creation with life. Every time we make the sign of the cross while reciting the names of the trinitarian persons we testify to this truth.

The Holocaust was never far from Moltmann's mind as he worked out this thesis. Here the theology of the suffering God receives its deepest significance: "there cannot be any other Christian answer to the question of this torment. To speak here of a God who could not suffer would make God a demon." In no way does this mean that the death camps can be justified. To the contrary, in relationship with the God of pathos we become compassionate resisters to all that desecrates and violates human beings. Far from inducing political passivity, in the end it is only the cross itself that seems able to bear up our active hope, so liable to drown in sorrow. With the resurrection of the gassed, the murdered, and the dead, God will turn this sorrow into eternal joy. Sustained by this hope, our desire to work for a better world flickers on. "God in Auschwitz and Auschwitz in the crucified God—that is the basis for a real hope which both embraces and overcomes the world, and the ground for a love which is stronger than death and can sustain death."

THE SILENT CRY

The relation of God to the mystery of suffering takes on a distinctly different cast in Soelle's work. While supporting the symbol of the suffering God, she is critical of Moltmann's narrative midrash. Yes, as opposed to the tradition of the a-pathic God and the concomitant ideal of a human life without tears, it is right to emphasize that God became poor, suffering, and defenseless on the cross out of love. But the idea that Jesus was deliberately handed over and abandoned by his Father to the fate of death is intolerable. When you think about it, what kind of Father is this? A sadist. Even Abraham drew back from killing his own son. This construal of the cross blames the Father for what in fact was done to Jesus by the history of human injustice. It schools people in patterns of thought that regard sadistic behavior as legitimate. When translated into spirituality, it encourages them to worship the executioner.

In crafting a way forward, Soelle argues that the suffering of the cross is not a sado-masochistic symbol of the relationship between Father and Son. Still, the antagonistic nature of reality means that suffering in this world is real. Against our cultural apathy we need to face it, articulate it, learn from it, and indict it. In this context, the cross shows that God is always suffering with the one who is suffering. We are called to join God there, to leave sadness and despair behind in serving the cause of life. Then the theodicy question becomes superseded in the mystical-resistance pattern of our lives of love.

Soelle makes a major contribution to the question of suffering with her work on divine power. Her journey through three theological positions offers a unique look at the possibilities: she went from classical theism's omnipotent Father who requires obedience, to the powerless God on the cross who models the impotence of love, to the crucified and risen Christ in whom the divine victory of life over death empowers our own participation in God's power of life.

First, in view of tradition's presentation of the omnipotent God, she queries why it is that the church encourages human beings to love and honor a God whose most important attribute is power, whose prime act is to subjugate, whose greatest fear is independence. This outsized father figure is really no more than a projection of men's fantasy of domination. It is imperialism writ large. Her wartime experience comes into play: "What comes to my mind when I think of male power? Yelling, giving orders, shooting . . . ." Submission and obedience to such a God destroys our potential as human beings to grow, be creative, take initiative. Speaking as a German after Nazism, Soelle maintains that far from being a virtue, obedience itself is a huge problem.

So she next curtailed omnipotence in her idea of God in order to emphasize the idea of selfless love. The cross stands at the center of this view. The Christian assumption that we recognize God most clearly in the figure of someone tortured to death goes completely against our fixation on power and domination. Shown in the gospels to be the man for others, Jesus has only his love. This leads him to die powerless on the cross, with no armies, no magic tricks to rescue him. His love is a nonviolent, weaponless power, and we are saved by loving in the same powerless way. Soon, however, this understanding of the cross in the language of powerless love raised problems of its own. For one thing, it can lead to a terrible passivity in the face of the world's suffering. For another, it does not tell the whole story. Christians believe in the resurrection too, which if it is anything is an event of God's power.

So Soelle kept thinking. She came finally to the realization that rather than being a dominating force or an ineffective form of love, divine power is a creative, noncompelling, life-giving good. This is power that flows through relationships bringing others to life, power as love. A homely analogy would be the power of the grass pushing up through cracks in the asphalt, a surge of life. In raising Jesus from the dead, God acted creatively and typically with this power. This was not a one-time act that gifted Jesus with a personal privilege for himself alone. It contains within itself hope for all, for everything, even the dead. "In this sense the resurrection of Christ is a tremendous distribution of power. The women who were the first to experience it were given a share in the power of life. It was the tremendous certainty of God that now entered their life," and their witness triggered the flow of this confidence in others. Divine power, then, is the silent cry of life in the midst of suffering.

None of this Christian theologizing is meant to remove the terror of the Holocaust of the Jews: "No heaven can justify Auschwitz." But the God who shared in the suffering and death of the cross and brought the power of life to bear in the resurrection of Jesus Christ was there, suffering in the death camps. Language about the suffering God who raises the dead to life is language about the power of God that seeks justice on behalf of those defrauded of their lives. Loving this God, sharing in the divine power to create life, gives us the possibility of a meaningful life of dedication to justice for others. And here, for Soelle, is the point: we can know God's love only when we become a part of it ourselves. We can know the God of compassion only in committed resistance to every form of unjust suffering inflicted on others.

PASSION FOR GOD

Metz parts company with Moltmann and Soelle in thinking that the symbol of a suffering God would help. This symbol, he thinks, offers too easy an answer. Among other problems, it eternalizes suffering by placing it in God; it gives suffering a certain splendor, making it secretly beautiful; it sneaks past the radical dissonance between God and suffering, reconciling them too smoothly; soothing our questions, it discharges the tension set up by the cries of the victims. In truth, there is no appropriate symbol, no tidy answer. Instead, theology should protect the radical question of suffering, clear a space for it, shelter it so it might continue to cry out in history and irritate our thought. Toward that end, Metz proposes two intertwined steps: remembering and lamenting unto God.

Remembering
"Do this in remembrance of me." At the center of Christian life is the memory of the life, passion, death, and resurrection of Jesus Christ. This becomes obvious in every eucharistic liturgy, where the central act recalls Jesus' self-giving the night before he died, a remembering that makes this self-giving present again through sacramental bread and wine. The primacy of the memory of the passion in christology and liturgy indicates that the kind of reasoning theology needs to use on the problem of suffering is not transcendental, the approach Metz learned from his teacher Rahner, but reasoning guided by narrative memory and solidarity. Metz introduces the category of "danger" to explore the dynamism at work here. Given Jesus Christ's solidarity with all of humanity, the pivotal act of remembering his death and resurrection brings in its wake the memory of all who suffer unjustly in history. Crosses keep on being set up in the world; the cry of abandonment echoes down through the centuries. To be faithful, theology remembers the cross of Jesus in solidarity with all the dead and those who suffer now in our world. Given that the crucified one is risen, remembering entails burning hope for their future.

Why is this dangerous? Breaking through our amnesia, remembering the victims has a double effect. First, by keeping alive their story against the inclination of tyrants to bury it, it robs the masters of their victory. History is written by the victors, who strut about as if the dead over whom they climbed did not count. But memory keeps the reality of their lives alive, in protest against their defeat and in commitment to their unfinished agenda. Second, by connecting their story with that of Jesus, memory awakens the realization that each one of them is precious, galvanizing hope that in God's good time they too will be justified. What there is at present, the victory of those who murder and harm, is not the last word. And so is set up a social counterforce to apathy; we do not act as if we were defeated by evil.

It is not accidental that in Metz's theology the practice of dangerous memory bests Marxism. Ascendant in European academic circles at the time, Marxist philosophy was content to forget the dead and leave their sufferings unrequited in the march of progress toward happiness for others. However, "ultimately no prosperity of the descendants can make up for the suffering of ancestors, and no amount of social progress can reconcile the injustice which befell the dead." Only universal justice, which is the final gift of God, can heal and save. Obviously, then, this is not a nostalgic kind of memory, but memory with the seed of the future in it. The dangerous memory of past suffering stimulates a hope for the future for all the defeated and the dead. In fact, Christians can risk looking into this abyss of pain precisely because they believe in God's eschatological promise. On the strength of this promise, dangerous remembering challenges modern society which tries to anesthetize people against the sufferings of others with a culture of consumerism, happy optimism, and breathtaking banality that irons all sympathy flat. In place of this trite form of life, it impels people of faith to a meaningful life through action that resists unjust, domineering actions that are creating a new generation of victims.

Lamenting

Dangerously remembering the dead in solidarity with their suffering and hope of future blessing needs to be accompanied by a mysticism of lamenting unto God. There is no positive meaning in unjust radical suffering that destroys persons. We must take the full measure of its negativity, refuse to ignore or spiritualize or glorify it. Then this affliction becomes a live question that must be addressed to God. In prayer we cry out, protest, lament, shout indignation, say this should not be. In its own way this prayer is a "suffering unto God," an active engagement with God uttered in anguished hope that there will be an answer. Rather than settle for neat theoretical solutions, it keeps the question open, living with the "not yet" of history while insisting on the promise of God.

Unfortunately this type of prayer has been excised from contemporary liturgical texts. One never laments or cries out in anguish during standard Eucharists. Such lamenting, however, fills the Bible in psalms and prophetic texts, wisdom writings and gospels. Metz finds the story of Job to be one of the best guides. Suffering an avalanche of troubles, his children dead, business ruined, body diseased, Job receives a visit from three friends. They mouth the standard explanation that his affliction is a punishment for sin and urge him to admit it so God will relent. Job refuses. Instead, he protests his innocence unto God. Over and over he presses his question why, insisting that God should answer, all the while clinging to the hope that he would be redeemed. Metz underscores the amazing point that in the end God affirms that it is Job, not his friends, who spoke rightly of God (42:7). It is no accident that Jesus' God-mysticism as heard in his final cry *"Why . . . ?"* is also part of this tradition. So too, suffering of past and present must drive us toward God protesting, complaining, lamenting, grieving, crying out of the depths, insistently questioning *"How long, O Lord?"* Rather than settling for rational explanations, lamenting unto God, unto *God* in spite of everything, keeps hope alive. Such prayer has the capacity to nurture ongoing resistance to the victimization of others, past and present.

Mystical and practical, Christian life then becomes a passion for God that encompasses the suffering, the passion, of others, committing people to resistance against injustice for the living in hope of universal justice even for the dead. The mystery of iniquity is not thereby resolved. Theological reasoning remains unreconciled to the surd of evil. It keeps on judging: this should not be. But God is love and has promised to prove it. The dangerous memory of the crucified and risen Jesus in solidarity with all the dead keeps the question open while laying down a hopeful, compassionate path for mature discipleship. Thus has Metz proposed that we speak of God with our face rather than our back turned to the terrible event of Auschwitz.

MYSTICAL-POLITICAL DISCIPLESHIP

The world is brittle, fragmentary, obscure, discordant, and opaque—in a word, sinful. The Holocaust and all other acts past and present that allow evil full play send the presence of God into eclipse. Peoples' lives become a hell. There is no logical or theological answer to the mystery of this suffering but there is a mystical-political way to live that goes on opening a pathway through the history of suffering. People can decide to oppose these wrongs in the public sphere, to practice justice and kindness, to aim at beauty and a full table of life's good for all. Within the anguished human context this brings a kind of meaning.

Post-Holocaust European political theology blazed a trail in this direction. The massive, unjust suffering of the Shoah broke into Christianity's usual way of thinking, shattering its received tradition and precipitating a religious crisis. The trio of theologians described here, among others, understood that this catastrophe belongs to the inner situation of Christian discourse about God. Starting with Auschwitz in particular and then widening their concern to the whole history of suffering, they formulated the God-question in its most contested form: from the perspective of those vanquished by unjust suffering. Agreed that even religion cannot answer the question, they pioneered a pattern of thinking and acting that honors the mystery of God in memory and hope. Whether one adopts the symbol of the crucified God, or the silent cry of life, or the compassionate God of promise to whom one laments, their work brings divine presence indelibly into the darkness of suffering that cries to heaven.

FOR FURTHER READING

There is no better introduction into the suffering of the Holocaust than the testimony by the young survivor, later Nobel Peace Prize winner, Elie Wiesel, *Night* (New York: Bantam Books, 1986; originally 1960). Jewish religious responses to the Holocaust are clearly laid out in Dan Cohn Sherbok, *Holocaust Theology* (London: Lamp Press, 1989). Christian wrestlings with the issue are collected in Elisabeth Schüssler Fiorenza and David Tracy, eds., *Holocaust as Interruption* (*Concilium* vol. 175; Edinburgh: T&T Clark, 1984); and Steven Jacobs, ed. *Contemporary Christian Religious Responses to the Shoah* (Lanham, Md.: University Press of America, 1993).

Abraham Heschel's influential discussion of the biblical God of pathos can be found in *The Prophets* (New York: Harper & Row, 1962).

The trio of German theologians discussed in this chapter have all published many books. The best place to begin reading their theology is with the single works enumerated here, from which the quotations in this chapter are also taken: Jürgen Moltmann, *The Crucified God: The Cross of Christ as the Foundation and Criticism of Christian Theology* (New York: Harper & Row, 1974), especially chapter 6; Dorothee Soelle, *Suffering* (Philadelphia: Fortress, 1975); and Johann Baptist Metz, *A Passion for God: The Mystical-Political Dimension of Christianity* (New York: Paulist, 1998); Matthew Ashley's introductory essay "Reading Metz" (pp. 7–21) is especially illuminating.

For the history of Christian teaching on God and suffering, see John Hick, *Evil and the God of Love* (New York: Harper & Row, 1978). A strong critique of the Enlightenment theodicy project coupled with theologizing from the perspective of the victims is presented by Terrence Tilley, *The Evils of Theodicy* (Washington, D.C.: Georgetown University Press, 1991). For contemporary wrestling with the issues, see John Thiel, *God, Evil, and Innocent Suffering: A Theological Reflection* (New York: Crossroad, 2002); and Jon Sobrino, *Where Is God? Earthquake, Terrorism, Barbarity, and Hope* (Maryknoll, N.Y.: Orbis Books, 2004).

4

LIBERATING GOD OF LIFE

CONTEXT: WRETCHED POVERTY

Consider the discovery that has burst on the world thanks to the encounter with God in the church of the poor. Pioneered in Latin America where it was first articulated as liberation theology, this view is now being expounded in Africa and Asia as well as by minority groups in economically developed countries, such as African American Christians in the United States. The original context is twofold: massive suffering due to poverty, coupled with struggle for the relief called justice. On this frontier it becomes clear that a particular care for the poor, for those being pressed toward a premature, unjust death, characterizes the living God whose heart is turned with mercy toward those who are oppressed by systemic forces.

Poverty, in the material sense of sheer lack of the physical necessities of life, is a brutal fact that afflicts millions upon millions of people in this world. Social analysis makes clear that this impoverishment cannot be attributed to indolence or vice on the part of the groups so afflicted. Neither is it a situation that has been produced randomly or by chance. Rather, in Latin America it is the result of historical decisions made by conquering European powers in the sixteenth century and continued by their descendants. These decisions had exploitation woven into their very fabric. They set up political, economic, and cultural institutions that de-humanized the indigenous peoples. As Archbishop Oscar Romero of San Salvador explained, over time individual egoisms carrying out the policies of the powerful crystallized into permanent social structures that in turn exerted oppressive power over the great majorities. Some few people benefit from these systems. Vast masses of people pay the price with lives of inhuman affliction.

For centuries the Catholic Church, which arrived with the Europeans, was complicit in this situation of injustice. Its official preaching and teaching favored those who ruled, despite outstanding individuals who excelled in charity toward the poor. In 1968 at a continental synod held in Medellín, Colombia, the Latin American bishops made the question of poverty and its causes, along with poor people themselves, the central focus of their teaching for the first time. Taking note of the many studies that describe the misery that beset large numbers in all their countries, they passed judgment with prophetic words: "That misery, as a collective fact, expresses itself as injustice which cries to the heavens." The salvific mission entrusted to the church by Christ requires commitment to redress this dire poverty out of love for our suffering brothers and sisters.

After a decade of ferment that saw this commitment being carried out at the popular, pastoral, and professional levels, the bishops at a second synod in Puebla, Mexico (1979) forthrightly declared, "we brand the situation of inhuman poverty in which millions of Latin Americans live as the most devastating and humiliating kind of scourge." Underscoring the systemic nature of this poverty and its unjust, sinful roots, they judged it to be a great scandal and a contradiction to Christian existence. Why? Because it is an instrument of *death*. Lack of food and drinkable water, lack of housing, education, and health care, exploitative wages or lack of employment opportunities, all add up to short lives of misery that give the lie to human dignity. In addition to material deprivation, poverty also means being marginalized from the corridors of power where decisions are made that affect the conditions of one's life. Social powerlessness, lack of political rights, and restrictions on freedom of expression conspire to maintain the status quo. This poverty, sedimented in death-dealing economic and political structures, constitutes a type of "institutionalized violence" that disrespects human worth. Death comes early to large numbers of infants. Death comes slowly, by inches, to young people and adults because the most basic needs of life are thwarted. And death comes quickly regardless of age, by overt violence, given the military repression necessary to maintain this structured inequity.

The Puebla Document painted word pictures of the faces of the poor to make the crisis graphic and concrete. The poor include the faces of young children, struck down by poverty in the womb that afflicts them with mental and physical deficiencies; the faces of vagrant children in the cities, often sexually exploited, sometimes murdered; the faces of young people, frustrated by lack of opportunity to build a future and robbed of hope in their own existence; the faces of indigenous peoples (Indians), disrespected and marginalized into situations where they can barely exist; the faces of peasants deprived of their land; the faces of ill-paid laborers and unemployed persons who have no options; the faces of women, old before their time in the struggle to feed their families, discriminated against because of their gender, or trafficked and prostituted; the faces of African Americans, descendants of slaves scorned because of their race; the faces of overcrowded dwellers in city slums whose lack of material goods is cruelly contrasted with the ostentatious wealth flaunted by others in the city; the faces of old people, cast off as no longer productive. Multiply by millions: an outrage that cries to heaven.

The world of the poor is more richly complex than this litany would suggest. Where communities hold together, this encompassing world also entails a way of being human, of thinking and loving, of sharing and being hospitable, of praying and believing in God. Daily struggles for survival manifest potent, tensile human strength. The characteristic communal way of celebrating expresses profound hope in life given as a good gift. Yet when the World Bank publishes data showing that worldwide there are twenty-five thousand children who die of starvation each day and more than one billion people who live on less than one dollar a day, a critical judgment becomes inescapable. The ship of concentrated poverty, built by systems that plunder the many to feed the wealth of the few and kept afloat by the denial of basic human rights, is laden with a cargo of grinding misery and cruel death. Thus depicted, poor people are the "underside" of history. They are "nonpersons" who count least or not at all. Not only in Latin America but among the six-plus billion people on this planet, their name is legion.

INTUITION OF GOD'S PRESENCE AND ACTION

Traditional Christian doctrine presented God as the Supreme Being who made all things and governed the world the way an all-powerful king ruled his realm, with authority. Although it did not address the question of grievous poverty, this teaching assumed that the situation, like all suffering, was somehow permitted by God's will. While the rich were encouraged to be charitable toward the poor, poor people were led to understand that bearing their suffering with patience, in accord with Christ's sacrifice on the cross, would lead to an eternal reward after they died. The popular customs of Holy Week, when statues of the dead Christ and his sorrowful mother are carried in procession through the streets, express this theology in a graphic way. God is in his heaven; he sent his Son to suffer for us; life is a vale of tears; our sufferings put us on the road to heaven. For poor communities there is a deep religious connection with Christ in his suffering: "he gets it," he knows what people are going through, and from this relationship they draw comfort and strength to struggle on. This theology, however, more often than not inculcates a resigned attitude toward the way things are. There is little motivation to change the social order.

Starting in mid-twentieth-century Brazil and quickly spreading throughout Latin America, a pastoral movement to revitalize faith among poor people began to gather them into small groups. Here they read scripture, prayerfully reflected on its meaning in relation to their situation, and began to act together for change. These *comunidades eclesiales de base*, or communities formed at the base of the church, became sites where poor people made the amazing discovery that they are beloved of God. Consequently, they saw that the immense suffering of poverty is against the divine intent for how beloved people should live. Taking organized action to transform the situation, they began to grasp their identity as active subjects who could shape their own history. In the process, they received the gift of a newly unfolding intuition of an ancient truth, namely, *in situations of misery God is not neutral.* As the Creator and ultimate ruler of this world, the God of life wants all creatures to flourish. When people are ground down, this violates the way God wants the world to be. In response, the living God makes a dramatic decision: to side with oppressed peoples in their struggle for life. In theological shorthand this is known as God's preferential option for the poor. The sole reason for this partiality is divine love, which freely sides with the poor not because they are more saintly or less sinful than others, but because of their situation. The purpose of this divine partiality is to heal, redeem, and liberate the situation so that the dehumanizing suffering will cease. Precisely in this partiality is the goodness of divine love revealed to be truly universal, because it includes the nonpersons whom the powerful and wealthy thought did not count.

"Liberation" becomes the language for exploring this precious, startling insight. God is a liberating God whose signature deeds set people free. Scripture provides compelling warrants.

Hebrew Bible

Liberation theology takes a major cue from the ground-breaking event of the exodus, in which the Israelite people, enslaved in a foreign land, were delivered into freedom. In a surprising way the God of the Hebrews here acts contrary to the usual alliance of deities with kingly power. In the ancient world the gods typically shored up the ruler, justified his status, and was even identified with the king. Instead of siding with the pharaoh of Egypt, however, the God of Abraham and Sarah deploys divine power on the side of the miserable slaves, agitating for their release. Speaking from the burning bush in the desert, the Holy One summons Moses to lead the struggle. The four verbs of this text are utterly revelatory of the heart of God:

> *I have seen the misery of my people who are in Egypt; I have heard their cry because of their taskmasters. I know well what they are suffering; therefore I have come down to deliver them.* (Exod 3:7–8)

The verb "to know" in this litany of divine compassion refers to an experiential rather than an intellectual kind of knowing, being the same verb that was used earlier for sexual intercourse: "*the man knew his wife Eve, and she conceived*" (Gen 4:1). This encounter reveals that the God of Israel sees, hears, and "feels" the affliction of these enslaved people, and so comes to set them free. No wonder the bush was on fire.

Throughout the Old Testament reams of texts bear witness to this truth that God's heart is set on justice for the oppressed. This is true to such an extent that "justice" can be called the love language of the Bible. With biting critique of social evil and consoling assurance of God's deliverance, prophets, psalms, and proverbs summon believers to side with God who sides with the poor. Forget about all those sacrifices in the temple, says the Lord in Isaiah, I am weary of them; but *"cease to do evil, learn to do good; seek justice, rescue the oppressed, defend the orphan, plead for the widow"* (Isa 1:16–17). Even more strongly in Amos, the Lord *hates* the burnt offerings and despises the festival music. What would please the Lord? *"Let justice roll down like waters, and righteousness like an ever-flowing stream"* (Amos 5:24). Not only public worship but private sacrifice such as disciplined fasting is rejected:

> *Is not this the fast that I choose:*
>   *to loose the bonds of injustice,*
>   *to undo the thongs of the yoke,*
>   *to let the oppressed go free*
>   *and to break every yoke?*
> *Is it not to share your bread with the hungry,*
>   *and bring the homeless poor into your house;*
> *when you see the naked, to cover them,*
>   *and not to hide yourself from your own kin?*
> *Then your light shall break forth like the dawn,*
>   *and your healing shall spring up quickly.* (Isa 58:6–8)

This insight into God's passion for the poor is linked with a rich understanding of what it means for God to be Creator. For if God creates the world freely, out of love, then divine glory and honor are at stake in the world's flourishing rather than its twisting up in misery. The human experience of creating out of love—a child, a work of art, a new school, a well of clean water, a beneficial theory—buttresses this idea, for those who create out of love want to see their handiwork thrive. In this light, poverty and oppression thwart divine intent for the world. The organic connection between creating and promoting the good is clear when in one breath Israel praises God:

> *who made heaven and earth,*
>   *the sea, and all that is in them;*
> *who keeps faith forever;*

> *who executes justice for the oppressed;*
> *who gives food to the hungry.* (Ps 146:6-7)

Anyone who says otherwise simply doesn't know the first thing about God. To know the true God as Creator is to understand divine passion for justice:

> *Thus says the Lord: Do not let the wise boast in their wisdom; do not let the mighty boast in their might; do not let the wealthy boast in their wealth; but let those who boast boast in this, that they understand and know me, that I am the Lord; I act with steadfast love, justice, and righteousness in the earth, for in these things I delight.* (Jer 9:23–24)

A simple thought experiment may bring home the depth of this biblical revelation about the nature of God. Is there a single text where in vigorous "thus says the Lord" fashion people are counseled to oppress the poor, to rob from the widow, to put on a big show of sacrifice at the expense of doing justice? Is there a text where God delights in seeing people—or any creatures—in agony? Suffering happens; indeed some texts interpret war and exile as divine punishment for the sin of the people as a whole, sin that includes precisely the acts of oppressing the poor. But even here, God's anger lasts for a moment, divine mercy for ten thousand years. Taken from start to finish, as a whole, the Bible reveals God as compassionate lover of justice, on the side of the oppressed to the point where *"those who oppress the poor insult their Maker"* (Prov 14:31).

New Testament

Liberation theology takes a second major cue from the gospel story of Jesus, whose entire life, death, and resurrection make clear that this same God of the burning bush is faithful in opting especially for those who are marginalized. For Christian faith, this story receives its power from the belief that here the transcendent reality of God draws radically near through incarnation into human flesh. The details of Jesus' historical life, then, matter, for Jesus reveals God's mercy in person. These details are telling. He was born into a poor family, was laid in an animal's feeding trough, and soon became a refugee fleeing from a ruler's murderous violence. In Gustavo Gutiérrez's memorable words, the advent of God in Jesus Christ is "an irruption smelling of the stable." At the outset of his ministry, Luke's gospel depicts Jesus reading from the scroll of Isaiah the following passage:

The Spirit of the Lord is upon me,
because he has anointed me
to brings good news to the poor.
He has sent me to proclaim release to the captives
and recovery of sight to the blind,
to let the oppressed go free,
to proclaim a year of the Lord's favor. (Luke 4:18–19)

What follows is good news in the concrete as sufferings of body and spirit, the evils of hunger and disease, the despair of the scorned religious outcast are met and transformed. The Messiah heals the sick, exorcizes demons, forgives sinners, and practices table companionship so inclusive that it gives scandal. Encounter with Jesus makes divine love experientially available to all who will listen, and in particular to the poor, the despised, the weak, those for whom living is a heavy burden. Illuminated by his thought-provoking parables centered on the reign of God, these merciful actions destabilize the prevailing norms of who is first and who is last. And they establish beyond doubt divine identification with those who lack basic necessities: "*I was hungry and you gave me to eat . . . I was hungry and you gave me no food*" (Matt 25:31–46). Neglect of "the least of these" means turning your back on God.

Nor are these blessings given only to men. In the Latin American culture strongly marked by *machismo*, poor women in the base ecclesial communities listen for a word that they too are included despite beliefs and practices that reduce them to insignificance. Biblical scholar Elsa Tamez enriches the picture by pointing out that glad tidings came to women not as a second thought in addition to Jesus' interaction with poor and oppressed men, but to both in equal measure, with attention to women's specific situation: to the widow mourning the death of her son, "*Do not weep*" (Luke 7:13); to the woman hemorrhaging, "*Daughter, your faith has made you well*" (Mark 5:34); to the foreigner seeking healing for her daughter, "*Woman, great is your faith*" (Matt 15:28); to the adulteress about to be stoned, "*Neither do I condemn you*" (John 8:11); to the faithful disciple weeping at his grave, "*Woman, why are you weeping?*" (John 20:13). Deeply affected not only by poverty but also by the sin of sexism in the structures of church and society, women, the excluded among the excluded, realize that God's preferential option for the poor is an option for poor women. In a context where they are reduced to insignificance they struggle on, as Ivone Gebara describes, hoping against hope that the last word on their lives will not be that of Pharaoh and his chariots but that of the liberating God of life.

As in the exodus story, Jesus' own bitter suffering and violent death dramatically reveal the God of Israel's option to be with the outcast. Rather than endorsing the judgment of the mighty rulers who found him guilty, God stands on the side of this particular crucified victim, unjustly executed by the power of the state. Precisely where one would not expect to find divinity—amid torture, weakness, suffering, and death—the gospel locates compassionate divine presence. The Holy One sees, hears, knows well what is being suffered on the cross, and comes to deliver. Even death is in God's hands.

The resurrection of Jesus to new life in the Spirit signals the liberating God's solidarity with this crucified one, and not only with him. The Easter *Alleluia* rings out because this deed is a saving activity of the God of life that anticipates what the future will be for all people and the cosmos itself. Read through the eyes of the poor, this event receives a special resonance. Not just anyone is raised, but Jesus, who lived in solidarity with the poor and as a consequence was unjustly crucified. In its historical context, the resurrection signals a victory not only of divine power over death but also of divine love over injustice. *Ecce homo*: behold the emaciated, tear-stained, terrified, face of Christ, desecrated in the masses of the world's poor, the crucified peoples. Precisely because God has raised this Jesus who was crucified, the crucified peoples of history can have hope. The resurrection irrevocably pledges that there will be a blessed future for all the violated and the dead, cast off as if their lives had no meaning.

THE GOD OF LIFE

In light of this history of revelation, liberation theology articulates a radical realization: liberation is the signature deed of the saving action of God in history. To liberate is to give life, life in its totality. Consequently it becomes clear that God does not want humankind to suffer degradation. Far from happening according to a divine decree, the sufferings of poor, oppressed, and marginal peoples are contrary to divine intent. The dehumanizing and death-dealing structures that create and maintain such degradation are instances of social sin. They transgress against the God of life, who creates the world out of love and glories when the beloved creation flourishes rather than when it is violated.

This rediscovery of the God of life is awash in the church-of-the-poor's experience that God is one who protects and defends those who have least life, journeying with them through history, at their side in their suffering, sustaining their struggle, awakening courage and hope. "We were discovering that God was different from what we had been taught," writes Luz Beatriz Arellano. "We were discovering God as the God of life, closer to us, as one who journeys with us through history . . . one who is immensely concerned for the poor and for the least, for those who have been left unattended, and it gave us a deep hope and a deep sense of having found something new." This is the axis that underpins biblical revelation, the poor have realized, the thread that runs through it as a whole.

On this frontier, liberation theology has explored the understanding of the God of life using creative interpretations of two traditional motifs: idolatry and mystery.

The True God against Idols

For decades the concern of European church leaders and theologians has focused on persons whose faith is threatened by the acid of secular, atheistic culture. In Latin America, by contrast, the focus is not on the nonbeliever struggling for faith but on the nonperson struggling for life. Here the central question is not whether God exists but how to believe in God amid such inhuman suffering. How does the church preach the God of love to people who are being crushed? The quest for an answer moves theology to proclaim the true God of life against false idols.

"*I am the Lord your God . . . you shall have no other gods before me*" (Exod 20:2–3). Idolatry entails putting alien gods before the true God of the Bible, worshiping something that is not divine. In the Latin American situation these gods are money, the comforts it brings, and the power necessary to make and keep it. Starting with the *conquistadores* and continuing for five centuries through successive ruling systems up to multinational corporations today, greed has divinized money and its trappings, that is, turned them into an absolute. Core transgressions against the first commandment have set up a belief system so compelling that it might be called money-theism, in contrast to monotheism.

Like all false gods, money and its trappings require the sacrifice of victims. Whether the poor are offered up indirectly through the economic conditions necessary to produce profit, or directly through the violence necessary to sustain these conditions, their lives are the sacrifice. What is most insidious is the way traditional preaching and theology put a superficial veneer of Christian belief over the face of these idols, naming God a king and lord objectively ruling the world. Neutral in the face of injustice, the racist, sexist, classist image of God perverts the actual contours of the living God of the Bible in the service of moneyed interests. This idolatrous image of God manipulates the God of the exodus, the God of Jesus Christ, into an ersatz deity of the oppressors, who then take the Lord's name in vain to justify their ways. "By deforming God we protect our own egotism," Juan Luis Segundo contends with startling insight. "Our falsified and inauthentic ways of dealing with our fellow human beings are allied to our falsification of the idea of God. Our unjust society and our perverted idea of God are in close and terrible alliance." The truth about God is twisted to justify human oppression, and companion creatures are demeaned in the name of a distorted view of divine will.

Revealed in a privileged way in the world of the underprivileged, the God of life liberates with an outstretched arm, does justice, faithfully defends the poor, and exposes the idolatrous character of construals of deity that deal death. The liberating God of the poor conflicts with "the god of the lords," and with the structural sin in which oblivious religious discourse and practices of dominant groups are embedded. If God is indeed Love, and if this Love is active in history to redeem from sin and death, then in situations where people encounter death, where they are impoverished and dehumanized, the divine option to see, hear, know, and come to deliver results in God's abiding, suffering, toiling, and pouring forth power in solidarity with the struggle for life. This rediscovery of the God of liberation and justice for the oppressed has been an ongoing joyful treasure in the experience of the church of the poor and contrasts profoundly with the deity who would inculcate punishment and passive resignation, the idol imposed by dominant groups in society and church. On this frontier a profound challenge goes forth to the whole church: stop trivializing the scandalous state-ments that scripture makes about God.

The God of Holy Mystery

God is not reducible to our manner of understanding but soars beyond-human imagination and our ability to comprehend or control. Traditional theology pegged this "always-ever-greater" quality of the divine to the lim-ited character of human intellect and will, which, being finite by nature, sim-ply cannot encompass the infinite. The modern European theology of Rahner and others connected divine incomprehensibility to the dynamic drive of the human spirit oriented to the infinite. The frontier of liberation theology opens up a new angle. Here the mystery of God is seen to reside not just at the end of an intellectual process but in the practical scandal of divine love. Divine transcendence as unutterable and unmanipulable mys-tery is not only a truth of reason but also a truth revealed in God's self-manifestation as God of the poor. As María Pilar Aquino dramatically puts it, ineffable mystery "erupts as love, liberating power, and hope among the poor and oppressed of the earth, among the outsiders in society and the church." In a world of power and wealth, who could have imagined this, that God makes an option for the poor, a decision to be in solidarity with their struggle for life? From this perspective the mystery of God must be appreci-ated anew.

Divine predilection for history's last, lowest, and least does not mean that God opts only for the poor. God's love is universal, not exclusive. But it does mean that God has a particular care for those who are suffering injus-tice and seeks to relieve their situation, which also means that in loving the oppressors God calls them to conversion. This insight comes to jubilant expression in Mary's song the *Magnificat*. Newly pregnant with the Messiah, she sings that God her Savior has scattered the proud, brought down the mighty from their thrones, lifted up the lowly, filled the hungry with good things but sent the rich away empty, all in fulfillment of the ancient promise of mercy (Luke 1:50–53). This is a liberating partiality. The goal is not to create a new situation of oppression by reversing who is dominant and who subordinate, but to create a new community on the model of the reign of God preached by Jesus.

Preferential option for the poor signals who ought to get first attention because their suffering is so great. The motive for this divine preference is what gives new color to the notion of God as holy mystery. This motive is nothing less than love, the free, gratuitous, unmerited character of divine love, which generously searches for those whom society marginalizes and which elects to be in solidarity with the weak and abused of history. Precisely through this particularity for the oppressed, God's love is revealed as universal—no one is left out, even the most socially outcast. The incomprehensible mystery of God is love beyond imagining.

FULLY ALIVE

Seeing God as the liberating God of life is a most practical insight, for it enlists the power of the Most High in opposition to whatever mars the divine image in women and men. Wherever persons are caught in the grip of unjust suffering, where the life of multitudes is throttled, gagged, slain, or starved, there the Holy One is to be found, in gracious solidarity with the poor, calling the oppressors to conversion, giving birth to courage for protest, struggling to bring life out of death.

With this vision, Oscar Romero, bishop and martyr, riffed on a famous proverb crafted in the second century by the bishop Irenaeus. In Latin this pithy, mellifluous maxim reads: *Gloria Dei, vivens homo*, which translated means, "the glory of God is the human being fully alive." The glory of God is *homo*, the human being, the whole human race, every individual person, *vivens*, fully alive. God's glory is at stake in the flourishing of people, every single one and all together. How could it be otherwise if the incomprehensible Mystery toward whom the human spirit dynamically tends self-communicates to the world in Jesus and the Spirit as absolute, challenging, sheltering love. In thus choosing to create, save, and dwell within the world, holy mystery has made the world and its inhabitants precious beyond all telling. Harming human beings, inflicting violence or neglecting their good, translates logically into an insult to the Holy One. The two are so tied together, by God's intent, that the glory of the One is at stake in the well-being of all others.

Archbishop Romero rephrased this axiom to declare what a treasure every poor person is in the eyes of God. He preached, *Gloria Dei, vivens pauper*: the glory of God is the *poor person* fully alive—*La gloria de Dios es el pobre que vive*. The claim of connection to God's glory is still made for *homo*, but is now made concrete precisely where abuse occurs. The glory of the liberating God of life is at stake in food, housing, work, land, medical care, education, and human rights for the poor person. By contrast, divine glory is trampled under foot wherever people suffer hunger, destitution, violence, and oppression. The ancient revelation comes alive with new momentum: God is a liberating God of people who loves and redeems their humanity. Faith then becomes the radical conviction that at the heart of the world this kind of love exists as a reality greater than any other, and this must be expressed in praxis that corresponds to God's own heart.

PRACTICE

PRAXIS OF BIBLICAL JUSTICE

Liberation theology has long insisted on the priority of praxis for right thinking. Rather than starting with a correct principle, whether of reason or of faith, you have to be walking as a disciple, placing your feet in the footsteps of Jesus and actively seeking to bring about the reign of God, in order for your thought to be true. Then, like an owl flying forth at dusk, theology arises as a second act that reflects on what has been learned in the heat of the day. This knowledge seeds and fertilizes a new day of praxis in an enriching cycle of ever-deeper understanding.

What praxis arises from the insight into the liberating God of life in the church of the poor? It is the praxis of justice. God simply cannot be separated from the reign of God, from the divine will that all should flourish. Thus, action on behalf of justice where structured inequity abounds and violence rages is a key concrete expression of faith. Situated in the framework of God's gratuitous love, it entails something different from works of charity. Dietrich Bonhoeffer provided a famous example: if a horse and carriage break loose and are careening down a main road running over people, what should one do? Bending over the injured to bind up their wounds is one necessary and noble deed. But to prevent continuing harm, someone has to grab the reins or jam the wheel spokes and stop the horse. The former is the work of charity; the latter, the praxis of justice. The goal is transformation of social structures, which, while it will never usher in the reign of God in a total way, will allow God's reign to arrive in fragments of human flourishing.

I write this in the United States, the wealthiest nation in the world and the world's only remaining military superpower, knowing what a counter-cultural challenge the praxis of justice raises up for myself and all Christians in our culture. One key reason for this is our consumer capitalist culture whose kudzu-like values and practices so crowd the landscape of daily lives that solidarity with others finds precious little ground in which to take root. But consider the champagne glass on the following page, which gives a graphic picture of the current distribution of the world's income.

Liberation theology is a gift from distressed Christians living in the stem of this glass. Jon Sobrino of El Salvador puts it plainly: Quantitatively, the most painful suffering on this planet is constituted by poverty, with death and very specific indignities that accompany it, and this poverty remains the world's most serious wound. While there are enclaves of wealth in poor countries and communities of very poor people in affluent nations, this deep wound appears far more radically in the third world than in the first. Merely by having been born in El Salvador, Haiti, Bangladesh, or Chad, human beings have incomparably less life and dignity than persons born in the United States, Spain, or Japan. "This is the fundamental wound today. And—let us recall it in Christian language—what is wounded is God's very creation."

Ignacio Ellacuría, S.J., the university president murdered for this praxis in 1989, spoke to first world Christians in dramatic words:

> I want you to set your eyes and your hearts on these peoples who are suf-fering so much—some from poverty and hunger, others from oppression and repression. Then (since I am a Jesuit), standing before this people thus crucified you must repeat St. Ignatius' examination from the first week of the Spiritual Exercises. Ask yourselves: what have I done to cru-cify them? What do I do to uncrucify them? What must I do for this peo-ple to rise again?

Removing the crucified people from their cross: make no mistake, this is not only ethics, though even if it were it would be a precious thing. Nor is this praxis based on human compassion alone, feeling the pain of others and

Global Income Distribution

World population arranged
by income

Distribution of income

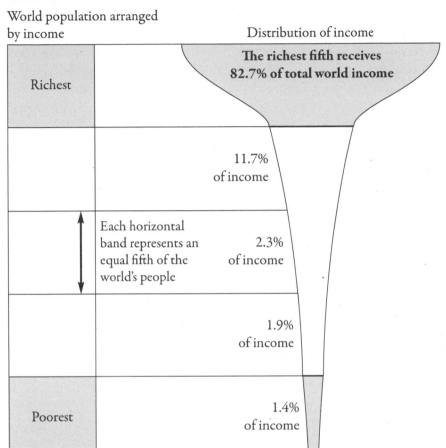

Figure 1. Source: United Nations Development Programme, *Human Development Report 1992* (New York: Oxford University Press, 1992)

seeking to relieve it, though this, too, is highly to be prized. The ultimate ground of praxis with an eye to the poor is nothing less than the living God. This action is rooted in God's love and arises in response to what is demanded by that love. How is the presence of God, precisely that God who delivered an enslaved people and became self-manifest in Jesus Christ crucified and risen, actualized today in a world of affliction? The answer: primarily through divine scandalous love for the poor and the intention that the poor should receive life. If this is the self-definition of God's heart, then knowing and loving God mean letting one's own life be configured to this shape of divine action in the world. In the midst of people suffering extreme poverty and premature, unjust death, it means letting one's own heart correspond to divine compassion, to love as God loves. When it is rooted in such corresponding, the practice of justice and peace actually *mediates* a profound experience of the mystery of God. We "know God" better in solidarity with the poor, as disciples recognized Christ in the breaking of the bread. Without care for those in anguish, by contrast, our relation to God is thinned and ruptured. The preferential option for the poor is an absolutely theocentric stance.

Naming God the liberator does not just craft one more symbol to add to the treasury of divine images. It puts a question mark next to every other idea of God that ignores the very concrete suffering of peoples due to economic, social, and politically structured deprivation. Thus, this call for the praxis of justice is important not just for the faith of Latin Americans but for the faith of the worldwide church. In a particular way it challenges the complacency of Christians in the affluent countries of the Northern and Western Hemispheres to acknowledge and take responsibility for our participation in institutional and structural injustice in the global economy.

The way Christians in affluent societies live their faith has repercussions, because it either reinforces or calls into question the systems responsible for the oppression of multitudes. It is all too easy for the economically well-off to be blind to these effects, even if they are of good will. On this frontier the God of life calls for the conversion of the middle class and the affluent. Either one enters into solidarity with the poor, joining with others who are trying in some way to stop the horse, or, even if one does not deliberately act unjustly, one lives in peaceful coexistence with policies that bring misery to millions. Precisely how justice can be done in different circumstances is a matter of ethical discernment and prudential judgment. People of good will can and do differ, vigorously, over which social policies and projects of social entrepreneurship will lead to the best outcomes. But the prophetic call of liberation theology ensures that in good conscience we can no longer separate God from the poor.

In basic terms, this is simply a restatement of Jesus' teaching to love God and love neighbor, the two being inseparably intertwined. As positioned in contemporary history, however, the praxis of justice forms the core of a new spirituality. A spirituality is a concrete way of living the gospel inspired by the Spirit and in company with others. A contemporary spirituality of liberation is characterized by conversion to one's neighbors who are exploited persons and despised ethnic groups. In addition to prayer and spiritual exercises, it entails social analysis and strategies of action. On this frontier, the life of faith commits one to discipleship in loving solidarity with all, especially the actual poor and dispossessed of this world.

In a true ecclesial sense, this praxis belongs to the central mission of the church. Carrying it out puts the church in alliance with the God of life who is found in compassionate solidarity with those who suffer from miserable impoverishment. Among Catholics there are still some who hesitate under the impression that liberation theology has been condemned by Rome. To clarify: in 1984 the Vatican did issue a document entitled "Instruction on Certain Aspects of the Theology of Liberation," which, although it affirmed that the mighty aspiration of people for liberation from traumatic destitution is a sign of the times to which the church must attend, also warned against an overuse of Marxist analysis and against reducing faith to a political, purely earthly dimension. But two years later, after much dialogue, Pope John Paul II addressed a letter to the bishops of Brazil in which he stated that liberation theology represents a "new stage" in the long evolution of theological reflection, and in the present historical situation it "is not only expedient but useful and necessary." In that same spirit, a new Vatican "Instruction on Christian Freedom and Liberation" in 1986 took a more comprehensively positive attitude toward the value of this approach. It is worth noting that rarely has the core project of a theology been so quickly and widely adopted into mainstream church teaching. While still opposed by some factions, the option for the poor, commitment to justice, and attending to the political dimension of the great truths of faith are now part of the social teaching of the church.

Unlike dualistic understandings of old that relegated redemption to the next world, the approach of liberation theology sees that saving grace applies also to this world. A realized eschatology requires that sacramental "foretastes" of the blessed future reign of God need to materialize even here, even now, in bread on the table, clean water for the children, and the challenging of unjust economic systems. This path of discipleship may well lead the church all the way to the cross. The vested interests at stake are powerful. Their defensive, diversionary tactics would reduce the church's business to a spiritualized discourse that has no impact on reality, thus making conflict inevitable. In our day a new treasury of saints and martyrs is growing, recipients of social scorn and rejection—to say nothing of imprisonment, abuse, slander, and even death—who have met their fate as a result of their loving commitment to the poor. In the darkness of suffering and lament, the God of life energizes resistance, courage, hope, and even hope against hope. Plunged into this struggle, the church itself, both as people and as institution, becomes open to being transformed. "Far from being incidental and adjectival for Christians, the option for the poor is central in the mission of the church, and this by reason of the fact that it is intimately bound up with the very heart of God and the center of revealed mystery" (Clodovis Boff).

A stunning example of the potential of the poor to evangelize the whole church, this insight calls to those of us swimming at the top of the champagne glass to find God where we had neglected to look: among the poor, history's insignificant ones. Thanks to their ecclesial presence and voice, it clarifies an insight into divine nature that we had forgotten to remember: that the God of life is bent with passionate care over those who suffer injustice. We can no longer separate our discourse about God from involvement in the historical process of liberation.

FOR FURTHER READING

A superb compendium of liberation theology is found in Ignacio Ellacuría and Jon Sobrino, eds., *Mysterium Liberationis: Fundamental Concepts of Liberation Theology* (Maryknoll, N.Y.: Orbis Books, 1993), with essays on all major themes including God, Christ, and spirituality; see especially Ellacuría, "The Crucified People," pp. 580–603. An engaging, grass-roots account that lets you eavesdrop on the biblical interpretations of the *comunidades* is Ernesto Cardenal, *The Gospel of Solentiname* (Orbis, 1976). An anthology of official church documents, including the Vatican's 1984 "Instruction," is gathered in Alfred Hennelly, ed., *Liberation Theology: A Documentary History* (Orbis, 1990).

Long respected as the first major theologian on this frontier (*A Theology of Liberation* [Orbis, 1973/1998]), Gustavo Gutiérrez has two meditative works that illuminate the question of God: *On Job: God-Talk and the Suffering of the Innocent* (Orbis, 1987); and *The God of Life* (Orbis, 1991). The powerful interpretations of Christ that have emerged to shape the understanding of discipleship include Leonardo Boff's *Jesus Christ Liberator: A View from the Victims* (Orbis, 1979); Juan Luis Segundo's *The Humanist Christology of Paul* (Orbis, 1986); and Jon Sobrino's *Jesus the Liberator* (Orbis, 1993) and *Christ the Liberator* (Orbis, 2001). For a beautiful analysis of the deeply-rooted spirituality of the base communities, see Sobrino's essay "The Experience of God in the Church of the Poor" in his *The True Church and the Poor* (Orbis, 1984), pp. 125–59. As sole Jesuit survivor of the 1989 massacre of the Jesuits, their housekeeper, and her daughter at the University of Central America in San Salvador, he speaks with unique authority about this whole subject in *The Principle of Mercy: Taking the Crucified People from the Cross* (Orbis, 1994).

María Pilar Aquino, *Our Cry for Life: Feminist Theology from Latin America* (Orbis, 1993) presents liberation theology from the perspective of women, oppressed not only by poverty but also by their subordinate position in a culture of *machismo*. See also Elsa Tamez, ed., *Through Her Eyes: Women's Theology from Latin America* (Orbis, 1989); Virginia Fabella and Mercy Amba Oduyoye, eds., *With Passion and Compassion: Third World Women Doing Theology* (Orbis, 1988), which carries statements from continent-wide conferences of women in Africa, Asia, and Latin America; and Ivone Gebara, *Longing for Running Water: Ecofeminism and Liberation* (Fortress, 1999).

White, educated, and privileged, Daniel Maguire details how solidarity with the poor can be lived by Christians who are not poor in *A Moral Creed for All Christians* (Minneapolis: Fortress, 2005); his challenging chapters on social justice, peace, and love are nothing short of lyrical. Susan Rakoczy explores spirituality in her beautiful study *Great Mystics and Social Justice: Walking on the Two Feet of Love* (New York: Paulist Press, 2006). Christine Hinze grapples with the ethical ramifications in her essay "Straining toward Solidarity in a Suffering World," in William Madges, ed., *Vatican II: Forty Years Later* (Orbis, 2006), pp. 165–95, from where I took the kudzu metaphor.

5

GOD ACTING WOMANISH

Consider the discovery that has graced the world thanks to women's encounter with the liberating God of life in our day. In this instance the context of new religious experience is not only the struggle against dehumanizing poverty, although that can play a significant role, but women's historic struggle against centuries-long discrimination on the basis of their gender. Simone de Beauvoir coined the memorable phrase "the second sex," meaning the inferior sex, to describe the status of women. The term points to the fact that, despite women's identity as human persons and the rich range of their gifts, their worth has consistently been subordinated and demeaned in the theories, symbols, rituals, and structures of both society and church, most of which they had no part in shaping. This bias is intensely exacerbated by prejudices of race and class, placing poor women of color on lowest rung of the social ladder. In the struggle for full and equal human dignity, women have glimpsed that the living God, who created women in the divine image and likeness, not only desires their flourishing but can also be reflected in their female ways.

Society
During the celebrations that marked the year 2000, the United Nations drew up a list of eight millennium goals that governments

and volunteer organizations pledged to try to achieve by 2015. Five of the goals, such as cutting extreme poverty and hunger in half and reversing the spread of diseases like HIV/AIDS, affect the whole community of men, women, and children alike. Three of these goals, however, deal specifically with females: to see that girls as well as boys receive a complete primary education; to reduce by three-quarters the deaths of women in childbirth; and to empower women economically, promoting equality between women and men. The fact that these goals need to be articulated at all reveals how lacking these social goods are in the lives of millions of girls and women.

Decades earlier the UN had compiled statistics that paint the broad background picture for these goals. While women make up one-half of the world's population, they work three-fourths of the world's working hours, receive one-tenth of the world's salary, own one one-hundredth of the planet's land, and constitute two-thirds of the world's illiterate adults. Together with their dependent children, they comprise 75 percent of the worlds starving people and 80 percent of homeless refugees. To make a dark picture even bleaker, violence stalks women's lives. Subject to domestic abuse and battering from husbands or boyfriends they do not please, they are also raped, prostituted, trafficked, and murdered by men to a degree that is not mutual. Factoring in race and class makes clear the complexity of forces against which women struggle for fullness of life. This is not to make women into a class of victims nor to deny women's agency, both sinful and graced, which is abundant. But it is to underscore statistics that make clear the inequity women face in society because of their gender. In no country on earth are women and men yet equal.

Church

In the church a similar situation exists. An early Christian hymn declares that the waters of baptism make people into a community of brothers and sisters bonded in mutual love: *"there is no longer Jew or Greek, there is no longer slave or free, there is no longer male and female; for all of you are one in Christ Jesus"* (Gal 3:28). Despite this theology rooted in the ministry of Jesus and the ongoing presence of the Spirit, and despite the irreplaceable participation of women in the founding and spread of the church, women were marginalized once the community became somewhat established. Barred from governing, women have for centuries had no voice in articulating the church's doctrine, moral teaching, and law. Banned from pulpit and altar, their wisdom has not been permitted to interpret the word of the gospel nor their spirituality to lead the church assembled in prayer.

The sheer fact of the omission of women from the public sphere led to the assumption that men have a privileged place before God. In this milieu theology developed grossly misogynist views about women's very nature. One New Testament writer triggered an appalling tradition with his teaching:

> *Let a woman learn in silence with full submission. I permit no woman to teach or to have authority over a man; she is to keep silent. For Adam was formed first, then Eve; and Adam was not deceived, but the woman was deceived and became a transgressor. Yet she will be saved through childbearing.* (1 Tim 2:11–15)

Notable thinkers throughout the tradition concurred. In the third century Tertullian viewed woman as a second Eve; just as she "softened up with her cajoling words he against whom the devil could not prevail by force," so too all women are "the gateway of the devil"; they tempt men, and because of their sin the Son of God had to die. Augustine, while affirming that woman is equal to man in her spiritual capacity, taught that in view of her body and social role, "she is not the image of God," but can be considered so only when taken together with man who is her head. The medieval period saw Thomas Aquinas define woman as a "defective male," misbegotten when the man performs with less than perfect vigor during intercourse. In the sixteenth century Martin Luther taught that a wife must live in obedience to her husband; while he goes off to the affairs of business and the state, she is to stay at home "like a nail driven into the wall," minding the house: "In this way is Eve punished." The litany could go on. Through the centuries the cumulative impact of these biased views coupled with exclusionary practices relegated women to "second-sex" stature in the church as well as society, with deleterious effects on their person and hence on the whole community.

"Woman, you are set free" (Luke 13:12)

The women's movement in civil society in the 1960s and 1970s galvanized women to analyze the causes of their subordinate situation and to strategize for change. This spilled over into women's religious lives, leading to something akin to a spiritual uprising. Gathering in North American prayer groups, book clubs, and political action committees; or in Latin American ecclesial base communities and mothers' clubs; or in Asian neighborhood associations and mutual aid societies; or in African community centers and health education partnerships; or in European retreat centers and ministerial support groups; or in Australian reform alliances, women came to grips with their subordination in church and society and critiqued it in light of the gospel. Silent and invisible for centuries, they began to stand up straight like the woman in Luke's gospel, bent over for eighteen years, whom Jesus declared to be free. Like her they found their voices and began to speak out in the midst of the assembly. Speaking critically, they examined the sin of sexism and exposed its abuses. In a more positive vein they probed the meaning of Christian faith, uncovering its rich emancipatory possibilities for themselves, their daughters, and the whole Christian community.

In the process, women have had the religious experience that, contrary to what has been said about them for centuries and contrary to what they have internalized, they are of inestimable worth in the eyes of God. The resulting surge of proper self-love leads to conversion, to turning away from assessments that trivialize their identity toward a profound affirmation of their human female selves in all diversity. Subsequently, some have left the church institution whose male dominance so distorted their religious experience; others have defected in place, remaining *in* but not *of* the system; still others remain with conviction to reform the church for the benefit of the gospel in coming generations. The ferment is stirred up by women's discovery that they are beloved of God, who desires fullness of life for them.

DIVERSITY

The theology being articulated with a view to women's experience was originally identified by the adjective "feminist," from the Latin *femina*, meaning woman. Pioneered in North America, this pattern of faith seeking understanding almost at once diversified into many different ways of thinking according to the political and philosophical commitments of its practitioners. Today we can point to liberal, social, cultural, radical, liberation, and postmodern feminist theologies, descriptive labels for work being done by white American women of Anglo-European descent. All draw from the teaching in Genesis that depicts women and men being created equally in

God's image; all in some way underscore divine solidarity with women's struggle for human dignity. Rosemary Radford Ruether gave classic expression to the criterion that guides this reflection when she wrote, "Whatever denies, diminishes, or distorts the full humanity of women is appraised as non-redemptive; . . . what does promote the full humanity of women is of the Holy, it does reflect true relation to the divine, the authentic message of redemption and the mission of redemptive community." Departing from male-dominated ways of interpreting society and the church, feminist theologies embrace an alternative vision of community, one of equality and mutuality between sexes, races, classes, all peoples, and between human beings and the earth, and actively seek to bring this vision into reality.

Unlike Anglo-European women, African American women find prejudice coming at them not only because of their sex but also because of their race. Class, more often than not, is also a factor. To signal that their struggle for life entails resisting predations to their human dignity on all these fronts, black women in the United States have named their project "womanist" theology. As defined by the novelist Alice Walker, the term "womanist" derives from the black term "womanish," which is opposed to girlish and means outrageous, audacious, courageous, or engaging in willful behavior. A womanist is a grown-up, the definition continues, and doesn't mind letting everyone around her know it; her love is universal, including men and women, music, dance, food, roundness, and the Spirit; she loves herself, "regardless;" she is committed to the survival of her entire people, male and female. In and through the liberation of the black community, the vision of womanist theology encompasses the goal of liberation for all who are oppressed by reason of race, sex, and class.

Women of Latin American descent in the United States also experience oppression due to ethnicity and class in addition to gender. Some theologians work under the banner of *mujerista* theology, from the Spanish *mujer,* meaning "woman"; others prefer the designation "Latina" or "Latina feminist." Doing *mujerista* or Latina theology is a reflective action that places women and the cultural specificity of their popular religion at the center of interpretation. In a parallel way, women of Asian descent in the United States probe the meaning of the gospel in the light of their distinctive heritage, which includes an admixture of the religious cultures, folk and formal, indigenous to Asia. Affirming the worth of women's daily lives, all these theologies seek understandings and affirm practices that nourish women's relationship to God while supporting their struggles for survival, which encompass the communities from which they cannot be separated.

Scanning beyond North America, we find women engaged in theology, often at great cost, wherever theological education has opened up to their presence and the economic situation allows. From India to Australia, Belgium to Brazil, Nigeria to Costa Rica, Italy to South Korea, their work seeks understanding that promotes the glory of God, which is tightly tied to all women—black, brown, yellow, red, and white, and especially women in poor, oppressed, and marginalized communities—being fully alive: *Gloria Dei, vivens femina*. These theologians addresses not only gender bias but all forces that rob women of human dignity. As Teresia Hinga of Kenya explains, "the phrase 'web of oppression' is used in African feminist discourse to describe the multiple and interlocking levels of oppression that women face as a result of racism, classism, colonialism, militarism, and sexism, a situation similar to that of all so-called 'Third World' women." To these oppressions a number of thinkers also add heterosexism, which uses the patriarchal lens to define lesbian women as less than fully, properly women because they do not desire men. With attention to these interlocking, overlapping forces, theology is now being expounded in women's voices on every continent.

Women's theology uses technical terms to single out oppressive patterns of social and mental behavior. *Patriarchy*, or rule of the father, refers to social structures where power is always in the hands of the dominant man or men. Under patriarchy women never have equal access to power in the social sphere. *Androcentrism*, or male-centeredness, refers to ways of thinking that privilege men; it makes men's way of being human normative for all human beings. In androcentric thinking women are always derivative, off-center, less than truly human. Today it becomes clear that the liberating goal of feminist, womanist, *mujerista* or Latina, and third-world women's theology is not reached by simply integrating women into a society and church where patriarchal structures and androcentric theory still prevail as a norm. This "add women and stir" recipe just results in further problems as women disregard their own gifts to try to fit into a male-defined world. Rather, the whole structure of church and society needs to be transformed to make space for a new community of mutual partnership. The goal is a new justice.

GLIMPSE OF DIVINE PRESENCE AND ACTION

On this frontier, theology glimpses an ancient, unassailable truth with new clarity: God loves women and passionately desires their flourishing. When violence is done to women, to their bodies or their spirits, it is an insult to divine glory. When liberating advances are made that overcome bias and promote the dignity of women, it is a victory for the reign of God. Struggling to claim their human dignity on every level, women find the God of life walking with them and supporting their efforts, for the Holy One who sprung the slaves out of Egypt and raised Jesus from the dead is unrepentant in siding with those deprived of fullness of life.

In the imagination of their prayer and spiritual life, women so engaged have experienced strong discomfort with the dominant images of God as father, lord, and king. This is more than simply a matter of words. While language reflects our world, it also shapes the way we construct our experience of the world. As hallowed by tradition and currently used, all-male images of God are hierarchal images rooted in the unequal relation between women and men, and they function to maintain this arrangement. Once women no longer relate to men as patriarchal fathers, lords, and kings in society, these images become religiously inadequate. Instead of evoking the reality of God, they block it.

Latina theologian María Pilar Aquino describes the shift that takes place: "Once women realized that their ancient oppression could be lifted, and moreover that God is on their side, this realization challenged the traditional view of God ruling in the male interest." The patriarchal lord who required their obedience began to be replaced by a God whose essence is love, "who freely conceives and creates, whose peculiar mode of being is compassion and mercy." From their own situation in life women sought new ways of understanding the divine that would bring mutuality into the relationship. They found God as lover according to the pattern of the biblical Song of Songs, where both woman and man take initiative in seeking each other and, once found, praise each other's beauty. They discovered God as a life-giving Spirit who can be encountered within themselves and everything that fosters life. Rather than a sovereign God who takes care of every problem, like a father or a big brother caring for a helpless little girl who in turn pleases him most by being quiet and dutiful, women emphasized the all-embracing love that liberates them into their own freedom. In this relationship they began to trust their own personal power as a function of womanliness in all its fullness. As Astrid Lobo, a scientist and active lay leader in the Catholic Church in India, remarked, "no longer do I see God as a rescuer. I see her more as a power and strength within me," who calls upon us to use our own resources. God is the creative force, befriender, friend, and companion who cherishes women in their gladness and pain, gratitude and anger, and ability to change the world.

By envisioning the incomprehensible mystery of God in such non-authoritarian ways, women come upon a further question. Holy mystery who is source, sustaining power, and goal of the world cannot be confined to any one set of images, but transcends them all. Should femaleness be an obstacle to naming the divine? Or can women's reality function as a sacramental sign of God's presence and action? If God created women in the divine image and likeness, theologians reasoned, then can we not return the favor and employ metaphors taken from women's lives to point to the living God? Can the living God not be spoken of in female terms?

The condition for this to happen is women's ownership of themselves as truly beloved of God. In a dramatic play about the dilemma of being black, being female, and being alive, Ntozake Shange captures the dynamism of this new religious experience. After roiling adventures of prejudice, hurt and survival, a tall black woman rises from despair to cry out, "I found god in myself and I loved her, loved her fiercely." It is this finding and fierce loving of the female self in relation to God that gives rise to rediscovering female images of God. These images, in turn, function to affirm the excellence of women's humanity on every level. Marked by sin and blessed by grace, women bear the profound dignity of God's image and likeness. Realizing this, the bells of their spirit ring changes in the traditional male image of God.

THE GRAVEN IMAGE

The background against which this glimpse of God stands out is the centuries-long practice of speaking about God in language descriptive of men in power. Exercising public authority in the church, men assumed the right to speak of God; their own privileged position then served as the chief model for the divine. As a result, verbal depictions of God in liturgy, preaching, and catechesis, along with visual representations in art, have forged a strong link in the popular mind between divinity and maleness. Take, for example, the ceiling of the Sistine Chapel in Rome, which has indelibly influenced the imagination of the West. From one end of the chapel to the other these well-known paintings depict God as old, white, well-fed, and male, the epitome of those who held power in Michelangelo's society. In one famous panel he reaches out his divine finger to create a young white man in his own image. Note that race and class as well as sex enters into this picture. Why could God not be depicted as young, or black, or female, or all three together? But the traditional image is tenacious. As Celie says in Alice Walker's *The Color Purple*: "Can't git that white man off my eyeballs." When it became public knowledge that the grandparents of Mikhail Gorbachev, then the head of the Soviet Union, had had him baptized when a baby, he was asked by an American reporter whether he believed in God. He replied, "Oh, I don't believe in him." Even atheists take it for granted that God is male.

The symbol of God functions. It is never neutral in its effects, but expresses and molds a community's bedrock convictions and actions. Women's groundbreaking work on this subject has made it piercingly clear that the practice of naming God exclusively in the image of powerful men has at least three pernicious effects.

First, because it offers no alternatives, it gets taken literally. Thereby it reduces the living God to an idol. Exclusively male language leads us to forget the incomprehensibility of holy mystery and instead reduces the living God to the fantasy of an infinitely ruling man. Once while Rosemary Radford Ruether was speaking about this issue during a conference, a theologian stood up to object. In great exasperation he argued, "God is not male. *He is Spirit.*" Ruether's response pointed out that if that were really the case, why all the fuss when feminine images or the pronoun "She" is used of God? The conflicts that break out over such naming indicate that, however subliminally, maleness *is* intended when we say God. More solid than stone, more resistant to iconoclasm than bronze, is the ruling male substratum of the idea of God cast in theological language and engraved in public and private prayer.

Second, in addition to this theological error, the exclusive use of patriarchal language for God also has powerful social effects. "One God, one pope, one emperor": from the time of Constantine onward these dominant-male images have functioned to justify patriarchy in church and society. In the name of the King of Kings and Lord of Lords who rules the world, men have assumed the duty to command and control, exercising authority on earth as it is in heaven. Mary Daly's succinct, inimitable phrase captures the rationale: "if God is male, then the male is God."

Third, by giving rise to the unwarranted idea that maleness has more in common with divinity than femaleness, exclusively male images imply that women are somehow less like unto God. Such language thus robs women of the dignity that would accrue if the gracious reality of God were addressed in their own womanly image and likeness. As Carol Christ astutely observed, a woman may see herself as created in the image of God only by abstracting herself from her concrete bodiliness. But she can never have the experience that is freely available to every man and boy in her culture of having her full sexual identity affirmed as being in the image and likeness of God. Thus is set up a largely unconscious dynamic that alienates women from their own spiritual power at the same time that it reinforces dependence on male authorities to act as intermediaries for them with God.

Prophets and religious thinkers have long insisted on the need to turn away from false idols and escape out of their clasp toward the living God. In this context, seeking the female face of God has profound significance. By relativizing masculine imagery it lassoes the idol off its pedestal, breaking the stranglehold of patriarchal discourse and its deleterious effects. God is not literally a father or a king or a lord but something ever so much greater. Thus is the truth more greatly honored. This is not to say that male metaphors cannot be used to signify the divine. Men, too, are created, redeemed, and sanctified by the gracious love of God, and images taken from their lives can function in as adequate or inadequate a way as do images taken from the lives of women. But naming toward God with female metaphors releases divine mystery from its age-old patriarchal cage so that God can be truly God—incomprehensible source, sustaining power, and goal of the world, holy Wisdom, indwelling Spirit, the ground of being, the beyond in our midst, the absolute future, being itself, mother, matrix, lover, friend, infinite love, the holy mystery that surrounds and supports the world. This naming, critical for the integrity of theology, also has the advantage in today's context of opening up rich new veins of justice.

Female representations of the abundance of God in creating, redeeming, and calling the world to eschatological peace function with prophetic power, challenging everyone to conversion in a new community where justice reigns. As the history of religions makes clear, God-language alone cannot bring about this transformation. Female deities and the subordination of women have and still do coexist. But in the context of the social movement for women's equality and human dignity, which now reaches around the globe, speech about God has a unique potential for effecting change at a deep and lasting level. If God is "she" as well as "he"—and in fact neither—a new possibility can be envisioned of a community that honors difference but allows women and men to share life in equal measure.

MOTHER GOD

One cluster of female images for the divine in scripture and tradition centers on women's experience of mothering. We need to be clear about the difficulties this metaphor trails in its wake. Not everyone has a good experience with their mother; there are wrathful, unreliable, moody, obsessive, addicted, inadequate, terrifying mothers. In addition, in patriarchal society a framework of distortions has defined the institution of motherhood, as opposed to the experience of mothering. Promoting the cult of motherhood, such society uses a sentimental rhetoric about women's mysterious and tender nature, establishing the idea that to be a true and fulfilled woman one has to have children. For those who do have children it promotes an ideology of serving and suffering to the point of encouraging women to be pathologically self-sacrificing. Its sentimental view of motherhood overlooks the fact that maternal thinking is a moral activity; the survival of others depends on her initiative and industry. For those who do not have children, whether by circumstance or choice, the rhetoric bestows a demeaning sense that they have not measured up. For all women, exalting motherhood to the exclusion of all other vocational options severely circumscribes the range of their life experience.

Despite these difficulties, however, imaging God as mother has great positive power to connote the creative source and origin of life. For the child, mothering is associated with primal human experiences of comfort, security, nurture, compassion; the security and assurance of being held, cradled, sheltered, and protected—the experience of being loved. For women too, when mothering is undertaken as an active experience of creative involvement, it can be one of the most ecstatic and rewarding experiences of their life. Since it is women whose bodies bear and deliver new persons into life and, as society is traditionally structured, are most often charged with the responsibility of nurturing and raising them into maturity, language about God as mother carries a unique power to express human relationship to the mystery who generates and cares for everything.

In the Bible a number of texts, especially of the prophets, depict the Holy One of Israel as a woman who is pregnant, crying out in labor, giving birth, breast-feeding, carrying her young, and nurturing their growth. The underlying point always seeks to convey the unbreakable compassion of God for the covenanted people:

> *Can a woman forget her nursing child,*
> *or show no compassion for the child of her womb?*
> *Even these may forget, yet I will not forget you.* (Isa 49:15)

The maternal metaphor continues in the New Testament, where Jesus compares himself to a mother hen gathering her chicks under her wings to protect them from harm (Matt 23:37).

Strongly associated with all these maternal images is divine compassion. Biblical scholars point out that the Hebrew noun for compassion or merciful love comes from the root word for women's uterus, *rehem*, which is also the root for the verb "to show mercy" and the adjective "merciful." Here the life-giving physical organ of the female body serves as a concrete metaphor for a distinctly divine way of being, feeling, and acting. When scripture calls on God for mercy, a frequent theme, it is actually asking the Holy One to treat us with the kind of love a mother has for the child of her womb. "To the responsive imagination," writes Phyllis Trible, this semantic connection "suggests the meaning of love as selfless participation in life. The womb protects and nourishes but does not possess and control. It yields its treasure in order that wholeness and well-being may happen. Truly, it is the way of compassion." Witnessing the biblical journey of this metaphor from the wombs of women to the compassion of God, one cannot help but think what a difference it would make if this knowledge became an explicit part of the teaching on divine love rather than being left tucked away in the text.

The mystical tradition in theology and spirituality has long articulated experience of God in maternal metaphors. The revelations of the fourteenth-century English mystic Julian of Norwich have become newly influential in our age. Writing of God's gracious courtesy, which bears and feeds us, educates and loves us as a mother, she taught:

> As truly as God is our Father, so truly is God our Mother . . . I understand three ways of contemplating motherhood in God. The first is the foundation of our nature's creation; the second is his taking of our nature, where the motherhood of grace begins; the third is the motherhood at work. And in that, by the same grace, everything is penetrated, in length and in breadth, in height and in depth without end; and it is all one love. (*Showings,* Long Text, 59th chapter)

A similar reference to divine maternity startled the world in 1978 when Pope John Paul I, comparing war to a fevered illness, said in a Sunday address:

> God is our father; even more God is our mother. God does not want to hurt us, but only to do good for us, all of us. If children are ill, they have additional claim to be loved by their mother. And we too, if by chance we are sick with badness and are on the wrong track, have yet another claim to be loved by the Lord. (*Osservatore Romano,* September 21, 1978)

Here the intensifier "even more" connects speech about God with a typical experience of a mother with her sick child to signify a certain kind of divine care for the well-being of those ill with sin, in which group the pope includes the world that keeps on going to war. With a mother's love God keeps vigil through the long night of our sickness and tries everything to break the violent fever and bring about peace.

In her major "thought experiment" on the model of God as mother, Sallie McFague's analysis makes an unexpected, beautiful connection between mothering and justice. Drawing on women's experience, she sees that mothering involves three elements. First of all, mothers give the gift of life to others and, when it appears, exclaim with delight, "It is good that you exist." In addition, maternal love nurtures what it has brought into existence, mainly by feeding the young and also by training the young to acquire personal and social behaviors. Finally, this love passionately wants the young to grow, to flourish, and be fulfilled; it rises up to defend against anything that would do them harm. Good paternal love does all of these things too. Parental love is the most powerful and intimate experience we have of giving love whose return is not calculated. But the irreplaceable role of women's own bodies in giving birth and their close connection with breast-nursing and child-rearing lend a special resonance to the maternal model.

The maternal love of the living God is characterized by these same three elements. Like a mother, God gives life to the world, nurtures this precious and vulnerable life, and desires the growth and flourishing of all. The practice of mothers everywhere shows that, far from being a passive relationship, this entails looking out for everyone in the household. If there is little food, a mother sees that it is fairly distributed. If one child has a special need, she tries to provide what is necessary. "The mother-God as creator, then, is also involved in 'economics,' the management of the household of the universe, to ensure the just distribution of good to *all*." God's preferential option for justice for the poor is the expression of a mother's strong instinct to care for the child most in need. And as mothers rise up to defend their young, so too when people do violence to one another, neglect the poor, aggrandize themselves through unjust systems of exchange, or ruin the ecological well-being of the earth, the maternal love of God is active to defend, seek justice, and heal. Like the mother bear in the prophet Hosea, God the mother rears up to protect her cubs, even tearing the attackers' hearts out from their chest (Hos 13:8). The wrath of God has a place in this maternal metaphor.

In relating to God, people need more than parental models, which, if used exclusively, can place us in the role of children rather than responsible adults. In addition to the idea of God as life-giving and nourishing mother, women's quest has discovered other metaphor clusters. One of the most important centers on the figure of Wisdom.

HOLY WISDOM

In a favorite Advent hymn, "O Come, O Come, Emmanuel," people sing words whose significance is not immediately obvious:

O come thou Wisdom from on high,
who orders all things mightily;
to us the path of knowledge show,
and teach us in her ways to go.

Hidden in plain sight in this hymn is a female image of God that runs like a golden thread through the whole Christian tradition.

The later writings of the Old Testament introduce a female figure of gracious power and might who approaches the world with creating, redeeming, and sanctifying activity. She is called *Sophia* in Greek, which translates into English as Wisdom. Jewish and Christian religious thinkers have long pondered her identity. Who is Sophia? Does her presence in scripture mean that Israel betrayed its heritage of monotheism and turned to love of the goddess? Some scholars thought to interpret Sophia as a feminine dimension of YHWH, or an angel or a messenger sent to the world. Elisabeth Schüssler Fiorenza and other women biblical scholars present a different interpretation. Given Sophia's activity, which is clearly proper to God alone, this figure is no angel or mere feminine aspect of the divine. Rather, Sophia represents Israel's robust God in active, redeeming engagement with the world, and does so a way that uses female images equivalent to the male images used elsewhere in scripture.

The book of Proverbs opens with Wisdom shouting out in the marketplace and at the city gates. She excoriates those who will not listen to her words of instruction but promises life to whoever listens and follows her way: *"whoever finds me finds life"* (8:35). Who else can make this promise but the living God? Sophia is present at creation, playing in delight with the newborn world (8:31). She walks the paths of justice, and kings who rule righteously do so by her light (8:15). In an act of surpassing hospitality, she prepares a feast and sets her table, sending her maidservants out to invite everyone, *"Come, eat of my bread and drink of the wine I have mixed. Lay aside immaturity, and live, and walk in the way of insight"* (9:5-6). The constant drumbeat of her words sounds the call to spiritual adulthood supported by the generous promise of her constant nourishment.

The book of Wisdom delineates Sophia's engagement with the world ever more clearly. Not only does she bring the world into birth, being, as Solomon says, the mother and fashioner of all things (7:12, 22), but she reaches from end to end of the universe, governing all things sweetly and mightily (8:1, the source of the Advent text). Being able to do all things, she uses her power to redeem. When the Israelites were enslaved in Egypt:

> *A holy people and blameless race*
> *Wisdom delivered from a nation of oppressors . . .*
> *she guided them along a marvelous way,*
> *and became a shelter to them by day,*
> *and a starry flame through the night.*
> *She brought them over the Red Sea,*
> *and led them through deep waters;*
> *but she drowned their enemies,*
> *and cast them up from the depth of the sea.* (10:15-17)

Her holy, intelligent, subtle, mobile, people-loving spirit pervades the world, renewing all things and making people into friends of God and prophets. Radiant and unfading, she is more beautiful than the sun and exceeds the brilliance of every constellation of stars. Most tellingly, while night overcomes day, *"against Wisdom, evil does not prevail"* (7:30).

The New Testament draws on this wisdom tradition for its interpretations of Jesus. Paul identifies the crucified Christ with the wisdom of God (1 Cor 1:24), thereby starting up the connection between the disgraced prophet from Nazareth and the one who establishes cosmic order. Matthew's gospel puts Sophia's words in Jesus' mouth and sees him doing her deeds (11:19). The prologue of the gospel of John tells the whole pre-history of Jesus as the story of Wisdom under the guise of the metaphor of Word. And when the Word/Wisdom was made flesh and dwelled among us, Jesus is identified as the human being Sophia became. His ministry is pervaded with themes from the wisdom literature, such as seeking and finding, bread and wine, light and darkness, life and death. *"I came that they may have life, and have it abundantly"* (John 10:10), words in the Johannine Jesus' mouth that play on Sophia's promise to give life. Indicating the importance of the identification of Christ with wisdom, the largest church in antiquity was dedicated to Christ under the title *Hagia Sophia*, Holy Wisdom; it still stands as a museum in Istanbul.

Far from pointing to a mere feminine dimension of the divine, language about Sophia bespeaks the unfathomable mystery of the living God in female imagery. While maternal love figures to a degree, Holy Wisdom expands beyond this to encompass governing, playing, teaching, walking with, justice-making, and life-giving in the public arena throughout the entire universe.

A SYMPHONY OF SYMBOLS

A veritable symphony of images in addition to mother and Wisdom enables women and girls to recognize themselves in language about God. The Spirit of God, named with the feminine noun *ruah* in Hebrew, is often depicted in Christian art as a dove, an ancient symbol of the goddess of love. Salted throughout scripture, depictions of her life-giving work include midwifing births, weaving connections, washing out stains, inspiring prophets, advocating for truth, awakening beauty, creating community, and renewing the face of the earth. There are representations of God as a woman kneading bread (Luke 13:18), or knitting (Ps 139:15), or pursuing her lover (Song of Songs), and as a mother bird hiding her brood in the shadow of her wings (Ps 17:8).

One precious image is the woman looking for a coin lost from her stash of ten silver pieces (Luke 15:8-10). This view of God was crafted by Jesus in a parable he told about divine care for those who have lost their way. The woman lights a lamp and searches high and low until she finds her money. When she calls her friends and neighbors together to rejoice, it is an image of the joy in heaven over one sinner repenting. In Luke's gospel this parable immediately follows the parable of the good shepherd, who leaves ninety-nine sheep to look for the one that strayed. Both stories depict the work of God the Redeemer—the imagery of one taken from men's world, that of the other from women's world of that day. Augustine once started a sermon on the parable of the lost coin by exclaiming, "Holy Divinity has lost her money, and it is us!" But over the centuries this seeker of money that is very important to her has not become a familiar image of the divine, unlike the good shepherd. She has even been disparaged. Once I heard a cardinal preach on this gospel, and he accused this woman of being "mercenary." Contrast this judgment with a woman in an ecclesial base community in southern Mexico who told me that this behavior is exactly what a poor woman would do who needed those pesos to buy tortillas for her children's breakfast.

In addition to lifting up biblical images, women today glimpse God reflected in their own contemporary experience. In the Hispanic community the *abuela*, the grandmother, is a key wisdom figure in the family, handing down traditions and keeping rituals alive. One young woman wrote that she sees God as her *abuela,* giving her courage in *la lucha* (the struggle), a sentiment echoed by many others. One ordained priest in the Anglican church worked with her parish in Vancouver to craft inclusive-language prayers for the liturgies of Sunday and major feasts. The prayer for Christmas Day reads:

> Maker of this earth our home,
> You sweep the heavens with your starry skirt of night
> and polish the eastern sky to bring light to the new day.
> Come to us in the birth of the infant Christ,
> that we may discover the fullness of your redemption throughout
>   the universe;
> Mother and Child of Peace bound by the Spirit of Love,
> One-in-Three forever. Amen.

In this and a host of other ways, women are exploring the frontier of their own interface with the divine, questing on many different paths for new expressions of religious language and celebration, new readings of the classic sources of religious traditions, and new patterns of spirituality that bless rather than demean the reality of being female. Awakening new appreciation of the profound mystery of God, the concepts that arise from this womanly imagery also transform traditional divine attributes by stressing the living God's relationship with the world, all-embracing immanence, deep maternal bonding with life in all its vulnerability and surprise, ability to suffer with others, power that empowers creative resistance to harm, and absolute compassion and inclusivity. No ally of oppressive structures, Wisdom's purpose is intent on life and liberation. Nor is this a matter of imagery alone. The dynamism of these female symbols, uttered in contexts of injustice and violence, empowers action for a new world where, as Korean theologian Chung Hyun Kyung writes, women no longer have to function as the moon reflecting the sun but can become "the sun that shines in its own light out of its burning core of life, fostering life on earth."

THE DANGER OF DUALISM

It is important to flag a danger to this enterprise. A number of theologians are utilizing these discoveries in their work by speaking of God having feminine "traits" or "dimensions" or "qualities," resulting in God the Father having a maternal side, so to speak. Behind such moves lurks the controversial idea of human beings stemming from the Greek philosophical tradition regarding matter and spirit. The idea is profoundly dualistic, making a strict separation between women and men. It starts with the obvious biological sex differences between men and women; then proceeds to assign predetermined personality traits to men and women on the basis of their roles in reproduction; and ends by extrapolating distinct social roles that must necessarily follow. In the concrete, this view identifies masculine nature with what is active, powerful, rational, able to give form—thus what is fit for leadership in the public arena. By contrast, women's feminine nature is identified with what is passive, malleable, emotional, receptive to form—thus what is meant for nurturing roles in the private realm.

The philosophical "myth" of gender dualism in ancient times was nourished by ignorance of reproductive biology. It saw the woman as merely the passive recipient of the life-shaping sperm, no one yet knowing about the existence of the female egg. Regardless of biological discoveries, however, dualism is still promoted by patriarchal culture with its stunted androcentric imagination. Scholars who take this route sometimes buttress their theories with Jungian ideas, associating the feminine with the unconscious, with dreams and fantasies, with *eros* (desire) rather than *logos* (reason), with darkness, death, depth, and receptivity, or with instinct, emotion, and bodiliness. When translated into actual practice, these definitions, taken to be "natural," mean that just as God (active and masculine) rules the world (receptive and feminine), so too the husband rules the wife, the father rules the children, the clergy rules the laity, the head rules the heart. Women are expected to submit to the authority of father, husband, and priest, or else they disrupt the divinely given order of the world.

When God is depicted in female images in this framework of gender dualism, the Holy indeed acquires gentle feminine characteristics. But these attributes do not suffice for governing the world and need to be complemented by the so-called masculine traits of reasonableness, power, justice-making, and headship. At the end of the day, God is still envisioned in the image of the ruling man, only now possessing a milder, sweeter side that offsets the harshness of the purely masculine model. The feminine is thereby incorporated in a subordinate way into a symbol of the divine that remains predominantly patriarchal. What we do not enjoy is a female icon of God in all fullness and strength.

Opposed to the old dualism is a new question: What indeed is woman's nature, and, even more critically, who gets to decide? Facts on the ground now far out-run traditional theory. Bursting out of gender dualism, itself a creation of patriarchy that maintains the status quo, and claiming the right to speak denied them for centuries, women are answering this question in their own voices. In all their differences they lay claim to the whole range of human qualities and urge men, too, to explore what they have lost under traditional biased descriptions.

Speaking of God, theologians underscore the truth that the Holy does not have dualistically arranged masculine and feminine traits, just as surely as God does not have animal traits (mother bear, hovering bird) or mineral traits (rock). Such an understanding tames the disruptive, stretching wisdom being discovered on this frontier. Rather, feminist, womanist, and Latina theologians around the world argue that women are capable of symbolizing the whole mystery of God in as adequate and inadequate a way as male images have done. In other words, women reflect God not only as mothering, nurturing, and compassionate, although certainly that, but also as powerful, taking initiative, creating-redeeming-saving, wrathful against injustice, in solidarity with the poor, struggling against and sometimes victorious over the powers of this world. Reorienting the imagination at a basic level, these female images open up insight into the maternal passion, fierce protectiveness, zeal for justice, healing power, inclusive hospitality, liberating will, and nonhierarchical, all-pervading relationality that characterize divine love. In the process, they carry back to women the stamp of divine likeness.

PRAXIS OF BIBLICAL JUSTICE FOR WOMEN

The still-developing historical struggle for women's equal human dignity is the context for the growing treasury of female icons of the living God who acts womanish: outrageous, audacious, courageous, willfully desiring the flourishing of women. The reflective, critical action that flows from this insight is the praxis of justice preferentially oriented toward those subordinated on the basis of gender. This is a social praxis governed by the principle that "women are fully human and are to be treated as such," as Margaret Farley succinctly puts it. As transformative action it seeks to make whole whatever demeans and violates the human dignity of women. God cannot be separated from the reign of God, from the divine will that all should be fully alive. Walking this path, Christian believers cast their lot with the liberating compassion of Sophia-God present in the midst of the silencing and degradation specifically of women. This entails that the church be called away from its own deeply ingrained patriarchy to build communities of the discipleship of equals, in Elisabeth Schüssler Fiorenza's apt phrase. It also challenges people of faith to collaborate in the struggle to transform society into a place where discrimination, exclusion, and violence against women and girl-children will cease and where women of all races and classes will be mutual partners with men rather than subordinate auxiliaries or marginalized objects.

Far from being silly or faddish, the theological approach women are pioneering goes forward with the conviction that *only* if God is named in this more complete way, *only* if the full reality of historical women of all races and classes enters into our symbol of the divine, *only* then will the idolatrous fixation on one image of God be broken, will women be empowered at their deepest core, and will religious and civic communities be converted toward healing justice in the concrete. Along the way, every female naming of the Holy produces one more fragment of the truth of the mystery of divine Sophia's gracious hospitality toward all human beings and the earth.

FOR FURTHER READING

The history of women's faith in tension with patriarchal definitions and exclusions is documented in Elizabeth Clark and Herbert Richardson, eds., *Women and Religion: The Original Sourcebook of Women in Christian Thought* (San Francisco: HarperSanFrancisco, 1996). A fine survey of basic concepts in systematic theology is given by Anne Clifford, *Introducing Feminist Theology* (Maryknoll, N.Y.: Orbis, 2001). Carol Newsom and

Sharon Ringe, eds., *Women's Bible Commentary* (Louisville: Westminster John Knox, 1998) contains rich resources for new biblical interpretation.

Early classics of Anglo-European feminist theology and its concern for God include Mary Daly, *Beyond God the Father* (Boston: Beacon, 1973), which sharply analyzes and rejects the patriarchal God; Rosemary Radford Ruether, *Sexism and God-Talk: Toward a Feminist Theology* (Boston: Beacon, 1983) which proposes a retrieval of the liberating God of the prophetic tradition; and Elisabeth Schüssler Fiorenza, *In Memory of Her: A Feminist Theological Reconstruction of Christian Origins* (New York: Crossroad, 1983), which develops the biblical symbol of Sophia.

In addition to women's work cited in the previous chapter on liberation theology, the global reach of women's theology can be seen in Ursula King, ed., *Feminist Theology from the Third World* (Orbis, 1994); Chung Hyun Kyung, *Struggle To Be the Sun Again: Introducing Asian Women's Theology* (Orbis, 1994); Mercy Amba Oduyoye, *Daughters of Anowa: African Women and Patriarchy* (Orbis, 1995); Mary John Mananzan et al., eds. *Women Resisting Violence: Spirituality for Life* (Orbis, 1996) (Philippines); Meehyun Chung, ed., *Breaking Silence: Theology from Asian Women* (Delhi: ISPCK, 2006); and Agnes Brazal and Andrea Lizares Si, eds., *Body and Sexuality: Theological-Pastoral Perspectives of Women in Asia* (Manila: Ateneo, 2007). A compendium of essays from around the world, including Europe and Australia, appears in Elisabeth Schüssler Fiorenza, ed., *The Power of Naming: A Concilium Reader in Feminist Liberation Theology* (Orbis, 1996); see especially Shawn Copeland, "Critical Theologies for the Liberation of Women," pp. 70–80; and Sallie McFague, "Mother God," pp. 324–29.

Key works that turn specific attention to the question of God-talk include the biblical studies by Phyllis Trible in *God and the Rhetoric of Sexuality* (Philadelphia: Fortress, 1978); the thought experiment by Sallie McFague, *Models of God: Theology for an Ecological, Nuclear Age* (Philadelphia: Fortress, 1987); and the systematic investigation by Elizabeth Johnson, *She Who Is: The Mystery of God in Feminist Theological Discourse* (New York: Crossroad, 1992). Mary Kathleen Speegle Schmitt, *Seasons of the Feminine Divine: Christian Feminist Prayers for the Liturgical Cycle,* 3 vols. (New York: Crossroad, 1993–95) contains the prayer for Christmas Day in vol. 2, cycle B.

The compendium *Womanspirit Rising: A Feminist Reader in Religion*, edited by Carol Christ and Judith Plaskow (San Francisco: Harper & Row, 1979) presents creative notions of the divine from both Jewish and Christian thinkers. The work of Catholic theologians gathers in Catherine LaCugna, *Freeing Theology: The Essentials of Theology in Feminist Perspective* (San Francisco: HarperSanFrancisco, 1993), especially LaCugna's essay on the Trinity, "God in Communion with Us," pp. 83–114; and in Ann O'Hara Graff, ed., *In the Embrace of God: Feminist Approaches to Theological Anthropology* (Orbis, 1995), especially Mary Catherine Hilkert, "Cry Beloved Image: Rethinking the Image of God," 190–205.

Continuing work in the field is presented in Susan Frank Parsons, ed., *The Cambridge Companion to Feminist Theology* (Cambridge/New York: Cambridge University Press, 2002); and Janet Martin Soskice and Diana Lipton, eds., *Oxford Readings in Feminism: Feminism & Theology* (New York: Oxford University Press, 2003).

6

GOD WHO BREAKS CHAINS

CONTEXT: WHITE PRIVILEGE AND RACISM

Consider the insight into God that emerged from the experience of African people enslaved in the "New World," an insight subsequently passed down through their descendants and now articulated anew by African American theologians. Starting in the sixteenth century and continuing for almost four centuries, an estimated ten million Africans were traded across the Atlantic Ocean to the Americas, a tragedy of such scope that it is difficult to imagine, much less comprehend. Stolen from their villages and transported across the ocean in crowded, horrific conditions, those who survived the Middle Passage then had to face the auction block, unremitting and unrequited labor on plantations and in white households, violent beatings, sexual assaults, hunger, and early death. Robbed of their freedom, slaves were brutally denied stable family ties; the master could break up kinship groups by selling individuals at will. For this economic system to work, the Africans were defined as property, not human beings.

Despite slave owners' efforts to eradicate African cultures, the religious beliefs and customs black people had brought with them persisted, centered in respect for spiritual power wherever it originated. Over time the slaves were exposed to the white community's religion, Christianity, which some had possibly already encountered in Africa. Two interesting things resulted. The enslaved people interpreted Christianity radically anew in the light of their own experience of oppression, finding God's liberating deeds in history at the core. And they expressed this faith in the rhythms, styles of worship, and fundamental perspectives of their own original African traditions. Transmitted by slaves to their descendants, this form of faith in the God of Jesus Christ sustained African Americans through centuries of slavery. After the Civil War (1861–65), it saw them through another century of segregation, Jim Crow laws, and lynchings, and through the civil rights movement of the 1950s and 1960s. It continues to sustain African American Christians today in an American society marked by the astonishing prevalence and persistence of racism among white people. A unique response to an egregious historic injustice, this faith gives strength to endure unspeakable sorrow, courage to resist forces of dehumanization, and hope that struggles through to freedom.

At its center is the God who breaks chains.

THE KERNEL

White slave owners and the preachers they supported taught Christianity to the slaves as a religion of law and order on earth under the one great Master in heaven. Docility rather than rebellion was the desired attitude. A biblical injunction reflecting the Roman empire's slave practices, *"Slaves, obey your earthly masters with fear and trembling"* (Eph 6:5), became a favorite text on American shores. Good slaves were supposed to be content with their lot, cooperative in carrying out commands, productive in the fields and house, and willing to wait until death made them free.

In actual fact, however, the enslaved Africans heard something else in the biblical stories told to them. Through their struggle against debasement they heard the potentially revolutionary doctrine that God is no respecter of persons but made and loves all people, all "his children." In resisting the staggering affliction of chattel slavery, they heard that Jesus died and rose again for all people, bond or free, black or white, rich or poor. By an amazing, vastly creative spiritual insight, they discerned the kernel of truth in the gospel, namely, that Jesus comes to set all people free. Consequently they saw the hypocrisy in their masters' practices compared with the deep heart of Christian faith.

In antebellum America this eye-opening situation resulted: the enslaved black "nonpersons" grasped and lived the Christian faith more truly than the respectable white slave owners. And they suffered for it. In his study *Slave Religion: The 'Invisible Institution' in the Antebellum South*, Albert Raboteau notes that if asked to discuss historical examples of the persecution of Christianity, a number of us would mention the early centuries of the church when many martyrs died at the hands of Roman authorities. We might also mention modern waves of persecution under Communist regimes in Eastern Europe and the Soviet Union. But few would name the suffering of African American slave Christians as the prime example of persecution of Christianity in the United States. Yet the extent to which their Christian faith was hindered and suppressed justifies seeing them as confessors and martyrs to the gospel. As Raboteau writes, "What the slaves affirmed and the slaveholders rejected was the belief that slavery and Christianity were incompatible—that a slaveholding Christianity was a contradiction in terms, in other words, a heresy."

The insight glimpsed by the enslaved Africans that God was a liberator of the oppressed gave them a powerful incentive to struggle for freedom, both spiritual and physical. At times their faith supported rebellion by escape; narratives tell of prayer before flight. At other times the very practice of religion was rebellious. While many masters encouraged their slaves to go to church for a dose of taming religion that would inculcate docility, others, fearful of religion's power to unify the slaves and thus enable them to resist, forbade their slaves to meet for worship. This led to clandestine prayer meetings at night in the woods, gullies, or ravines, in the full knowledge that discovery would result in severe beatings. Former slave Sarah Rhodes speaks of those clandestine gatherings, aptly named "hush harbor" meetings, in this way:

> We used to steal off to de woods and have church, like de Spirit moved us —sing and pray to our own liking and soul satisfaction—and we sure did have good meetings, honey - baptize in de river like God said. We had dem spirit-filled meetings at night on de bank of de river, and God met us there.

God met us there. This was a defiant faith that moved them to disobey their masters in obedience to their God. It kept them in touch with an inner world opposed to slaveholders' treatment of them as property. It empowered them silently but obstinately to refuse to participate in their own dehumanization. Out of slave religion with its pain and break-out joy arose a living tradition that stood in profound, prophetic challenge to standard American Christianity.

IDEA OF GOD

Faith in a power higher than themselves and higher than those who enslaved them gave African Americans a base from which to deal with both grinding institutional oppression and the psychological oppression—including despair and feelings of personal worthlessness—it created. To say that God is my Creator is to say that white slave masters are not the ground of my being. A certain moral autonomy of myself as a human person results. More specifically than this, however, slave religion was shaped by two particular biblical events of suffering and liberation: the exodus of the Israelites from Egypt and the cross and resurrection of Jesus.

Expressing the divine will made known to him in the burning bush, Moses confronted the Pharaoh with the unforgettable demand, *"Let my people go"* (Exod 5:1). After many trials and tribulations the Israelites' bondage came to an end as they crossed the dried-up sea into the desert. Divine victory is achieved in freedom for the people who now set out for the promised land. African American slave religion creatively appropriated the Exodus to an extraordinary degree. The slaves identified themselves with the children of Israel enslaved in Egypt immediately and intensely. The cries of the Hebrew slaves under the Egyptian taskmasters were *their* cries; the yearning for deliverance was *their* yearning; the outcome of the story assured them that God was on *their* side. Narrating and singing this story was a way of keeping meaning going, finding purpose in their chaotic experience, and gaining hope by projecting a radically different future. God would break their chains.

Emphasis on the death and resurrection of Jesus has at times led to a passive acceptance of suffering and an otherworldly hope, which preachers exploit to the detriment of the oppressed. Slave Christianity found another, more dangerous interpretation. Having suffered himself, Jesus knows what they are suffering better than anyone. There is an intimacy in pain that bears them up in the midst of anguish. His resurrection from the dead conveys hope in God not in a way that transfers loyalty from earth to heaven but in a way that empowers meaningful struggle against iniquity now. As African American theologian James Cone encapsulates the logic, "to believe in heaven is to refuse to accept hell on earth." For the slaves to envision the future as revealed in the resurrection of Christ was also to see the contradiction between the earthly injustice they suffered and the way God intended them to live in Christ. Heaven meant they would be coming home. This promised, meaningful future not only staved off despair; it also rooted their resistance to the present order because the humiliation of slavery is inconsistent with the crown to come. This radiates out from the songs they created:

> Oh freedom! Oh freedom!
> Oh freedom, I love thee!
> And before I'll be a slave,
> I'll be buried in my grave,
> And go home to my Lord and be free.
> (American Spiritual)

SPIRITUALS

No other legacy from this bleak period carries forward the idea of God as breaker of chains better than the religious music fashioned by the slaves themselves. Known as spirituals, these songs express the sustaining truth of their faith not in rational discourse but in moving, colloquial, and often dramatic terms. Combining African rhythms, chants, and patterns of lament with biblical themes from European Christianity, spirituals were performed in flexible and improvisational ways: words were often added as the tunes unfolded; they could be accompanied by rhythmic hand-clapping, foot-stomping, and ring-dancing. They were the medium of communal worship, sung in churches, at prayer meetings, in the slave quarters, and hummed in fields under the hot sun.

Spirituals had extraordinary power to shape the slaves' experience and identity. Expressing moods of sorrow, fear, joy, and hope, they bore up the souls of black folk in the face of almost unbearable degradation. As James Cone explains, in the spirituals God's own Spirit was entering into the lives of the people, "buildin' them up where they were torn down and proppin' them up on every leaning side." The songs gave rise in the community to a palpable feeling that God was with them and would provide them with the courage to make it through:

> O my Lord delivered Daniel
> O why not deliver me too?

Suffused with pain, the lyrics sounded a note of salvation, heading "across the river Jordan, onto Canaan's bright shore." On that day when the people reached the promised land, they would be home at last, everyone able to "sit at the welcome table."

In a powerful way characteristic of the music of oppressed people, some spirituals conveyed veiled social commentary and criticism. Themes of freedom and going home frequently appear, longed-for goals that were not just reserved for a future in heaven but could be gained even now through struggle and escape. Diana Hayes makes the connection this way:

So they sang of Canaan and ran away to Canada. They sang "Steal Away to Jesus" while they stole away North, and "Wade in the Water" while they walked across the Ohio, the Delaware, the Mississippi Rivers. The masters and overseers may have been fooled, but the slaves were not.

While spirituals could have this double meaning, and did, especially in situations where the attempt to break loose was imminent, Raboteau cautions against seeing them mainly as political freedom songs, vitally important as these are. It is true that throughout the grinding centuries freedom from slavery on earth was always seen as a key element in the redemption won by Jesus Christ. Still, with no realistic prospect of this happening today or tomorrow, the spirituals' relevance to the situation of chattel slavery transpired at a profoundly religious level. The songs coded resistance to dehumanization and helped the slaves make meaning in the midst of their suffering. Themes and events from the Old and New Testaments, from Genesis to Revelation, were used to interpret their own experience by measuring it against a wider system of meaning. Characters whose faith had been tested

—Jacob wrestling with the angel, Moses confronting Pharaoh, Daniel in the lions' den, "weeping Mary" before the empty tomb, "sinking Peter" on the waves of Galilee, "doubting Thomas" in the upper room—became alive in the present with encouragement to hang on and struggle through. In the process, the biblical symbols were translated into beacons of help amid the slaves' own hard daily experience. Contact with God then became a communal experience at worship and praise services, where these symbols uplifted the spirit. For the vast majority of slaves, who could not read, spirituals were their channel to the word of God. And "for a time at least, the sorrow and toil of the individual's life were assuaged and given meaning." The spirituals provided not an answer but a way of getting through and affirming that your life was valuable, regardless.

One of the secrets of the spirituals' power lies in the way they explicitly name the suffering that the slaves endured. Life was a valley of tears, a road of sorrow, weariness, and toil:

> Sometimes I'm up, sometimes I'm down,
> Sometimes I'm almost on de ground.

Faith elicits a note of joy, even so; the above verse appears in a spiritual whose repetitive refrain connects the suffering closely with Jesus:

> Nobody knows de trouble I've seen,
> Nobody knows but Jesus,
> Nobody knows de trouble I've had,
> Glory hallelujah!

The slaves knew that on earth Jesus had used his power to help the lowly. They knew, too, the details of his suffering: "dey whupped him up de hill . . . dey crowned him wid a thorny crown . . . dey nailed him to de cross . . . ." Far from being a glorification of pain, references to the passion of Christ told of God's love compassionately involved with the human condition. They intuitively grasped that in this event God had entered into solidarity with them, giving them a dignity that slavery denied. Their worth was not defined by white slave owners, but by what Jesus said and did for them. This was an awesome insight, which came pouring out in the enduring lament:

> Were you there when they crucified my Lord?
> Were you there when they crucified my Lord?

Oh, sometimes it cause me to tremble, tremble, tremble,
Were you there when they crucified my Lord?

The cross enabled the slaves to see that their life had meaning despite servitude. Since their future was in the hands of the one who died on Calvary, a "hallelujah" could round out the story of their trouble:

Sometimes I hangs my head an' cries,
But Jesus goin' to wipe my weepin' eyes.

The reason for this hope lies in the end of the story, with the great Lord Christ risen from the dead. The victory of God over death resounds with the call to dry their tears:

Weep no more, Marta,
Weep no more, Mary.
Jesus rise from the dead,
Happy morning!,

a victory very rightly connected with the earlier Passover event:

O Mary, don't you weep, don't you moan,
O Mary, don't you weep, don't you moan,
Pharaoh's army got drowned
O Mary don't you weep.

The slaves' grasp of Christ's cross and resurrection made it possible for them to see that their dignity, their worth as human beings was not to be equated simply with their present situation, ensnared in the evil and danger of slavery. Divine redemption affirms that no chain shall hold their humanity down forever:

I'm a chile of God wid my soul set free,
For Christ hab bought my liberty.

The theme of freedom flows through the spirituals, coming to a crescendo with the symbol of heaven. This is no pie-in-the-sky-when-we-die kind of symbol, but a powerful marker of limit to pain, thanks to God who overcomes. Salvation was coming, whether in the form of a ship, a train, or a sweet chariot to carry them home. Jesus was coming, and expectation of his arrival discloses such hope:

I'm going back with Jesus when he comes,
I'm going back with Jesus when he comes,
O He may not come today
But He's coming anyway,
I'm going back with Jesus when he comes.

And we won't die anymore when He comes,
And we won't die anymore when He comes,
O He may not come today
But He's coming anyway,
And we won't die anymore when He comes.

No more "master's hollerin, driver's drivin, missus' scoldin"; all at the table, taking their ease; tears dried away; one long sabbath without end, an everlasting day of rest: all these imaginings of heaven's happiness added to the store of life symbols by which the slaves expanded the horizons of their present suffering. Ordinary historical observation would say their case was hopeless. But visions of a new heaven and a new earth had a powerful impact on their spirit, enabling them to live along the underside of history without being conquered by it.

One of the most poignant images of heaven was that of reunion. In heaven, parents and children, lovers, relatives, and friends would meet again —a devout hope for people who had seen their loved ones forcibly sold away with no hope of reunion in this world. One slave narrative described a departure scene where, as those who had been sold to another owner began to walk away down the road, those remaining on the plantation ran along inside the fence: ". . . some were yelling and wringing their hands, while others were singing little hymns that they had been accustomed to for the consolation of those who were going away, such as:

When we all meet in heaven,
There is no parting there;
When we all meet in heaven,
There is parting no more.

The spiritual was embedded in the anguish of this forced separation. The hope that they would meet again by God's design held their humanity together in the midst of the unjust brokenness of black slave existence.

On that morning "when the stars begin to fall" not only glory but also judgment would arrive. Vengeance was not a large part of the religion of the slaves. But it did not escape their notice that sheep and goats would be separated, with evildoers going to a punishment decreed by divine justice. Belief in God was not sentimental. Divine love entailed righteousness, and a wrath that would settle accounts with the slavers in God's own way.

The spirituals are unique religious creations that enabled an oppressed people to experience God sustaining their spirit in wretched places. Their question was not whether God exists, but whether God was with them in their struggle. They knew that over the long haul they could not trust their own strength to survive, let alone break the chains of slavery. Songs of God's liberating dealings with people in the past opened up a hopeful vision of the future, which kept their human dignity alive in the present. *"Let my people go"*: thus resounded the pledge that God will liberate the weak from the injustice of the strong. Divine presence thereby became a "rock in a weary land," a "shelter in the time of storm," a hand to hold "lest I fall." In an economic, legal, and social system that treated these human persons as property for monetary gain, spirituals nourished their humanity on the long road to freedom.

> Slavery chain done broke at last, broke at last, broke at last,
> Slavery chain done broke at last,
> Goin' to praise God til I die.

BLACK LIBERATION THEOLOGY

The religious heritage generated by the slaves flowed down through succeeding generations. Pressing to establish civic and legal equality for black people and thereby to end a century of violent post–Civil War segregation, the civil rights movement drew in powerful measure on this legacy, present now in the black churches. With black sermonic style and prophetic acuteness, a key leader, Martin Luther King Jr., memorably drew on this tradition in the struggle for freedom. His speeches and writings were rich with hopeful images of roads made straight, mountaintops scaled, flickering lamps restored, righteousness flowing like a mighty stream, being bound for glory; rich with prophetic visions of a world where all God's children will dwell in peace; rich with laments over the dream of freedom denied: "How long, O Lord...Not long!"; and rich with passion for the story of exodus including, poignantly, the night before King was murdered in Memphis, the promised land: "I may not get there with you, but I want you to know tonight that we as a people will get to the promised land. . . ." This was the heritage that brought him face to face with agony and despair, but also with the joyful hope that justice was arriving. Because God was on the side of righteousness, "we shall overcome."

As part of this movement and its aftermath, theologians from the black community have brought this faith vision into explicit, systematic language, crafting a black liberation theology in a North American context. Like all liberation theology, this work, in the words of a leading contributor, James Cone, "is a rational study of the being of God in the world in the light of the existential situation of an oppressed community, relating the forces of liberation to the essence of the gospel, which is Jesus Christ." It puts into ordered speech the meaning of God's activity in the world, which is liberation. In this instance, theology has as its bedrock the biblical theme grasped by the slaves, that the revelation of God takes place in the freeing of the oppressed Israelites from Egypt and in the strongly compassionate life, death, and resurrection of Jesus Christ, who was always on the side of the marginalized. Active throughout history, this is still a God who participates in the liberation of the oppressed of the land, now taking place in the struggle of black people for freedom. Filled with the Spirit, the black community is empowered to work to break the humiliating chains that hold them down, whether political, economic, legal, or cultural.

The problem, though, is that white people, too, from slave owners to the privileged of society today, believe in this same God of Jesus Christ. They invoke this God for a blessing, but do so in a society that is racist, with its institutions constructed so as to favor white people and discriminate against black people because of the color of their skin. This pattern is so insidious that white people do not even realize how privileged they are. Whiteness is pervasively normative, whereas the marker "black" gets added to people who deviate from that norm, a small point that signifies a lifetime of difference. All adherents of the Christian religion claim to be for God, with white churches taking the lead. But ungodly acts against black people have been perpetrated in the name of this God. Even in the absence of physical violence, which is, however, never far from the surface, the forces of institutional violence wreak havoc with the lives of black people. Black experience means daily existence in a system of white racism. Therefore, the question for black theology from the perspective of the black community necessarily becomes, "How can we speak of God without being associated with the oppressors of the land?"

To solve this dilemma black liberation theology, in addition to reflecting on the creating, redeeming, inspiriting God whose action is liberating and who promises a future to all the oppressed, makes a very specific move. It is convinced that "in a racist society, God is never color blind," which would mean being blind to injustice, blind to the difference between good and evil. Seeing clearly, God takes the side of those who are suffering, namely, black people. Black theology puts the new wine of this insight into the new wineskin of the symbol: *God is black*. As Cone declares, "The blackness of God, and everything implied by it in a racist society, is the heart of Black Theology's doctrine of God."

The significance of this image becomes clear when set in its social context of a dominantly white society and church. In this setting, unfortunately, preaching and catechesis have interpreted the gospel according to the political and cultural interests of the majority race. White American theologians, too, because of their identity with the power structure, analyze the nature of God in the interest of white society as a whole. Largely boxed in by their own cultural history, they rarely cross over to analyze the gospel in the light of the consciousness of black people struggling for human dignity, equality, and freedom. While theologians, along with most people, if asked, would acknowledge that God has no racial characteristics, the prevailing image in church and society is that of God as an all-powerful white man. This white God is an idol created by racism, and it functions to support the dominant status of white people in society. Prophets have always been called to the iconoclastic task of smashing false images. Declare "God is black," and a new vision of reality springs up.

To say that God is black means that God takes the oppressed condition and makes it God's own condition, something that is clear from the story of the exodus and the life story of Jesus. The Bible reveals that God self-identifies with people who experience humiliation and intense suffering. It means, furthermore, that divine solidarity does not show itself in pity without activity. Rather, God's signature deed is liberation. There is no God except the God who participates in the liberation of the oppressed of the land. In solidarity with black people's struggle for freedom, therefore, God is not the complacent, deeply racist white God of the dominant society. Nor is God simply colorless, a condition that would not challenge and contradict a society where people suffer precisely because of their color. Opting for black people, linking their destiny with the victory of divine glory, God is black.

Consequently, to be faithful believers "we must become black with God." For black persons, this means rejecting the white ideal imposed upon them and loving themselves as they are in all their physical blackness. As black Catholic theologian Diana Hayes notes, this entails "celebrating God's image in our blackness," being confident in our self-understanding as sons and daughters of God while affirming that all human beings are beloved by the Author of life. For white persons, this means being converted from the deep racism that pervades their religion and society and receiving the gift of salvation, which is love of God and a true love of neighbor, which reorients their life. For all Christians, knowing the Wholly Other God who is black entails being on the side of those who suffer, participating in the historic struggle toward the goal of liberation.

The symbol of the black God carries over into christology. In place of the honey-haired, blue-eyed, white Jesus whose image adorns churches, homes, and greeting cards, Christ is black. This is not necessarily a biological claim, though some would argue that a bit of Jewish-African intermarrying may well have occurred in Jesus' ancestry. And this, by the crazy calculus of American racial definitions, which finds even one drop of Negro blood enough to remove one from the white race, would make him black. The crucial import of the blackness of Christ is not genealogical, however, but religious. In his birth, ministry, and death, and in his presence in the community now, the black Christ's existential commitments ally the saving power of God made flesh with the despised of the land. This symbol evokes the truth that Christ takes on as his own black peoples' experience of racism, their protest against it, and their struggle for life and wholeness.

By using the religious experience of black people as a prominent source of theology, black liberation theology shows that this people's historical life of travail and joy provides valuable insight into the nature of God. Carrying forward the religious heritage of enslaved African people into a new era of struggle against white racism, this theology offers the whole church a challenging glimpse of the Holy One active in history: "the God of the oppressed is a God of revolution who breaks the chains of slavery."

WOMANIST SURVIVAL THEOLOGY

Not all African American theologians have been content to leave the matter there. While acknowledging that liberation theology and the symbol of divine blackness do articulate the community's glimpse of God in the face of racism, women in particular have shown that there is more to the story than this. Womanist analysis makes clear that in addition to racism, black women also suffer from bias against them due to their sex. To be a person who is black and female is thus to contend with both white racism and patriarchy that comes in all colors.

Bias against black women pervades the black community and the black churches themselves, which are deeply patriarchal. Struggling today to make a way for themselves and their children, black women live a religious experience that is not adequately captured in the theology of liberation or the symbol of the black Christ.

There are other biblical paradigms for encounter with God, however, which do speak to black women's experience. One of the most far-reaching surrounds the biblical figure of Hagar, who has been passed along in sculpture, poetry, and preaching in the African American community for generations. Richly reinterpreted in the work of Delores Williams, Hagar's story, emphasizing as it does female activity, has become widely influential. The key movement here is not exodus from slavery to the promised land but sojourn in the wilderness. The primary motif of God's activity is not liberation but survival.

Hagar's tale unfolds in Genesis chapters 16 and 21. She was not a Jew, a member of the people chosen by God, but a female slave of African descent. Twice she had dramatic encounters with God over matters of life and death; once she took the initiative to name the Most High. As an Egyptian enslaved to Sarah, the wife of Abraham, she kept finding ways around roadblocks thrown up in her situation to forge a path toward the future. Similarities between her experience and that of black women both under slavery and in the time since are striking.

The story opens with Sarah, not being able to conceive an heir, encouraging her husband to lie with her slave woman. When their union issues in Hagar's becoming pregnant, tension between the two women flares. With Abraham's agreement, Sarah treats Hagar harshly. The slave woman resists this brutality with courage: she runs away. In the wilderness this pregnant woman encounters the Holy One. What is the divine response to her predicament? Rather than encourage her liberating escape, God issues a startling instruction: "Return." This mandate is accompanied by a many-layered promise. She will give birth to a son and call him Ishmael; her descendants would multiply so greatly that they cannot be counted; in effect she would be the mother of a great people. Hagar named the One who spoke to her *El-roi*, the God of seeing, which name still attaches to the life-sustaining well in the wilderness where her encounter took place. The point Williams notes is that in some circumstances divine presence prompts women to take action to survive and safeguard the thread of life into the future, rather than seek freedom at the risk of death as a paramount value. Since the best resources for the child's being born and growing up healthy lay in the house of Abraham and Sarah, Hagar acts according to God's prompting for survival.

This motif is reiterated when Hagar finds herself exiled in the wilderness a second time, now with her son in tow. After the birth of Abraham's firstborn son by Hagar, Sarah finally conceived her own child, Isaac. Watching the two boys play, she feared that Ishmael would share in Abraham's inheritance, so she cast the boy and his mother out of the household. Without sufficient resources to survive in the bleak, dry wilderness, Hagar and her child were near death from hunger and thirst. She placed the boy under a bush so she would not have to watch him die. Weeping, she then heard the voice of the angel of God reiterating the promise that Ishmael would become a great nation. "*Then God opened her eyes and she saw a well of water. She went, and filled the skin with water, and gave the boy a drink*" (Gen 21:19). This encounter with the Holy One prompted life-giving vision for Hagar. Once again she saw what was needed for survival and acted. Years later she arranged a marriage for Ishmael with a woman from Egypt, and the divine promise was off and running through history.

As Williams notes, God's response to Hagar's crises, both times, prompted her to survive and develop a quality of life appropriate to her heritage and situation. Congruent with many African American women's situation in the past and even today, Hagar faced slavery, poverty, ethnic prejudice, sexual and economic exploitation, rape, surrogate motherhood, domestic violence, homelessness, and single-parenting. They find themselves, like Hagar, in the wilderness, resources exhausted, looking for water. In the midst of this turmoil, they hear the voice of the angel of God. "Over and over again, black women in the churches have testified about their serious personal and salvific encounters with God, encounters that helped them and their families survive." Strengthened by this encounter, they figure out how to make a way out of no way.

The story of Hagar in the wilderness directs attention to African American women's history of survival intelligence using a variety of silent, subtle, and dramatic strategies. Holding onto life in the face of formidable forces, they find ways for their families to survive and grow. The insights of black theology are thus twofold. In addition to the liberation tradition, which views God as Liberator leading the oppressed to freedom, there is the survival tradition, which sees God as Sustainer in the wilderness. Liberation is the ultimate goal, but along the way the Spirit of God supports daily efforts to stay alive, helping people to see new resources, promising a future for children: *"in the wilderness I will make a way"* (Isa 43:19).

A SHARPER FOCUS

Using the experience of African American women as a source for theology brings new insights to perennial issues.

 Regarding images of God, the question is not only how women can consider themselves made in God's image if the metaphors most often used —father, lord, and king—are predominantly masculine. But the question also arises as to why black women should relate to a God identified in this way, since these names connote power over others and elicit a corresponding fear of authority in those whom such power has abused. While it might help to know that if God is Lord then the slave master does not have final say over my being, the image by its very nature transfers a defective earthly model to heaven. As Patricia Hunter observes, "The patriarchal titles of

Lord and Master do not conjure loving or kind images for those whose history includes enslavement."

⟨ Similarly, for all its power to resist white racist assumptions, the symbol of the black Christ does not confront the oppression of women within the black community, adhering as it does to a male-identified image of Christ. Only when women are seen as the icon of Christ, Kelly Brown Douglas argues, will the sustaining, liberating, prophetic presence of the Christ who is black serve the growth of the whole community. We need to learn to see and honor the face of Christ in the faces of the poorest black women, in the faces of a Sojourner Truth, a Harriet Tubman, or a Fannie Lou Hamer as each one struggled to help the black community survive, in order for this symbol to release its blessing.

⟨ Black women's experience of surrogacy brings a critical sensitivity to interpretations of the cross. Under slavery, women were coerced into surrogacy roles in households (the mammy nurturing the white mother's children), in the fields (80 percent of female slaves plowed, planted, and harvested, work normally consigned to men), and in the beds of the slave owners (raped to provide pleasure not available from the white wife). Female slaves had no power to refuse these roles, for they were property. The experience left a deep suspicion about standing in for another, since substitutionary roles formed such a unique dimension of domination in black women's lives.

Traditional theology of the cross makes Jesus a surrogate figure, teaching that in death he suffered the punishment that sinful humanity deserved. The fact that he took on himself human sinfulness, thereby removing the burden from us, shows his deep love and makes him our Savior. This construct, however, is deeply flawed. Redemption can have nothing to do with a bloody act of one person being killed in place of another. Such substitution is repugnant. Rather, through Jesus' ministry, with its hopeful healings and its preaching about the kingdom of God, and through his resurrection and the consequent flourishing of the Spirit in the world, God gained victory over the evil that tried to kill the gift that Jesus brought. Theology of the cross today needs to employ different sociopolitical models, Williams argues, showing black women, "that their salvation does not depend upon any form of surrogacy made sacred by human understandings of God." Otherwise the repugnant slave-master image of God looms again.

¶ The history of slavery also limits the usefulness of the religious idea of being a handmaid or servant of the Lord. "Some folk are more servants than others," observes Jacqueline Grant ironically, noting that while members of the church hierarchy call themselves servants of God, they are likely to be male, educated, and economically well-off. Meanwhile, the persons who actually are servants, both domestically and in service industries, are likely to be women of color, poorly educated, and on the lowest rung of the economic ladder. In place of servanthood as a religious ideal, indeed one that abets and does not resist sinful social situations, Grant argues that discipleship is a preferable model for the human–divine relationship. God is not honored by any master–slave relationship, nor does divine activity in the world result in subordination. Being a disciple, by contrast, empowers women both in their personal lives and in their participation in the church to take ownership, take initiative, take charge.

Thus does black theology bring the wisdom of just dealings to theological discussions.

PRAXIS OF RACIAL JUSTICE

Glimpses of God who liberates the oppressed and makes a way in the wilderness where there is no way have also emerged with vigor in the black theology forged in South Africa under apartheid and in theology done from the experience of aboriginal people in Australia. In each case the juggernaut of white colonialism wreaked havoc on the lives of people whose skin is a darker color. Amid intense suffering, misery, and death, black people have glimpsed a God different from the one who arrived with the conquerors, namely, a God who participates in their struggle to survive and get free. Out of the history of America's "original sin" of slavery, African American theology is making its own distinctive contribution in the voices of black people to the church's understanding of God.

What kind of praxis flows from this insight? The praxis of racial justice in the social and personal spheres. To be black in America is still too often to be discriminated against because of one's color and what that color signifies to white people. This continued presence of racism, subtle or overt, in society is a bitter sin whose damage tears at the soul of the white community, the perpetrators, even as it inflicts dehumanizing harm on the black community. Doing racial justice runs counter to this violation. In one of his speeches Martin Luther King explained beautifully, "Justice is love correcting that which revolts against love." For people of faith, acting justly in race matters expresses a love of specific neighbors that is utterly interwoven with belief in the living God. Doing justice is intrinsic to faith because the God who points out springs of water in the wilderness cannot be separated from the one who wanders there; the God who breaks chains is forever in solidarity with those marching toward the promised land.

> Children we shall be free,
> When Jesus, he shall appear.

FOR FURTHER READING

A beautifully written work of original research on the religion of the slaves is Albert Raboteau, *Slave Religion: The "Invisible Institution" in the Antebellum South* (New York: Oxford, 1978, 2004). It studies the spirituals, setting them in their context. For a theological assessment of these songs, see James Cone, *The Spirituals and the Blues: An Interpretation* (New York: Seabury, 1972; reprint, Maryknoll, N.Y.: Orbis 1991).

Resonant with biblical references, the key speeches, sermons, and writings of Martin Luther King Jr. have been collected in *A Testament of Hope: The Essential Writings and Speeches of Martin Luther King, Jr.* (New York: HarperCollins, 1991). See David Garrow, *Bearing the Cross: Martin Luther King Jr. and the Southern Christian Leadership Conference* (New York: Wm. Morrow, 1986) for King's story, including his roots in the black church.

For an overview of the development of black voices in theology, see James Cone and Gayraud Wilmore, eds. *Black Theology: A Documentary History*, vol. 1, *1966–1979* (Orbis, 1979); vol. 2, *1980–1992* (Orbis, 1993). A leading thinker of black liberation theology is James Cone, whose most influential works are *A Black Theology of Liberation* (Philadelphia: Lippincott, 1970; reprint, Orbis, 1986), and *God of the Oppressed* (San Francisco:

Harper & Row, 1975; reprint, Orbis, 1997). The work of J. Deotis Roberts places more emphasis on reconciliation of the black community with white people; see *Liberation and Reconciliation: A Black Theology* (Philadelphia: Westminster, 1971). The books of both authors have extended reflections on God and Christ as black. Diana Hayes, *And Still We Rise: An Introduction to Black Liberation Theology* (New York: Paulist, 1996) provides a fine overview of the field.

The theology of survival from the perspective of black women's experience was first worked out by Delores Williams, whose book dialogues critically with the shortsightedness of the theology of both black men and white women: *Sisters in the Wilderness: The Challenge of Womanist God-Talk* (Orbis, 1993). A creative womanist work on God is Karen Baker Fletcher, *Dancing with God: The Trinity from a Womanist Perspective* (St. Louis: Chalice Press, 2006). Kelly Brown Douglas, *The Black Christ* (Orbis, 1994) expands the Christ symbol by taking into account the existence and experience of black women. A womanist approach to christology in contrast to feminism's critique is worked out in Jacqueline Grant, *White Women's Christ and Black Women's Jesus: Feminist Christology and Womanist Response* (American Academy of Religion Academy series 64; Atlanta: Scholars Press, 1989). For a superb set of essays that deal with the slave heritage in the light of black women's experience of struggle today, see Emilie Townes, ed., *A Troubling in My Soul: Womanist Perspectives on Evil and Suffering* (Orbis, 1993), especially M. Shawn Copeland, "Wading through Many Sorrows," pp. 109–29.

The growing Catholic voice in black theology is heard in Diana Hayes and Cyprian Davis, eds., *Taking Down Our Harps: Black Catholics in the United States* (Orbis, 1998); Jamie Phelps, *Black and Catholic: The Challenge and Gift of Black Folk: Contributions of African American Experience and Thought to Catholic Theology* (Milwaukee, Wis.: Marquette University, 1997)(also published as electronic book); and Peter Phan and Diana Hayes, eds., *Many Faces, One Church: Cultural Diversity and the American Catholic Experience* (Lanham, Md.: Rowman & Littlefield, 2005).

7

ACCOMPANYING GOD OF *FIESTA*

CONTEXT: *LA LUCHA*

Consider the insight into God's holy mystery that has arisen among peoples with ancestral Latin American and Caribbean roots who are living in the United States. These communities themselves are widely diverse, hailing from different countries of origin and carrying forward different local customs. In the year 2000 the national census revealed that collectively these peoples comprise 13 percent of the U.S. population, now forming the largest minority. The census further identified six subgroups ranging numerically from the largest to the smallest, from Mexico, Puerto Rico, Central America, South America, Cuba, and the Dominican Republic, respectively. The term Hispanic, put into service by the U.S. Census Bureau and often used in common parlance to describe these communities, tends to flatten out differences in what is actually a flexible and dynamic identity shared among peoples of diverse ethnicity, race, and nationality. One alternative coming into use among scholars is Latino or Latina, often written in condensed form as Latino/a, which, although it has the advantage of being a self-chosen designation, is also marked by many of the same ambiguities.

Whatever the appellation, and this chapter uses the terms interchangeably, statistics indicate that in terms of economic and educational status, two-thirds of the people of these communities are at the lower end of the scale. The majority being poor and poorly educated, the group as a whole is underrepresented in institutions that run society. General underclass status also means that mainstream U.S. culture tends to ignore, disparage, or misunderstand their culture, considering it not quintessentially "American." For the majority, to live means to engage in the struggle, *la lucha*.

Two Conquests

The back story of Hispanic peoples and their religious wisdom is bloody and violent, marked by two conquests. The first was Spain's conquest of the lands and peoples of the "new world" discovered by them in 1492. On the hunt for gold and riches, Spain placed indigenous populations into servitude, killed their leaders, appropriated their land and natural resources, and broke the backs of their cultures. Twenty-three million people died in the space of fifty years in Mexico during the early colonial period. It was in this state of vanquishment that people first heard the word of Christianity from the missionaries who arrived with the *conquistadores*. Experiencing slavery, plunder, rape, and oppression, their suffering gave a particular cast to the way they heard the "good news."

The second conquest happened in the nineteenth century, when the United States expanded its national borders by military conquest, annexation, and purchase. The largest disruption occurred in 1848, when Mexico, defeated in war, ceded approximately one-half of its own country to the United States. This vast territory included the present states of California, Arizona, and New Mexico plus large sections of Colorado, Nevada, and Utah. The treaty of 1848 also approved the United States' prior annexation of Texas. The presence of Latinos and Latinas in the southwest today happened not because of migration but because centuries-old settled communities were engulfed by the United States and its "manifest destiny." As Gary Riebe-Estrella makes clear, "Our presence in this country historically happened not because we crossed the border but rather because the border crossed us." The United States had earlier purchased Florida from Mexico. War with Spain in 1898 resulted in U.S. hegemony over Cuba and Puerto Rico, though these islands were not incorporated as states. This second conquest resulted in the imposition of political, economic, and social systems that marginalized the Hispanic populations. It also brought them and their religious traditions face to face with Protestant Anglo Christianity, whose vanguard evidenced persistent disdain for these "papist, degenerate, and mixed-blooded" people (Elizondo). The second conquest placed Latino and Latina people in a minority position within a ruling nation that cared little for their history or well-being.

Mestizaje/Mixing

The result of this cruel history is a people formed, like a new river, out of two previously separated streams. The concept of *mestizaje,* or mixing, was first worked out by Virgilio Elizondo to identify the specific and special identity of these two streams. As he describes it, *mestizaje* represents a border reality where people have a foot in two worlds, blending together in themselves different races, cultures, and religious traditions.

❧ Racially, the mixing of indigenous and Spanish people that occurred in the first conquest is itself a complex phenomenon. Amerindian ancestors emigrated from Asia and ended up in different native population groups such as the Taínos, Caribs, Aztecs, Mayas, and Incas. The Spanish themselves combined Iberian, Greek, Arab, Goth, and gypsy genes in their makeup. The mixing of these two strains produced persons referred to as *mestizo* or *mestiza.* The Spanish also engaged in the slave trade; the mixing of their biological heritage with peoples of African descent produced persons referred to as *mulato* or *mulata.* Out of this conflictive history of *mestizaje/mulataje* have come the U.S. Hispanic peoples, racially the descendants of both the conquerors and the conquered.

❧ Culturally, the original mixing of Spanish Mediterranean traditions with Amerindian and African traditions produced a people whose positive characteristics include a gift for celebration, strong connection to family, and a passionate zest for life dramatized in community. On the negative side the culture may inculcate a certain fatalism or passivity in the face of life's afflictions and, with its emphasis on *machismo,* promote oppressive family structures and a restricted sense of self among women. The second conquest further positioned this already blended people between two disparate cultures, southern and northern. This social context is often conflictive, the values and expectations of one culture being disappointed by the performance of the other.

❝ Religiously, the worldview of the indigenous peoples of Mesoamerica was imbued with the presence of the sacred, which was ritualized in visual, musical, and dramatic symbols. At key moments in the year's cycle the people engaged in extended religious pageantry in public places such as town squares or the tops of pyramids. Small clan altars or family altars provided local access to the sacred on a daily basis. The Iberian form of Christianity brought with the *conquistadores* and implanted on this indigenous soil was itself deeply symbolic. In a series of careful, insightful studies, Orlando Espín has demonstrated that this Christianity was medieval in form, predating the split occasioned by the Protestant Reformation and thus untouched by the new patterns established by the Catholic Church at the Council of Trent. With roots in the patristic and medieval church, it was premodern Christianity as it existed before the West even knew the words Protestant and Catholic in their current divided senses. Its religious vision knew nothing of the later division between secular and sacred, for the world of the spirit was present everywhere. Its style was profusely sacramental, approaching the sacred through images, stories, and popular rituals based on the belief that such created things can mediate between the visible and invisible worlds and convey grace.

Both Amerindian and medieval European religion addressed a largely illiterate population, and consequently depended on visual and oral means of teaching and celebrating the faith. The mixing of the two yielded a new form of *mestizo* Iberoamerican Christianity, not tied to the religious problems of Europe that produced Protestantism and Tridentine Catholicism, nor beholden to modern Western ways of knowing. Rather, as the inheritor of two great mystical traditions, it became an embodiment of the faith of the suffering poor in the new world. The addition of religious traditions of Africa into the mix strengthened in its own way the accent on visual, oral, dramatic mediation.

POPULAR RELIGION

In subsequent centuries this inculturation of Christianity developed not according to the models of the church in Europe or the United States but "in accordance with the inner dynamics of the Spirit actively at work" in the people, as Elizondo argues. Its ultimate center of attention is the mystery of God who walks with the people in everyday life, *lo cotidiano*. This divine presence is mediated in graphic, tangible ways. Ubiquitous home altars, simple affairs set up in a nook, with a cross, statues, or pictures of Jesus, Mary, or the saints and adorned with flowers and votive candles, manifest that God is there for the people in their own homes, accessible morning, noon, and night in a relationship of mutual commitment and responsibility. The rosaries hanging from car mirrors, images of Guadalupe tattooed on the bodies of young men and painted on the walls of *barrios*, the ex-votos (texts of thanks) and *milagritos* (charms depicting body parts) brought to places of pilgrimage in gratitude for healing, the public religious *fiestas,* Christmas *posadas*, and Good Friday processions that punctuate the year, all serve to express a strong sense of connection to the Holy in polyvalent, imaginative ways pervaded with a profoundly affective flair.

This is "popular religion," so-called not because it is approved by a large number of folks but because its creators and practitioners are the people. It is the work of the community, the people's way of appropriating the traditional beliefs of Christianity and expressing them in their own everyday spiritual practices. Sixto Garcia's definition underscores the context: popular religion is "the set of experiences, beliefs, and rituals which more-or-less peripheral human groups create, assume, and develop . . . to find access to God and salvation which they feel they cannot find in what church and society present as normative." It is a lived faith that encounters and names God "from within their experiences of life and death, word and silence, joy and suffering, liberation and oppression," as María Pilar Aquino describes it. Its practices express a strong spirituality that recognizes the presence of the divine in the routines and surprises of everyday life.

This style of Christianity is unrepentantly incarnational, passing on core knowledge in an experiential way. Unlike the systematic logic of the modern West, it thinks with a rationality structured around relationships. Knowledge is acquired through affective participation in the symbols and rituals, yielding not primarily cerebral knowledge of doctrines, although its doctrinal repertoire is broad and deep, but personal trust and love of God, who is the source of the community's existence. Compared to the more sedate pattern of the Christianity of northern climates, its expressions are exuberantly imaginative. Sociologists have studied them as instances of

exotic or folkloric customs. But far from being a collection of colorful odd-
ities, this constellation of practices and the worldview they bear are a form
of living religion. Shaped in a matrix of suffering and abuse, this religion
comprises a network of beliefs, ethical expectations, rites, and prayerful
experiences that together convey the vibrant presence of God in the midst
of daily life. Rather than being restricted to the institutional church's sacred
place (the consecrated building) and sacred times (formal worship led by
the clergy), here divine presence migrates into the community to be with
people in their homes, streets, and main plazas of the towns.

A notable aspect of this peoples' form of Christianity is that its obser-
vance is accessible to all, being lay-led rather than organized by the ordained
or professional clergy. In the colonial period there were good reasons for
this: vast geographic distances, large populations, European clergy relatively
few in number, and ecclesiastical racism that would not allow indigenous or
mestizo/mulato men into seminaries (not to mention women). The result
has been a cultural-religious pattern that diminishes the importance of the
institutional church, making intimate relationship with God rather more
accessible in daily life than in official liturgies. Speaking of the *abuelitas,* the
wise older women present in his childhood community, Elizondo writes
that when no clergy were present to minister to their needs, "our grand-
mothers were around to bless us, to pray for us, and to offer a *velita* (candle)
as the sacrifice of the poor." As for the public religious rituals of the community, Elizondo, himself now a Catholic priest, writes approvingly that
"they are truly the faith celebrations of the people of God in which the bishops, clergy, and religious are most welcome, but not missed if they are not
around."

The fact that the majority of people deal with poverty and second-class
status gives this whole design a tone of struggle and hope. Both historically
and in contemporary life, conflict and injustice shape people's experience.
How can they maintain their spirit amid this matrix of suffering? Popular
religion answers meaningfully—through daily life with its religious practices that confront sin and affirm that God is walking with them. *Mujerista*
theologian Ada María Isasi-Díaz points out the special relevance this pattern has for poor women and children who, while their primary language is
neither English nor that of academic theology, can discover and be blessed
by the presence of God in the marginalized private space of their own home,

however substandard. Popular religion has salvific value, Aquino argues, "because God dwells therein, among the scorned of the earth."

Far from being a mere vestige of Christianity, popular religion is a robust way of relating to reality and of living the gospel that carries forward the medieval sacramental pattern of Christian faith inculturated within Amerindian and African sacral worldviews. While different from the contemporary Western style of faith practiced in Europe and the United States, it is a configuration that brings God into the daily life of the poor while interpreting and transmitting Christian revelation in a significant way. U.S. Hispanic theologians note that, as with all religion, there are limits. Popular religion is mediated through a culture that is wounded and in need of healing and correction. Discernment is necessary to make sure the gospel is communicated in all its strength, including the call to leave passive quiescence for hopeful resistance in the social sphere. Still, this faith of lived intimacy with God, based on confidence that the divine is accessible in the midst of suffering, and culturally salted with symbols of compassion and hope, has for centuries sustained the lives of millions of people with beauty and joy. "As long as human beings desire to make contact with the transcendent dimension of everyday life," declares Roberto Goizueta, "as long as we seek to find meaning in life and death, as long as we strive to express the ineffable and to relate religious belief to everyday life—which is to say always—there will be popular religion."

DOING THEOLOGY *LATINAMENTE*

Traditionally overlooked in history books, the presence of Hispanic peoples with their popular religion is one of the oldest on the U.S. landscape. Theology done *latinamente* in organic connection with these communities, however, is relatively young. Dating from the early 1970s, it began when some few members of the community trained in theology began to focus on the lived faith of the people and began to make the argument that their popular network of religious customs receives, believes, and passes on the Christian truth about God and the world in a legitimate manner.

This theology should not be confused with the liberation theology that originated in Central and South America. While the two have many points in common, especially appreciation for God's special care of the poor, they have arisen in distinctly different historical contexts. In its struggle for the presence of God amid economic injustice, liberation theology could at least take its own cultural context, including language, for granted. By contrast, U.S. Latino and Latina theologians seek to give voice to the faith of peoples deeply shaped by their Latin American heritage while they live, whether by birth or immigration, in a very different, English-speaking dominant society. To do so, they interpret the "big story" of the Christian tradition as mediated through the "little stories" that comprise the daily lives of the people. Despite the pain and brokenness of their experience, people survive, using cultural/religious practices to build lives of love, beauty, and joy. Attending to this, Latino and Latina theologians not only make an option for the poor. They also make an option for the *faith* of the poor, to coin a phrase, seeking to interpret the meaning of popular religious practice with a fresh and original voice. Befitting their membership in the community, they often work together, *en conjunto*, making theology a shared endeavor with the goal of religious relevance, pastoral care, and the implementation of biblical justice in society.

To back up this approach, Orlando Espín appeals to the classical teaching on the *sensus fidelium*, the sense of the faithful. This is the teaching that the body of the faithful as a whole, baptized, anointed, and moved by the Spirit, has an intuitive grasp of matters of belief that is ultimately reliable. Believing in the word of God, the Christian people can sense that something is true or not true according to the gospel, and can know in their bones what encourages right conduct, prayer, and witness. Consequently, along with the magisterium, the liturgy, official teaching, and theologians, the people are bearers of tradition, to be consulted, as Cardinal John Henry Newman famously noted, in matters of doctrine.

In the present context, this means that popular religion, the people's lived religiosity, is a constitutive element of the church and an indispensable source of insight into God. Yes, it is culturally specific, keeping faith alive not solely by dogmas and official liturgies, but also by great symbols and rituals that engage the imagination, emotion, and the heart. But every instantiation of the gospel from the beginning has been culturally specific; there is no other possibility for an incarnational faith that stays alive in history. Functioning in deep contact with myths, graphic visual imagery, stories, and celebrations, popular religion has functioned for centuries as an indispensable bearer of tradition. The God it cherishes is "a God who defends, protects, corrects, and nourishes the very same social groups the world disdains," Aquino underscores. To date, Hispanic theology has achieved its distinct profile by taking popular religion seriously as a fruitful source for theological reflection.

Our Lady

One important area of work that has surprisingly far-reaching implications for the theology of God deals with popular devotion to *la Virgen*, a widespread and deeply felt Catholic phenomenon that raises consternation among mainline Protestant, evangelical, and Pentecostal Christians who today also comprise the broad Hispanic community (European divisions have caught up with the New World). Each national group has its own version of the Marian symbol accompanied by stories that show the care of the Mother of God for their struggles. The most well known is Mexico's Our Lady of Guadalupe, whose appearance to a poor Indian shortly after the Spanish conquest is a brilliant instance of religious *mestizaje*, fusing Christian and indigenous symbols. Flowers and song, symbols of the divine in Amerindian religion, attended the Lady's coming. She appeared on Tepeyac hill, the site of the recently suppressed sanctuary of the beloved goddess Tonantzin. Most striking, the image of her face left on Juan Diego's homespun cloak is indigenous, giving rise to the affectionate name *la Morenita*, the little brown one. Her presence and consoling words served to promote the human dignity of defeated people at the time of conquest and have continued ever since: witness César Chávez, whose 1970s marches for justice for immigrant farm workers in California stepped out under the banner of Our Lady of Guadalupe. Whatever the image and title, the Marian devotion of popular Catholicism is warm and loving, relating to the Mother of God as a tangible manifestation of care. She "walks-with persons who have been culturally marginalized," explains Miguel Díaz; "as she looks at, welcomes, and assumes the cultural face of those who have been rejected, forgotten, and oppressed, they are welcomed, remembered, and resurrected."

Latina and Latino theological reflection in the United States is virtually unanimous in interpreting the figure of *la Virgen* in their communities as a symbol of divine love, and people's devotion as a mediated encounter with divine compassion. One group of theologians questing for understanding goes further and queries the knot tied so tightly between Hispanic images of the Virgin and the actual first-century Jewish woman Mary of Nazareth, mother of Jesus. Orlando Espín, for one, argues for a different interpretation. "When I am confronted by the depth of trust and affection that Latinos have for the *Virgen*, and when I see the beautiful, reverential relationship they nurture with her, and also how deeply touched and empowered they are by her, then as a theologian I have to wonder." His wonder leads him to suggest that instead of an encounter with Mary, what is taking place is a superbly inculturated experience of the Holy Spirit.

Espín is not implying that Mary *is* the Holy Spirit, or that in some way she mediates the feminine face of God. He is arguing that the historical Mary has nothing much to do with this phenomenon at all. It is not the Jewish woman Miriam of Nazareth whom Latinos and Latinas venerate in their devotion to *la Virgen de Guadalupe*. It is rather the Holy Spirit of God, expressed not in the categories of Greek myth or European culture and philosophy but now in categories fused from conquering Spanish and conquered Mesoamerican peoples. Ecclesiastical authorities in colonial times insisted on a Marian interpretation in an understandably defensive move to protect doctrinal purity, since the only female imagery for the divine that they knew was associated with the religion they were trying to stamp out. Besides, too much talk of the Holy Spirit could bring on the unwanted attention of the Inquisition. But in the experience of the people then and now, references to the Mary of the gospels are notably absent in connection with devotion to Guadalupe. What is mediated instead is a profoundly engaging experience of sacred love and compassion that gives heart, wisdom, and fortitude to adherents. Therefore, might it not be the case, reflects Espín, that "what we have here is not mariology but pneumatology in an unexpected and brilliantly achieved cultural mediation?" The Marian practices of Hispanic Catholicism may thus come to signify an orthodox pneumatology, superbly inculturated.

THE GOD WHO ACCOMPANIES

Unlike the inadequate idea of God in modern theism that prevails in major portions of U.S. society, the glimpses of God caught in Hispanic communities are rich in immanence and relationship. This is a God who is *with* people, sustaining and strengthening them wherever they go, especially in the midst of *la lucha*. The people relate not to a metaphysical reality or to a distant deity but to a personal and communal God of great compassion. Experiencing the Creator of heaven and earth as a loving and affectionate friend, people may call upon the divine as *Diosito*, a term of endearment for One who is known intimately: dear little God. This protective, supportive Holy One walks every day with the community. In turn, and not insignificantly, the living God is known by the company Love keeps.

The metaphor of accompaniment plays a central role in articulating the peoples' experience of the holy mystery who journeys with them in daily life. Its meaning gains depth and clarity when placed in the framework of the peoples' experience of "being with" on the human level. One of the most significant characteristics of Hispanic culture has to do with the meaning of the individual. In this culture, the fundamental unit of society is envisioned as a group, primarily the family. The identity of the individual emerges from his or her membership in the group. In this cultural perspective, as Gary Riebe-Estrella explains, "human persons mature by recognizing their place within the group and by refining to some extent the mutual obligations and rights which that place entails." In this "sociocentric organic" culture, a person's identity is intrinsically relational, always bounded by the group. A folk axiom puts it succinctly: tell me who you walk with and I'll tell you who you are. By contrast, the modern liberal anthropology of U.S. mainstream culture envisions the fundamental unit of society as the individual. Human persons mature by distancing themselves from others in order to discover their own abilities. "When this identity has achieved sufficient strength and form, the individual freely associates with others for mutual benefit in the lifelong developmental task of intimacy." The relationship is contractual, dependent on mutual consent. Thus, the model can be characterized as "egocentric contractual," with priority to the individual over the group. To date, the sociocentric organic pattern of Hispanic culture has persisted through second and third generations in the United States, even amid financial and social success.

Such cultural analysis provides a helpful framework for interpreting the notion of the God who accompanies. Just as Latinas and Latinos understand themselves communally, finding the fullness of their identity by walking together, so too they envision that God is walking with them, gifting them with life and strength. The many rituals of popular religion, especially those surrounding the birth and death of Jesus, are indications of this co-walking, enacting the realization that God understands: the struggles, sufferings and joys of human existence are not alien to the divine, but rather the site of divine solidarity and care.

❧ *Posada.* This pre-Christmas ritual reenacts the Bethlehem story with emphasis on the search for shelter, there being no room at the inn. Accompanied by the community, the individuals embodying Mary and Joseph walk from house to house in the neighborhood looking for hospitality. Repeatedly turned away, they keep searching for a place to stay until a (pre-designated) family finally takes them in, at which point refreshments are shared all around. This ritual procession makes vividly present the truth that the God of heaven and earth was walking with this poor couple. Indeed, the poor girl from Nazareth is now the place where the Holy One dwells in the flesh. Those who take part in the procession understand its strong resonance with the migration, homelessness, and rejection all too well known in the community. The celebration that follows affirms that Emmanuel comes to abide among those whom the world rejects, which is cause for joy.

❧ *Good Friday processions.* It is a paradox that among those who most agonizingly know the power of death we find the most stubborn faith in the power of life. This faith is enacted in the customs of Holy Week, which locate divine presence on the road not to birth but to death. To well-established persons, Hispanic emphasis on the cross in graphic art and religious theater might seem morbid. But to those whose foundational experience was vanquishment and whose daily life is filled with struggle, only a suffering God who walks to the cross can give meaning to the painful absurdities that life multiplies. Roberto Goizueta's haunting depiction of the Good Friday reenactment at San Fernando Cathedral in San Antonio, Texas, conveys its energy:

> At 10:00 A.M. a loud trumpet signals the entrance of Pilate onto the stage to confront Jesus of Nazareth. From this point on, the words and actions follow the gospel passion narratives, with San Fernando parishioners playing the parts of the different characters in the passion story. Pilate sends Jesus to Herod, who in turn returns him to Pilate for judgment.

After the crowd calls for the release of Barabbas, Jesus is flogged and crowned with thorns. Pilate presents the beaten and broken Nazarene to the people—that is to the assembled crowd in San Fernando/Jerusalem —who cry out for his crucifixion. The scene can only be described as eerie: this is not an event that happened two thousand years ago, but an event taking place today and in which we are actively participating.

The event continues out of doors as Jesus carries his cross down the crowd-lined city streets to Calvary. Shopkeepers close their stores and stand at reverent attention. Women reach out to whisper consoling words to Jesus' sorrowful mother as she passes by. A little boy unexpectedly runs out to kiss Jesus after he falls.

The symbolic resonance of the entire passion play reverberates with the experience of the marginalized people who participate in it. Their sufferings become visible in the broken humanity of Jesus. "Jesus the Christ is our brother in sorrow and oppression," explains Sixto García, "and we can touch him, mourn with him, die with him, and yes, also hope with him." What is so valuable about the reenactment is not just that the story ends in victory on Easter morning, but that even along the way of the cross divine mercy strengthens and sustains Jesus in his victimization. This is at the center of Hispanic popular religion's insight into God.

Three Principles

Virgilio Elizondo's work in christology gives further precision to the intuition of God's accompaniment. According to the gospels, Jesus was a Galilean Jew. In Elizondo's analysis this fact has great theological significance. Whereas the center of Jewish culture and religion was Jerusalem, with its wealthy elite and priest-attended Temple, the northern region of Galilee was an outpost of poor, rural people. Its villages were despised—"*Can anything good come out of Nazareth?*" (John 1:46). This Galilee was a marginal place, a center of neither religious nor intellectual nor political influence: "marginality as symbolized by Galilee is one of the key functional concepts of the inner dynamism of the gospel." As a crossroads of commerce in goods and the movements of people, it was also a place where various cultures intermingled. Infiltrated by exposure to outsiders, it was far from being a place of pure Jewish culture.

As a Galilean Jew, Jesus, the Word and Wisdom of God, was marginal like his region. His humanity was a product of *mestizaje*, culturally mixed, linguistically bilingual, with even his birth and parentage suspect, many undoubtedly assuming he had a Roman father (taking the infancy narratives and later Jewish legend as part of the story). In his final trip to Jerusalem he encountered failure, rejection, and the violent treatment meted out by great powers to those who are politically insignificant. But God was with him all the way.

From this interpretation of the historical, geographic, and cultural coordinates of Jesus' life, Elizondo culls three principles applicable to the Hispanic community. First, the Galilee principle: what human beings reject, God chooses as his own. Second, the Jerusalem principle: God entrusts the rejected with a mission, to confront the powers of this world in order to transform society. Third, the resurrection principle: out of the suffering and death that this entails, God brings life, overcoming evil by the power of love. These principles spell out the divine way of acting in the world made known in Christ. In truth, they are a scandal to the important, well-qualified, well-installed, honorable people of society. But they are good news to poor, marginalized peoples of *mestizaje* heritage who recognize here how God walks with the poor.

This glimpse of the accompanying God is filtered through the lens of Jesus, the suffering human brother and Word of God. In Jesus, Latino and Latina peoples grasp that divine presence has not fled because of pain, but rather is supportively there. And because God walked with Jesus all the way through death to risen life, people can sense that the present situation does not have the final word. Hope arises, a trust that divine providence will bring about alternatives, new life, change. Active hope for the future keeps spirits from flagging even as the struggle continues. Festive, poetic elements result. The idea of God-walking-with-us that this approach discovers arises with flower and song out of the suffering of the people.

THE GOD OF *FIESTA*

The Amerindian ancients looked to beauty as a reflection of the presence of the divine. Their intuition survives in the Spanish phrase *flor y canto*, flower and song, a translation of the pre-Columbian Náhuatl metaphor for the truth of the spiritual world. Not only did beauty signify the blessing of divine presence, but indigenous ancestors historically used flower and song to communicate back with the Sacred. This approach reveals an aesthetic conception of the universe that approaches philosophy through poetry, conflating truth with beauty. Rather than arriving at truth through universal, abstract concepts governed by linear logic, the mind grasps truth intuitively through the imagination of the heart: "to know the truth was to understand the hidden meaning of things through 'flower and song,' a power emanating from the deified heart" (Léon-Portilla). In this context the details of the Guadalupe event reveal their true significance:

> In the Náhuatl world of Juan Diego, beauty *is* truth and truth *is* beauty: *flor y canto.* It is in the singing of the birds, in the aroma of the roses, and above all in the encounter with the Lady of Tepeyac that Juan Diego comes to understand the truth of who he is, who she is, and who God is. (Goizueta)

This sense of beauty, intertwined with divine truth and goodness, animates awareness of God in the spiritual imagination of Hispanic communities. The glimpse of God discerned in popular symbols, rites, music, dance, enactments, and stories is simply pervaded with an overarching aesthetic sensibility. Without it, talk of God seems cold and irrelevant. With it, an experience of the sacred attracts the whole person in an open, creative, and searching way.

This beauty does not invite the community into a purely aesthetic experience devoid of the experience of suffering and the concomitant concern for redemptive justice. One example of how the two are always interacting can be found in *la pastorela*, the shepherds play, a quintessential piece of Christmas theater with roots in the Middle Ages brought to the Americas by the missionaries. On their way to the crib after the angels' announcement, the shepherds get distracted by Satan. With biting, insulting humor, the play depicts one temptation after another that keeps them from arriving. Basically a commentary on evil, the play teaches that Christmas is not just about joy, but about joy that occurs in the midst of struggle. It sees deeply into the tragic nature of human waywardness, while discerning hope at the center. Finally, the shepherds are shepherded toward the crib by the angel Gabriel, who instructs them to pick all the flowers in the field as their gift:

repentance begins with a gathering of flowers! Their arrival in the presence of the Savior makes clear that Jesus' birth humbles the evil spirit without violence, "as a beautiful reality humbles a lesser vision," by the sheer power of its attraction, writes Alejandro García-Rivera. Through the story God is revealed to be a "Passionate Lover of Beauty" who creates the world as a unique and beautiful whole and, laid in a manger, comes in love to restore its wholeness.

The aesthetic quality of relationship to the sacred comes to full expression in the *fiesta*, an essential part of the life of Hispanic communities. A festival filled with merriment and music, the *fiesta* is not just a party. Held to commemorate a founding event of the civic or religious community or a significant moment in an individual's life, it is a collective mystical experience that celebrates life. Theological analysis points out that the *fiesta* is deeply rooted in the sense that life is a gift; that the Source of this gift is the Creator; that the first act of the human being is to receive this gift and respond with thanks. This is done in community, with others aware of the pain and tragedy that mark their history but aware, too, that the joy experienced now points to a fullness still to come. In this sense the *fiesta* "expresses life in the subjunctive mood," as Goizueta elegantly puts it, meaning the mood of desire and future possibility as compared to the indicative mood of factuality that controls economic life in society.

Inspired and challenged though it may be by Latin American liberation theology, U.S. Hispanic theology finds that its southern colleague falls short on precisely this point. Dealing with forces that crush the life of the poor, liberation theology envisions the human person as *homo faber*, the maker. To be human is to be engaged in the transformation of society, to become an agent of change. Since popular religion does not immediately lead to such action, liberation theology has been inattentive to the value of celebration, ritual, and family life in the ongoing struggles of the poor. While the sociopolitical implications of faith are indeed crucially important, Latino and Latina theology emphasizes that the human person is also *homo ludens*, the player. To be human is to celebrate, to cease being a maker of quantifiable products and become connected to the deep meaning of life. This is what *fiesta* accomplishes. Drawing on the affective, imaginative, aesthetic resources of the community, it enables a "feeling" of being at one with God, the others, the cosmos, oneself. Not based on rational discourse nor oriented to timely, efficient action, it "represents precisely that attitude of trust in the ultimate goodness of life, both as a reality in the present and as an unrealized future that challenges and subverts the status quo" (Goizueta). The community is not just a doer, but a receiver and grateful responder to the gift of life. Once this is in play, then the commitment to social justice receives a wellspring of motivation. As Ada María Isasi-Díaz stresses from her work with circles of Hispanic women, the commitment to justice will not survive without love and tenderness in people's lives to sustain them.

As "an aesthetic praxis," the *fiesta* and the glimpse of God it embodies have much to offer the dominant society. By celebrating the goodness of the gift of life even in the midst of suffering, its *flor y canto* joyfully express the beauty of God's love unto a new creation. Linking the sociopolitical approach of liberation theology with the aesthetic approach of prayer and celebration, Roberto Goizueta sums up this insight when he underscores that for the U.S. Hispanic community and the theology that reflects upon its faith, "God is known in the form of the Beautiful." Journeying with the people through the many dislocating migrations of history, the accompanying presence of God bears them up through the myriad daily practices of popular religion, most especially through the beauty of *fiesta*.

TO THE FUTURE

As a young endeavor, U.S. Latino and Latina theology has not yet developed its insights into the accompanying God of *fiesta* in any extended systematic fashion. With some few fine exceptions, its main focus to date has been on theological anthropology, seeking to define the human reality of Hispanic communities and their religious vision, values, and experience of grace. In the 2006 *Handbook of Latina/o Theologies,* for example, the lead essay on God quickly announces that it will consider how Hispanic peoples are created in the image of God, which then quickly devolves into a discussion of the importance of the language of family origin; the entry on the Holy Spirit transmutes into a discussion of pastoral ministry among urban communities; and the essay on the Trinity sets out to understand this doctrine with an existential aim, seeking its practical ability to empower the community. There is as yet little discussion of how these insights impact doctrine or systematic theology of God as such. What has been done to date, however, shows that this theology has much to contribute to worldwide theological wisdom. We look forward to the richness still to come.

Meanwhile, the present moment is rife with change for communities of Latinos and Latinas in the United States. Many are migrating from the countryside to urban centers, disrupting older patterns of community typical of smaller towns or villages. Many more people of Latin heritage are migrating across the U.S. border in circumstances of danger into unstable, low-wage jobs. Contact with today's wired form of mainstream U.S. culture is pressuring everyone to migrate from premodernity to modernity and postmodernity in short order. The young in particular are adapting more or less rapidly to dominant mores that depart from traditional patterns of life. Amid this flux, the understanding of God in Hispanic theology flows into a praxis that harmonizes beauty with justice, ethics with enjoyment. The preferential option for the poor in economic and social terms is accompanied by an option for the faith of the poor, which can quench the thirst for the Sacred in all who pay attention. As Miguel Díaz writes, the traditional way of expressing hospitality is to say, *mi casa es tu casa*, my house is your house. He invites, "Come into our home, sit at our table, hear our story, and share your story of what it means to be human." Conversing about how we have encountered the experience of grace, we walk in solidarity toward hopeful social action.

FOR FURTHER READING

The two revered pioneers of U.S. Hispanic theology are the Catholic theologian Virgilio Elizondo and the Protestant church historian Justo González. Among their works that break new ground and give the flavor of this approach are Elizondo, *Galilean Journey: The Mexican-American Promise* (Maryknoll, N.Y.: Orbis, 1983), and González, *Mañana: Christian Theology from a Hispanic Perspective* (Nashville: Abingdon, 1990), both written in accessible fashion.

The next generation has worked vigorously *en conjunto* to develop basic themes. For Catholic theology, see the indispensable essays in Orlando Espín and Miguel Díaz, eds., *From the Heart of Our People: Latino/a Explorations in Catholic Systematic Theology* (Orbis, 1999); the present chapter quotes from the essays by María Pilar Aquino, "Theological Method in U.S. Latino/a Theology"; Alejandro García-Rivera, "The Whole and the Love of Difference"; Roberto Goizueta, "Fiesta"; Gary Riebe-Estrella, "*Pueblo and Church*"; and Jeanette Rodríguez, "*La Tierra.*" A valuable companion work in Protestant theology is José David Rodríguez and Loida Martell-Otero, eds., *Teología en Conjunto: A Collaborative Hispanic Protestant Theology* (Louisville: Westminster John Knox, 1997); the present chapter quotes from the essays by Teresa Chavez Sauceda, "Love in the Crossroads: Stepping Stones to a Doctrine of God in Hispanic/Latino Theology"; and Loida Martell-Otero, "The Ongoing Challenge of Hispanic Theology." The essays that appear in Allan Figueroa Deck, ed., *Frontiers of Hispanic Theology in the United States* (Orbis, 1992), especially Sixto García, "U.S. Hispanic and Mainstream Trinitarian Theologies," and Arturo Bañuelas, ed., *Mestizo Christianity: Theology from the Latino Perspective* (Orbis, 1995) are solid and enlightening. Reading these collections is like picking flowers in a field: each one different, all together a beautiful bouquet of insight.

Original theological reflection based on women's experience is given voice by Ada María Isasi-Díaz, *En La Lucha: A Hispanic Women's Liberation Theology* (Minneapolis: Fortress, 1993), and her *Mujerista Theology: A Theology for the Twenty-First Century* (Orbis, 1996). The collection gathered by María Pilar Aquino, Daisy Machado, and Jeanette Rodríguez, eds., *A Reader in Latina Feminist Theology: Religion and Justice* (Austin: University of Texas Press, 2002) displays the diversity of concerns and insights of a broad spectrum of religious scholars.

While popular religion is the common thread that links all of these works, some books delve deeply into one or other aspects of the people's faith in a more foundational but still generally accessible way. Particularly helpful are Roberto Goizueta, *Caminemos con Jesús: A Hispanic/Latino Theology of Accompaniment* (Orbis, 1995); Orlando Espín, *The Faith of the People: Theological Reflections on Popular Catholicism* (Orbis, 1997); and Miguel Díaz, *On Being Human: U.S. Hispanic and Rahnerian Perspectives* (Orbis, 2001).

The most comprehensive history of Hispanic Catholicism in the United States up to the end of the twentieth century is Jay Dolan, Allan Figueroa Deck, and Jaime Vidal, eds., *Hispanic Catholic Culture in the U.S.* (3 vols.; Notre Dame, Ind.: University of Notre Dame Press, 1994). The work of Ana María Díaz-Stevens and Anthony Stevens-Arroyo, *Recognizing the Latino Resurgence in U.S. Religion* (Boulder, Colo.: Westview, 1998) provides insightful sociological analysis. A comprehensive overview of the state of discussion is provided by Edwin David Aponte and Miguel De La Torre, eds., *Handbook of Latina/o Theologies* (St. Louis: Chalice Press, 2006).

The *Journal of Hispanic/Latino Theology,* begun in 1993 and now available online (www.latinotheology.org), and the journal *Apuntes,* begun in 1981, open a window on current research.

8

GENEROUS GOD OF THE RELIGIONS

CONTEXT: RELIGIOUS PLURALISM

Consider the insight into God growing ever clearer wherever people wrestle with the meaning of their religious faith in the light of the different religious traditions of others. In our era of global communications, planet-wide travel, widespread immigration, and millions of refugees, religious traditions are jostling against each other as never before. While the world has always known religious diversity, many peoples long experienced a strong link between living in a specific place and holding a particular religious worldview. That link is now eroding as a pluralism of religious beliefs forms the ordinary matrix of daily life. However committed persons may be to their own faith, they are regularly confronted with people whose commitments offer a different claim about what is worth believing.

Take the United States as one example. Most of the religions of the world are now practiced in this country. In addition to the indigenous religions of the Native Americans and the homegrown religion of the Mormons, there are Christians of Catholic, Orthodox, and Protestant persuasion; Jewish, Muslim, Hindu, and Buddhist communities; groups that follow Zoroastrian, Jain, Sikh, Confucian, Daoist, Shinto, and Baha'i traditions; and religions from the Caribbean such as Santería and Voo'dou. While directing the Pluralism Project at Harvard University, religion professor Diana Eck discovered that today there are Hindu and Buddhist temples and Muslim mosques in virtually every American city, most of them largely invisible because they are in homes, office buildings, movie theaters, or former churches, but some visible as majestic and imposing edifices. Besides building houses of prayer, these religions celebrate annual festivals and engage in charitable, educational, and cultural activities that promote the vibrancy of their traditions. As Eck observes in her book *Encountering God*, religiously faithful Hindu Americans are becoming our surgeons, engineers, and newsdealers; Buddhist Americans our bankers and astronauts; Muslim Americans our teachers, lawyers, and cabdrivers.

One sign of this multifaith shift occurred in 1991 when the U.S. House of Representatives invited a Muslim religious leader to conduct its daily opening prayer for the first time. Another occurred after September 11, 2001, when many of the public memorial services featured Catholic, Protestant, Jewish, Muslim, Hindu, and other religious representatives who offered prayers from their respective traditions. The annual Thanksgiving holiday sees many interfaith services at the grassroots level with an orientation toward helping those in the neighborhood who want for food. Around the country, bookstores are stocked with paperback books about the world's religions side by side with copies of their sacred texts: the Bible, the Holy Qur'an, the Bhagavad Gita. By now we are all virtually next-door neighbors.

This changed religious landscape elicits different reactions. The issue is not only political, in the sense of how to tolerate difference so that all can cooperate for the common good in the civil arena. Without doubt this is the most vital concern, given the history of violence that religions have triggered, collaborated with, or been used to promote. But intertwined with this is a burning theological question, namely, how to be faithful to one's own beliefs while making space for the undoubted difference of others. One response, the fundamentalist one, circles the wagons tightly to defend one's identity by declaring all others simply in error. Another response, relativist in character, flattens out differences, thinking it doesn't much matter which religion people choose since all are variations of a common essence. Seeking to avoid both hostility and relativism, yet a third response is dialogic. Here people engage each other with critical respect and affection, learning the different religious wisdom of others and sharing that of their own tradition.

The encounter inevitably circles people back to their own faith with desire to account for what they have discovered.

For Christians this option, practiced by both individuals and institutional churches, places the God of revelation in a new context. The deep spiritual wisdom, practice of goodness, and undoubted devotion of people of the world's religions makes clear that, while in Jesus Christ Christians have a unique encounter with God's ways in the world—who else holds dear such belief in incarnation, ministry, crucifixion, resurrection!—we do not have a monopoly on either truth or virtue. The question becomes: What has God been up to outside our tribe? The incomprehensible mystery of the living God shines ever brighter as the God of Abraham and Sarah, the God of Jesus Christ, meets Allah, Brahman, Krishna, Kali, Sunyata, Kwan Yin, the Buddha, the Tao.

THE BACK STORY IN CHURCH TEACHING

In the Roman Catholic Church the theological evolution of this issue can be charted in three great and shifting questions. Can individual persons who are not Christian, that is, who are not baptized and do not believe in Jesus Christ, be saved? If yes, are they saved through the practice of their religion or despite it? If through their religions, then do these religions enjoy a positive meaning in God's one plan of salvation for the whole human race? The sequence entails making a theological assessment of religious pluralism in the light of the universal significance of Jesus Christ at the core of Christian faith.

First Question
The question about the possibility of individual salvation can be considered settled in the affirmative. For centuries theology, while affirming divine mercy, held a largely pessimistic view. It was hard even for members of the church to get to heaven let alone those without benefit of the true faith, although the idea of "implicit faith" held the door slightly ajar for those outside the church. The Second Vatican Council was a watershed for this question. Without ambiguity it endorsed an optimism of grace. The Dogmatic Constitution on the Church teaches:

> Those also can attain to everlasting salvation who through no fault of
> their own do not know the gospel of Christ or His Church, yet sincerely
> seek God and, moved by grace, strive by their deeds to know His will as
> it is known to them through the dictates of conscience. Nor does divine
> Providence deny the help necessary for salvation to those who, without
> blame on their part, have not yet arrived at an explicit knowledge of God,
> but who strive to live a good life, thanks to His grace. (*Lumen Gentium*
> 16)

In similar fashion, after describing the mystery of salvation that benefits
Christians, the Pastoral Constitution on the Church in the Modern World
makes clear:

> All this holds true not only for Christians, but for all persons of good will
> in whose hearts grace works in an unseen way. For since Christ died for
> all people, and since the ultimate vocation of the human race is in fact
> one, and divine, we ought to believe that the Holy Spirit in a manner
> known only to God offers to every person the possibility of being associ-
> ated with this paschal mystery. (*Gaudium et Spes* 22)

"The Holy Spirit in a manner known only to God . . .": thus did the church
let go of its traditional pessimism regarding salvation and point to the living
God, whose mercy reaches wide beyond Christian word and sacrament.

Second Question

What role, then, do the religions play in the salvation of individuals? Are
they positive paths, neutral institutions, or downright obstacles? Here con-
ciliar teaching, while less definite, points to a positive assessment, at least
implicitly. It acknowledges that "this universal design of God for the salvation of the human race is not carried out exclusively in the soul of a person
with a kind of secrecy" (*Ad Gentes* 3). Rather, salvation is accomplished by
endeavors that include the practice of religion, wherein "elements of truth
and grace" can be found (ibid., 9). In fact, when Christians are pervaded by
the Spirit of Christ and knowledgeable about the people with whom they
live, "they themselves can learn by sincere and patient dialogue what trea-
sures a bountiful God has distributed among the nations of the earth,"
including other religions (ibid., 11). This positive view comes to a climax in
the famous statement of the Decree on Non-Christian Religions. Noting

the "profound religious sense" of people of Hindu, Buddhist, Muslim, and Jewish faith and appreciating the role of their teachings, rules of life, and sacred ceremonies, the council declares:

> The Catholic Church rejects nothing which is true and holy in these religions. She looks with sincere respect upon those ways of conduct and of life, those rules and teachings which, though differing in many particulars from what she holds and sets forth, nevertheless often reflect a ray of that Truth which enlightens all people. (*Nostra Aetate* 2)

Consequently, church members are exhorted to a course of action:

> prudently and lovingly, through dialogue and collaboration with the followers of other religions, and in witness of Christian faith and life, acknowledge, preserve, and promote the spiritual and moral goods found among these people, as well as the values in their society and culture. (*Nostra Aetate* 2)

On the one hand, this amounts to a positive assessment of the presence of grace in the beliefs and rituals of other religions. On the other hand, even though divine providence allows that the religions may guide people to God, the council views them as doing so only partially, for a time. According to the fulfillment model that shaped the council's thinking, all religions are meant to reach their true fulfillment in the one church of Jesus Christ.

Catholic thinking on this second question developed rapidly after the council, with a diversity of positions being endorsed. The argument crafted by Karl Rahner remains highly influential. Given that human beings are not pure individual spirits but embodied spirits-in-the-world with a social nature, all their relationships are mediated through the structures present in their society at any historical moment. The same holds true for relationship with God. It is quite unthinkable that salvation could be achieved as a private, interior reality outside of the religious bodies in the environment in which people live. Since experience of the divine is embodied in the creeds, rituals, and moral codes of religious traditions, these concrete religions necessarily become the mediation of salvation in various cultures.

Later church teaching continues to endorse this insight. In a major encyclical on the church's mission, for example, Pope John Paul II clearly states that the presence of the Spirit also affects religious traditions themselves: "The Spirit's presence and activity affect not only individuals but also society and history, peoples, cultures, and religions" *(Redemptoris Missio* 28). Very explicitly this encyclical affirms the presence of God in the religions, stating that God "does not fail to make himself present in many ways, not only to individuals, but also to entire peoples through their spiritual riches, of which their religions are the main and essential expression" (ibid., 55). The answer to the second question, while not definitive, would appear to be heading in the direction of yes—thanks to the presence of God's own Spirit, people are saved through the practice of their religion, not despite it.

Third Question

Shifting from *whether* others are saved and *how* they are saved in the concrete, the debate now turns lively over the question of how, then, to understand the religions in God's will to save the human race, given the central role Christians believe Jesus Christ to have in that same design. In the West, labels were at first used to pigeonhole positions: exclusivist, for those like Karl Barth who because of Christ refuse to allow the religions any lasting legitimacy; inclusivist, for those like Rahner who see the grace of Christ operative everywhere and in all the religions; and pluralist for those like John Hick who posit the various religions as beneficial ways of life apart from Christ and the church. In time these labels themselves have been judged to be inadequate for dealing with the complexity of the issue. Still, there is need to keep track of the different positions being taken in the conversation. One fruitful proposal comes from Paul Knitter, who suggests that we think of Christianity's relation to other religions in terms of the replacement model, the fulfillment model, the mutuality model, and the acceptance model, as helps to clarity.

For all the intensity of theological exchange in the West, the nerve center for groundbreaking reflection on this question has been Asia. There Christians number roughly 3 percent of the population of 3.5 billion people. More than half of the Christian population of Asia lives in the Philippines, so bracketing that country for a moment leaves Christians as 1.5 percent of Asian people, scattered over that vast continent. Embedded in ancient cultures imbued with Hindu, Buddhist, Confucian, Daoist, Shinto, Islamic, and indigenous beliefs, this tiny Christian minority has necessarily lived their faith rubbing shoulders with the surrounding religions. Observing the evident goodness of many of their neighbors, they interact with them in a dialogue of everyday life and action. Friendships form; mutual appreciation deepens.

The pioneering theological work resulting from this context has made its way into church documents authored by the Federation of Asian Bishops' Conferences. Founded in 1972, this group is comprised of the Catholic bishops of fourteen countries including India, Japan, Philippines, and Vietnam, among others, and is rounded out by ten associate member nations, mostly from central Asia. They see the church as a small group living amid a teeming mass of people many of whom are worn down by dehumanizing poverty yet rich in cultures and religions that give them dignity. The burning question is how to witness to Christ amid crushing poverty and competing religious systems. Rather than putting the institutional church at the center of Christian life and working to "plant the church" by conversions, although such are welcome, the bishops propose that the church's mission to proclaim Christ can best be carried out by promoting the kingdom of God, the reign of God's compassionate justice and peace. A huge shift of focus, this entails first and foremost a dialogue with the poor, their cultures, and their religions. As one Indian bishop put it, "This dialogal model is the new Asian way of being Church, promoting mutual understanding, harmony, and collaboration." It commits the church to the work of liberation with the poor, to the task of inculturating the church's Western patterns into Eastern forms, and to interreligious dialogue at every level.

Based on their experience with this open approach, Asian Catholic people with their theologians and bishops have inclined toward a positive assessment of the religions in God's continuing plan of salvation. The episcopal conference of India argued that, since hundreds of millions of our fellow human beings find salvation channeled to them through their religious traditions, we cannot deny a priori a salvific role for these religions in God's plan. The bishops conference in Korea called for recognition of the part played by the great traditional religions of their country in the salvific economy of God. The Filipino bishops called for open and humble exploration of the revelatory nature of the distinguished ancient religions in Asia. The "new way of being church" is bringing new discoveries of divine presence beyond church boundaries.

Brakes   (RATZINGER)

In the midst of this ferment, the Vatican Congregation for the Doctrine of the Faith raised a red flag of warning in its declaration *Dominus Iesus* (*The Lord Jesus* [2000]). Concerned that appreciating religious pluralism may well lead to relativism, it sets forth what must be upheld. Most centrally Christians need to maintain the salvific role of Jesus Christ, which is "unique and singular, proper to him alone, exclusive, universal, and absolute" (par. 15). The complete character of revelation in Christ, furthermore, entails that the Catholic Church alone is the universal sacrament of this mystery, having an indispensable relation to the salvation of every human being.

From this standpoint, *Dominus Iesus* then draws conclusions about the other religions. They are not complementary to the Catholic faith. It may not be said that their sacred texts are inspired. The Holy Spirit does not work salvifically in them apart from Christ. Regardless of what one might think at first, this does not lessen the church's sincere respect for the religions of the world. Citing Vatican II's teaching about their holiness and truth, the document acknowledges that various religious traditions "offer religious elements which come from God" (par. 21). Some of their prayers and rituals may open the human heart to the action of God. Some of their sacred texts are "instruments by which countless people throughout the centuries have been and still are able today to nourish and maintain their life-relationship with God" (par. 8). Still, regarding the religions themselves, this document made a negative judgment: "*objectively speaking* they are in a gravely deficient situation" (par. 22 [italics in the original text]).

This declaration met with a decidedly mixed reception. Many commentators applauded its emphasis on the saving centrality of Christ and its call to avoid responses to religious pluralism that would water down Christian faith. But the torrent of criticism from religious leaders and scholars across a broad spectrum shows that something essential was seriously missing. The vexation stemmed mainly from the way it denigrated the value of other religious traditions beyond the Jewish-Christian axis, although it did not do justice to Jewish and Protestant Christian religious communities either. Virtually all critics noted that this declaration seemed to come out of a vacuum, displaying no concrete knowledge of others gleaned from interreligious dialogue that might have tempered its judgments. Some noted a certain illogic: if the grace in sacred books comes from Christ, as *Dominus Iesus* maintains, then the grace contained in the Sūtras and the Upanishads, the Qur'an and the Dao-de-jing must be from Christ, and these texts cannot be mere human inventions, as the declaration also asserts. If the religions contain elements that "come from God," then does not the judgment that they are "gravely deficient" rebound to insult the divine manner of acting in the world? For all of its positive statements about the presence of the Spirit in other religions, this declaration's negative assessment of their identity before God was seen by many engaged in interreligious dialogue to be deeply wounding, rife with potential for violence, and in need of correction.

As the argument over *Dominus Iesus* shows, there is no consensus on the vital issue of what God intends by the existence of multiple religious paths. *Dominus Iesus* is one way to interpret the religions in light of faith in Jesus Christ, but people in dialogue who themselves confess Christ as the Way have experienced a reverence for other religions that points to a broader, deeper, wider play of God's merciful ways. The third question emerges with all its complexity: holding faithfully to Jesus Christ, how does one make room theologically for God's handiwork in the other religions? And what glimpse in turn does this open onto the living God?

GLIMPSE OF GOD FROM DIALOGUE

The aim of this chapter is not to resolve this controversy, nor even to present all the relevant positions. Rather, it seeks a glimpse of God being discovered in the encounter of religions. Accordingly, it lays out one line of thinking taken by those committed to dialogue, since this is the frontier where new insight is emerging. To begin, recall the age-old truth that the incomprehensible mystery of God lies beyond all human control and understanding. Rather than signifying divine absence, this points to a divine overabundance that fills the world to its depths and then overflows. There is no end to the being and fullness of God, who creates heaven and earth and is continuously present and active throughout the world, in all ages and all cultures. Throughout history this gracious mystery approaches us with little theophanies, signs and revelations and events that invite us into relationship. As Jeannine Hill Fletcher suggests, this is the starting point for Christian response to religious diversity. At the outset it opens the possibility that others might have distinct encounters with the divine that can be new resources for Christian exploration into the overabundance of God. To put it simply, the living God is not a Christian. Rather, the incalculable mystery, which the Christian scripture dares to call love (1 John 4:8 and 16) is not constrained in loving but freely pours out affection to all and each one.

Specifying this starting point within a trinitarian framework, a number of theologians in dialogue now reason that theology's lens for reflecting on this issue should be a theology of the Holy Spirit. The actual presence of God drawing near and passing by throughout the whole world, the Spirit is the giver of the inmost, divinizing gift of grace to all human beings. Every personal encounter of God with human beings occurs in the Spirit, and it is in the Spirit that people make their response. This presence of the Spirit is a power and a joy, an outpouring and a gift. It is not controllable by any institution or community but is effective beyond the confines of the church, bringing forth fruits of holiness in people who do not partake of Christian word and sacrament. Writing of the ability of the great religious traditions of Asia to draw people to God, for example, the Catholic Asian bishops expressed appreciation for the fruits of the Spirit evident in the people who follow these paths: a sense of the sacred, a thirst for wholeness, an openness to renunciation, compassion over suffering, an urge to goodness, a commitment to service, a total surrender of the self, and an attachment to the transcendent in their symbols and rituals. Like the wind blowing where it will, the Spirit creates authentic experience of the one God's saving presence throughout the world wherever people live their lives, and most explicitly in their religions.

Once thinkers espy the Spirit at work in the other religions, then they circle back to gain a renewed understanding of Christian belief in Jesus Christ within this perspective. In a problematic way, theology has often subordinated the mission of the Spirit to Christ, thereby tying salvation very tightly to the church, which carries forth Christ's mission in the world. In truth, the crucified and risen Word of God and the church that proclaims God's mercy in him are normative and constitutive for the salvation of all. In Jesus Christ, God's saving activity reaches its greatest intensity in history in the concrete. But the manifestation of God's presence and activity in the religions cannot be limited to what has been revealed in Jesus Christ and proclaimed by the church. Although such manifestation would never be contradictory to Christian revelation—God being faithful and not two-faced—it might be different. Michael Amaladoss of India put it this way: "The Spirit is the Spirit of Jesus. But she does not just repeat what Jesus has done in the Christian community. Otherwise the other religions would not be different."

For many moons of centuries, theology dismissed other religions as pagan inventions or condescended to them as deficient ways people had of stumbling toward the divine. Actual dialogic encounter with other religions leads to a different view. Assuming that the real presence of grace and truth can only have a divine origin, the religions can be seen as God's handiwork. In them we catch a first glimpse of the overflowing generosity of the living God who has left no people abandoned but has bestowed divine love on every culture. This is the grace of our age: encountering multiple religious traditions widens the horizon wherein we catch sight of God's loving plenitude. Thus we are enabled to approach the mystery ever more deeply. In the words of Jacques Dupuis, "More divine truth and grace are found operative in the entire history of God's dealings with humankind than are available simply in the Christian tradition."

The experience of dialogue is responsible for opening minds and hearts to this way of thinking. Dialogue has such a powerful effect not only because one is exposed to new ideas intellectually but also because spiritually, in the words of John Paul II, "by dialogue we let God be present in our midst; as we open ourselves in dialogue to one another, we open ourselves to God." Borrowing an idea from the Vatican's Pontifical Council for Interreligious Dialogue (the former Secretariat for Non-Christians—the name change captures a deep theological shift), the Asian bishops frequently teach about four types of dialogue, each essential to the mission of the church. Illustrating them will allow the glimpse of God being encountered to emerge more clearly.

DIALOGUE OF LIFE

This dialogue takes place wherever people of different faiths live and work side by side in amicable relationships. An effective means to correct biases and to open minds and spirits, it takes place informally in families and neighborhoods, in interfaith marriages and social gatherings, in workplaces and the marketplace. Occasionally, motivated by the desire to understand one another, to promote mutual interests, or to resolve conflicts, people may speak explicitly about matters of religious significance. More often, though, this dialogue entails making friends with people of other religions, sharing problems and preoccupations, lending a hand and receiving help in turn, sharing joys and sorrows, participating in rituals at weddings or funerals, and in general just living with mutual respect. In the process people come to discover a plenitude in the divine that they would otherwise never know existed.

Diana Eck captures the experiential depth of this dialogue of life when she speaks of her friend Ranjini. Every Saturday morning Ranjini attends services at the Hindu temple in Ashland, Massachusetts, singing hymns of praise to Vishnu and touching her forehead to the base of his great granite statue. She does not consider this statue to be an idol, of course, but a residence of the divine, thanks to the priestly ceremony that established "spirit" in it. The image is a lens through which her vision of God is directed and through which her service to God is offered. She has a smaller version in a cupboard-size shrine in her kitchen. The gracious presence of Vishnu, a living reality in her life, inspires Ranjini's goodness toward others. As a scholar of religion, Eck pursues technical questions such as: how does a Hindu think of Vishnu in relation to the other gods of India? But as a Christian she also raises personal questions, pondering what her own faith in God means in light of her encounter with the rich religious life of her friend.

DIALOGUE OF ACTION

This dialogue transpires amid the common struggle of people to better their lives. The harsh realities of poverty intertwined with the exploitation of earth's natural resources elicit the desire to act to change the situation. Wherever more than one religion exists, this often becomes a multifaith endeavor. The Asian Catholic bishops encourage this cooperation, writing: "Since the religions, as the Church, are at the service of the world, interreligious dialogue cannot be confined to the religious sphere but must embrace all dimensions of life: economic, sociopolitical, cultural, and religious. It is in their common commitment to the fuller life of the human community that they discover their complementarity and the urgency and relevance of dialogue at all levels." Concretely working together on a shared project, people of different religions enter a process of mutual discovery.

At the outset people analyze the situation and plan practical efforts to remove the causes of suffering. The sense of togetherness grows as action proceeds. When they encounter obstacles from privileged, powerful groups, the prophetic strands of their religious heritage help them to go on. Shared action, the point of departure, then becomes a springboard for ongoing dialogue and growth in understanding as people speak about what animates them. As Samuel Rayan describes the experience in India, "In the process of a liberating, whole-making collaboration with God and neighbor, the different spiritualities progressively discover one another, discover themselves with their weaknesses and strengths, and encounter more intimately the Mystery they bear, symbolize, and convey." Having heard and actually seen how the Four Noble Truths enable Buddhist partners to participate in the transformation of village life in Sri Lanka, Christians come to appreciate this path in new and fruitful ways. Correspondingly, Buddhists gain a better grasp of Christians' belief in the death and resurrection of Jesus, seeing how such commitment sustains efforts to transform society even in the face of apparent hopelessness.

In some locales people form "base human communities," committed gatherings of those struggling for justice, similar to the base ecclesial communities pioneered in Latin America but now with an interfaith character. Here poor people themselves become the active subjects of dialogue. Sharing a common plight and a common program gives rise to an experience of practical and spiritual communion. Speaking of such base human communities of Buddhists and Christians in Sri Lanka, Aloysius Pieris explains, "Here co-pilgrims expound their respective scriptures, retelling the story of Jesus and Gautama in a core-to-core dialogue that makes their hearts burn." When faiths commit themselves together to promote justice, what results is more strength for the struggle, a deep cordiality that generates mutual understanding, and new insight into the wide mystery of God that sustains them all.

DIALOGUE OF THEOLOGICAL EXCHANGE

This dialogue occurs when specialists such as theologians, monks and nuns who follow the monastic vocation, or pastoral leaders speak face to face, seeking to explore one another's insights and values while sharing their own. Religious bodies may sponsor such dialogues, selecting participants, paying for their travel, and receiving back reports. Whenever they are fruitful, all of these exchanges take place in an atmosphere of respect imbued with hope for greater understanding.

One enlightening example is the ongoing dialogue between Buddhist and Christian scholars on the nature of ultimate reality. Unlike Christian thought, which perceives God as Creator and therefore connects the idea of God with personal being and actuality, Buddhism understands the Ultimate to be absolute nothingness (*Sunyata*). The basis of Buddhism is not faith in God who faces us and can be addressed as "Thou." Rather, the basis is awakening to the *Dharma* (truth) that *Sunyata* is nothingness or emptiness or voidness. Perhaps these are not good terms with which to translate *Sunyata* into English, conjuring as they do stagnation, boredom, a great lack. The term intends to signify that the Ultimate is entirely unobjectifiable, indescribable, and unattainable by reason or will. Within the framework of nondualist philosophy, it is not a substance, not any "something" at all. In fact, it is not even emptiness as opposed to fullness. Hence, it cannot be thought of as somewhere outside of or beyond oneself, or inside oneself. Perhaps it would help to think of it as a verb, not a noun—a terrifically dynamic movement with no fixed center that spontaneously contains all opposites within itself. In this positive sense, the emptiness of *Sunyata* can be called "suchness." Living with this truth calls for spiritual awakening to the impermanence of everything, which is essentially insubstantial and transient. Open-handedly one aims to live in a nonclinging stance that empties oneself of binding attachments.

Dialogue led the Japanese scholar Masao Abe to make an interesting connection. Listening as a Buddhist, he hears a trace of *Sunyata* in the central Christian affirmation that the story of Jesus Christ entails *kenōsis*, a divine self-emptying:

though he was in the form of God, did not think equality with God a thing
to be clung to, but emptied himself, taking on the form of a slave . . . , and
became obedient unto death, even death on a cross. (Phil 2:5–8)

Abe suggests that this is not just a historical statement but refers to the very
nature of Ultimate Reality. The Messiah is self-emptying, self-abnegating,
and this belongs to the very nature of God, who is love. When *Sunyata* as the
Buddhist Ultimate encounters the kenotic God made known in Christ, the
result is so beyond the Western notion of God as Being Itself, Creator of all,
that Abe can suggest that God is a great zero, as free from "one" as from
"three." This calls for a deep spirituality coherent with Jesus' central wisdom
that losing one's life is the path to finding it.

    Participating in this dialogue, Catholic theologian David Tracy
acknowledges that "Masao Abe helped me change my Christian understanding of God in ways that needed changing." The Buddhist view loosens
the grip of images that can cramp the human spirit and confine the divine.
It puts Tracy in mind of the often neglected Christian tradition of radical
apophatic theology expressed in the medieval Meister Eckhart's words, "I
pray to God to free me from God," that is, from all-too-narrow language and
doctrines. Western theology tends to many wordy affirmations. Dialogue
about *Sunyata* reminds us that discourse about God is adequate only so long
as it is aware of the gripping and releasing, the affirming and negating, the
speech and the silence, which together lead us reverently into the heart of
this holy mystery.

    That said, Tracy argues vigorously for the Christian idea of God as full-
ness rather than emptiness. Radical negation, while important, is but one
moment in the larger movement of language that affirms. This is because
the core religious experience for Christians is shaped by the event of God's
self-manifestation in Jesus Christ, which opens out into awareness of God's
active presence in Word and Spirit throughout history. Here for Christians
are the central clues that guide their necessarily partial understanding of the
divine. Any good Christian theology of God is trinitarian, moving in an
intrinsically dynamic, relational, dialectical way toward the affirmation-in-
negation of unfathomable divine love. Hence, nothingness is encompassed
in ineffable Being who is Love.

    This example of interreligious dialogue among scholars, easy to access because it leaves a strong paper trail, is typical of countless others. The goal is neither conversion of each other nor arrival at some least common denominator. Rather, each is seeking understanding through the filter of the other's tradition. For Christian theologians who engage in this practice, an interesting dynamic ensues. They endeavor to witness to the truth of God made known in Jesus Christ, giving explanations of Christian belief in ways that the dialogue partner may understand. At the same time, deep listening entails that they "pass over" to the viewpoint of their dialogue partners, endeavoring to see, savor, grasp the world from a different perspective. Genuine appreciation often develops as they discover the acutely intelligent, highly moral, deeply theological, and profoundly spiritual dimensions of the tradition they are encountering. Having learned from the wisdom of the other, they return "home" to find that the experience affects their Christian understanding in two ways: it enriches, transforms, and deepens the meaning of what faith holds dear, while it also purifies what may be prejudicial, arrogant, narrow, and ignorant.

One variation of this kind of dialogue occurs when scholars, rather than engage in live conversation, buckle down to study a sacred text of another tradition. Dealing with a text and its commentaries in their original languages, this work seeks to grasp the concrete message of this one little piece of a greater tradition and to bring it into dialogue with its Christian counterpart. In the process, scholars forge what has come to be called comparative theology, which Francis Clooney characterizes as an "interreligious, comparative, dialogic, yet still confessional theology," venturing new interpretations of Christian faith in light of these widened boundaries.

Clooney's work on texts about Antal, a popular female saint in south India, is a good case in point. This young poet, who lived in the ninth century, was distinguished by her intense love of God, the Lord Narayana. In one key incident, Narayana chooses her for his bride. On the way to the wedding at the great temple at Srirangam, her women companions are skeptical that the Lord would approach any human being this way, let alone select someone like Antal as his bride. In response, Antal sings:

> Whichever form pleases his people, that is his form;
> Whichever name pleases his people, that is his name;

Whichever way pleases his people who meditate without
  ceasing, that is his way,
That one who holds the discus.

Translating, teaching, and thinking about this text and its commentaries in
Hindu theology, Clooney connected it with the wisdom of the *Spiritual
Exercises* of St. Ignatius Loyola. According to these *Exercises*, individuals
who wish to meditate are invited to picture a gospel scene, place themselves
within it, and interact with Jesus about pressing issues in their lives. With
their creative imagination and affections thus engaged, they become disposed to greater love and service of God. This is because, as Ignatius intu-
ited, God accommodates these various imaginings, using them as vehicles of
divine grace. The play of imagination in meditation thus not merely forges
a connection with ancient gospel events but becomes the means of a deeply
personal encounter with God, different for every person who meditates.
Drawing the wisdom of Hindu Antal and Catholic Ignatius comparatively
together, Clooney constructs a beautiful thesis. In imaginative contemplation we walk a path toward God that suits our own spiritual needs at any
given moment. Amazingly, God agrees to meet us there. "As we love God,
God adjusts and comes to us accordingly; if someone loves like a bride, God
comes as a groom."

James Fredericks provides another skillful example of comparative theology with his work on the story of Krishna and the *gopis*. According to this
popular Hindu story, Krishna, the deity who represents the sweetness and
passion of divine love, comes to a village late one night, playing enchanting
music on his flute. All the milkmaids (*gopis*) awaken and join in dancing
with him. Then jealousy sets in as each wants him for herself alone. Krishna
disappears. Moved by their sorrow he reappears with his music, this time
multiplying his presence so that for every *gopi* there is Krishna gazing into
the eyes of his beloved. Krishna's love is such that there is enough to go
around, no matter how many milkmaids join the dance.

In Fredericks's analysis, Christians have been no strangers to the fault of
the milkmaids, seeing themselves as possessing God's love to the exclusion of
Jews, the pagans, the "others." The obvious point is that those who try to
possess divine love for themselves alone succeed only in making it disappear

from their own lives. We cannot hoard; we can only dance. This wisdom deepens when the *gopi* story is read in tandem with Jesus' well-known parable of the Prodigal Son. Here the father is extravagantly generous but the elder brother, like the milkmaids, resents that love is being lavished on another and claims his own superior right to it. Jesus' parable suggests that there is enough of God's forgiving love to go around. The God of Jesus dances with tax collectors, plays the flute for sinners. In the end we are left with the elder son, confronting a decision: to go into the banquet, sharing the love poured out on good and bad alike, or to stay out in the cold, nursing our resentment.

At times claims do conflict, and the dialogue of theological exchange requires that the truth of one's own tradition cannot be bartered away. But even stubborn points of religious difference remain places where the heart can listen and the mind can think. The effort infuses new vitality and insight into Christian faith, leading as it does to deeper, more appreciative knowledge of the expansiveness of a loving God.

DIALOGUE OF RELIGIOUS EXPERIENCE

Prayer, fasting, community ritual, pilgrimage, and individual devotions of all kinds characterize religious traditions. The dialogue of religious experience takes place when people share in these spiritual practices, tasting each other's prayer and ways of communing with God or the Absolute.

A colorful panorama occurred on October 27, 1986, when Pope John Paul II invited leaders of diverse religious communities to gather in Assisi, Italy, and join in a world day of prayer for peace. Native Americans with feathered headdresses and peace pipes, Orthodox patriarchs, Buddhist monks, Muslim imams, Jewish rabbis, Hindu priests, and a multitude of others in various garb moved in procession and prayed. They did not say the same prayer, however. According to their respective traditions they turned toward whomever or whatever they considered to be Ultimate, praying that the world would stop violence, ravaging, disharmony, and war and enjoy the gift of peace. Interpreting this festival of tongues, which showcased so dramatically the diversity of human religious practice, one might conclude that there are many gods, each with his or her own set of devotees, making religion an endless source of division and conflict among people. This in fact is a sorry feature of the history of religions. Another interpretation, sensed by many participants and observers, is also possible, namely, that the mystery of the living God transcends the different religious ways and unites them at some profound level for the common good. The latter position was taken by John Paul II, when, responding to criticism of this event, he explained his rationale in an address to members of the Roman Curia. A "mystery of unity" unites all peoples, who from the point of view of Christian doctrine are one in creation, redemption, and eternal destiny. This unity exists despite differences in the circumstances of their lives; indeed, the unity is "radical, fundamental, and decisive." Noting that all the participants at Assisi had prayed for peace in accord with their own religious identities, the pope continued that nevertheless the gathering had been a "wonderful manifestation of the unity which binds us together beyond the differences and divisions which are known to all." The reason for this is radically theological: the presence of God. "We can indeed maintain that every authentic prayer is called forth by the Holy Spirit, who is mysteriously present in the heart of every person." Over time this papal interpretation has led to the Assisi gathering's being seen as a theatrical manifestation of what the living God has been up to in the religions of the world, summoning all to stand against killing in favor of the bounty of peace. As such, it has become a powerful symbol of religious cooperation.

The dialogue of religious experience more often entails not only praying side by side as at Assisi but also entering into the spiritual practices of another religious tradition. Some Christians who live high-pressure lives, for example, have discovered the serenity of spirit that comes from the disciplined Buddhist practice of Zen sitting. Diana Eck's account of attending a Hindu ritual conveys the spiritual depth that such experience may bring. Born in Montana, Eck is a Methodist Christian by upbringing and by choice, committed to the church and its service to the world. On one occasion, after two months of research in southern India, she was permitted access to a temple of Vishnu as the time approached for the evening offering of oil lamps. With hundreds of other women she moved in concentric circles through hallways of approach toward the inner sanctum, the walls shifting with the flickering light and shadow of the lamps. When they finally arrived at the center, to the sound of beating drums, clanging bells, and reedy melody, the central pair of doors to Vishnu's chamber were flung open to reveal the middle part of the huge, reclining, eighteen-foot image. Then the doors to the left were opened to reveal the face, followed by the doors to the right revealing the feet. Amid the press of bodies and wavering soft lamplight, as the music reached a crescendo, Eck felt a sense of an enormous presence, accessible only partially and through suggestion. When the priest brought out the last lamp presented to Vishnu and offered it to the people, "four hundred pairs of hands stretched out to touch the flame and then touch its blessing to the forehead. Mine was among them."

Was this idolatry? Eck argues that for Hindus engaged in this devout exercise, the image of Vishnu was no more an idol than the cross is for Christians. The Hindu image needs to be blessed before it can function in ritual, and once blessed it becomes a window onto the divine. The people do not worship the image, but the deity to whom it points. Upon reflection, Eck recounts that her experience of this ritual could be described only as worship. While her framework as a Christian was different from the Hindus pressed around her, she shared with them a sense of delight as the doors were opened to reveal three glimpses of a God larger than one could fully comprehend, accompanied by a sense of awe before the majesty and mystery of the divine. "I thought of nothing at the time. It was a moment of total presence, not reflection." But later pondering led her to think about the Trinity, the threefold Christian confession of God as creator, redeemer, and spirit, the one God whose self-revelation still leaves us with the overwhelming sense that no vantage point could enable us to see the whole. She realized that she recognized God's presence in a Hindu temple only because through this trinitarian formula of God, Christ, and Spirit she already had a sense of what divine presence is like. "Recognition means that we have seen it somewhere before." Not every ritual, place, or community provides this experience of recognition; critical religious and ethical criteria need to be used. Nor are all these visions of God the same—they are not. Yet being open to encounter, being on the track of the Spirit in the world, so to speak, has a profound result: "The image of Vishnu at Padmanabhaswamy both challenged and enlarged my own concept of God."

A personal vignette may illustrate yet another way this dialogue can take place, namely, through inculturation, the practice of translating Christian faith into the cultural and religious symbols of non-European traditions. In the mid-1990s I traveled to India for a Vatican-sponsored conference on Jesus Christ amid the savior figures of the world's religions. One day during the conference the Catholic participants celebrated the Eucharist in a new rite recently approved by Rome. Using symbols drawn from Hinduism, this liturgy had a distinctly Eastern cast. The presiding priests wore saffron shawls; both they and the congregation sat on pillows in the lotus position (if one could manage it!). The opening penitential rite ended with forgiveness being signified as we each received the *bindi,* or red dot, placed between the eyes as symbol of a third eye that seeks wisdom within. Before the gospel was read we swallowed a spoonful of rose-scented water, which became a cushion within us where the word of God could enter and dwell. After the consecration of bread and wine we chanted the Sanskrit acclamation *"Om, Shri Yeshu Khristaya namaha . . . Om,"* over and over again, and then lapsed into a profoundly quiet, peaceful, meditative silence. At the kiss of peace we bowed toward each other with folded hands as is the custom in India. Throughout the Mass there was abundant use of Indian musical instruments and chants, incense, and marigold flowers, as one would find in Hindu temple service.

I have never been at a liturgy like this. Its effect was profoundly calming and strangely awakening. It was obviously still a Catholic Mass, but the power of the Hindu symbols had a transforming effect. Upon reflection I realized that these symbols, pressed into service to celebrate the death and resurrection of Jesus Christ, came already saturated with millennia of religious feeling and significance. They conveyed into this Christian sacrament a spacious sense of the divine, the God profoundly within and beyond all imagining. The experience loosened the grip of my predominantly Western imagination which, despite all talk of God as mystery, is still fundamentally anthropomorphic. Now it was as if the God of traditional Western theology, even the compassionate God of liberation theologies and the relational God of feminist theologies, was freed by this evocation of the nonpersonal nature of absolute being in Hindu sensibility to become the mystery of the God beyond all telling, yet ever more profoundly near.

The dialogues of life, action, theological exchange, and religious experience allow Christians to glimpse the God we know through the windows framed by other peoples' faith traditions and to share our own precious heritage in exchange. The public effects are far-reaching. Mutual understanding coupled with growing friendships set up possibilities for a new relationship among the religions themselves. The personal effects are equally significant. Glimpsing the Holy through the religious experience of peoples of other faiths, Christians grow in knowledge and love of the great mystery of the living God. Reflecting on his own experience of dialogue in India over almost four decades, Jacques Dupuis noted, "Personal commitment to one's own faith and openness to the faith of others need not be mutually exclusive; rather they ought to grow in direct proportion." If one has an ear attuned to the Spirit's presence, then one hears the music, even if it is being played in a different key. And one's repertoire consequently expands.

A BOUNTIFUL GOD

An old hymn sings the words, "There's a wideness in God's mercy . . . ." The practice of interfaith dialogue opens broad and deep vistas onto God's unspeakable generosity to the human race, pressed down and flowing over. To explore this further, Dupuis, in his book *Toward a Christian Theology of Religious Pluralism,* suggests that we perform a thought experiment: try to take a God's-eye view of history. Admittedly this is impossible, not to say presumptuous. But if we could see the sweep of history from God's point of view, what would be the meaning of the plurality of living faiths with which Christians are surrounded? If there is only one God, then presumably there is one plan by which providence intends to bring all people into saving union. This plan presumably has an internal consistency, God not being scatter-brained. By this line of thinking we may reach the realization that the divine design for the salvation of the world is *multifaceted*. This design reaches its highest historical density in Jesus Christ with significance for all. Yet the eternal Word of God is not constrained, not exhausted, not all used up in this one particular history, nor is the Spirit of God thereby limited in her outpouring into the world. Rather, thanks to God's gracious initiative, different paths have been laid down in different cultures, times, and places inviting people to share divine life. Thus, the religions with their saving figures and sacred texts, their creeds, moral codes, and rituals, may be seen to be channels of God's word and grace set up by divine providence. Put plainly, the religions can be nothing less than the work of God present in the world through Word and Spirit: "Other religious traditions represent true interventions and authentic manifestations of God in the history of peoples." Their very existence reveals the overflowing generosity of God, who before, during, and after the coming of Christ approaches all people with the invitation to divine life. Their very variety manifests the bountiful depths of the living God, which is never spent. This dazzling discovery of the diversity of divine patterns of engagement throughout history affords a glimpse of incomprehensible mystery greater than we could have imagined by ourselves.

Jesus Christ

Placing Christian faith in this broader theocentric framework expands our notion of God at the same time that it calls for new vision about the meaning of Jesus Christ. Disputes about how to reconcile core Christian affirmations about the salvific role of Jesus Christ with the validity of other religions are numerous. There is as yet no theological consensus. One promising way forward can be forged by combining three elements of standard christology into a new configuration that sees Jesus as the incarnate Word, crucified and risen, who, instead of lording it over other manifestations of God in the world, washes feet.

☙ *Kenōsis.* From the Greek word that means self-emptying, this term is used in the scripture to describe Christ's method of coming into the world. The incarnation was an act of humility. Refusing to cling to divine glory, Christ divested himself and became like a lowly slave (Phil 2:5–11). Paul's insistence that Jesus' role as savior is tightly tied to this act of self-emptying undergirds the self-giving manner of Jesus' ministry in the gospels. It gives a specific shape to divine love.

☙ *Reign of God.* A rich symbol that appears at the center of Jesus' preaching, this points to the situation that will prevail when God's will is done on earth as it is in heaven: the lion will lie down with the lamb; men will beat their swords into ploughshares; the woman will find her coin, the shepherd his sheep; the blind will see, the lame walk; daily bread will be given; the oppressed will be set free; there will be no more tears or mourning. In a word, the blessing of life will prevail for the earth and all its inhabitants. The gospel accounts of Jesus' words and deeds show how this promise is worked out in the concrete, linking his salvific role with practices of service: feeding, healing, teaching all who would listen, challenging the oblivious and scornful powers-that-be. The disciples are called to do likewise. In these ways the reign of God already began to take root in the lives of those who heard and loved him.

❧ *Sacrament.* Originating in God's loving desire to communicate with people in a saving way, specific things such as persons, events, texts, and rituals become bearers of the power of this desire in history. Through them God approaches; through them people become conscious of divine presence and make their response. In Christian faith, Jesus Christ is *the* sacrament of this two-way encounter. Wishing to unite with the human race in its joys, sinfulness, and terrible suffering in order to save, the Word became flesh and dwelt among us as a human being. Through his life, death, and resurrection God has forged a saving bond with the human race that cannot be broken. The cross brings God's love into the depths of our death; Christ's risen humanity is the pledge of life for all into the eternal future. God thereby posits the incarnate Word in history in order to signal a broader economy, the presence of God's saving will coextensive with the history of humankind.

❧ *Configuration of all three.* It is odd, when you think about it, that for centuries belief in Christ was used to obscure the work of God in other religions rather than to expand appreciation of it. An imperialist framework for christology made it appear that since the Word is incarnate in Jesus, then God is not present elsewhere, or at least not so truly and lovingly. A hierarchal pattern of thinking led to the conclusion that since Christ is number one, no other religion is all that worthy of attention. Not only was divine presence denied elsewhere, but Christ the Way, the Truth, and the Life was brandished triumphally like a stick to render others inferior. The God of Jesus Christ became a figure of closedness rather than openness.

Understanding Jesus Christ as the sacrament of God's saving will enfleshed in history under the sign of *kenōsis* and interpreting his universal significance in the light of his preaching the reign of God make possible a more generous view. Christians need not, indeed must not, abandon the faith that Jesus is in person Wisdom made flesh, whose advent holds saving significance for the whole of humankind, nor stop explaining to others the beauty of the gospel and its effect on our lives. This is the treasure entrusted to our hands in the living tradition of Christian faith. But in the midst of earth's history, which limits every divine manifestation and human insight, this proclamation should be done in the spirit of the same humble self-emptying that we are talking about. As Joseph Hough put it, "It is essential for Christian faith that we know we have seen the face of God in the face of Jesus. It is not essential to believe that no one else has seen God and experienced redemption in another time and place." When placed within an expansive appreciation of what the Holy has been up to, even the doctrine that Jesus Christ has a salvific role that is "unique and singular, proper to him alone, exclusive, universal, and absolute," as *Dominus Iesus* phrases it, need not, indeed must not, mean that other traditions have been deprived of God's gracious presence and action. Holding our truth as absolutely true does not mean we have to consider ourselves in possession of all the truth worth having. For God "is greater than our heart" (1 John 3:20) and claims the freedom to be Love at work in all lives and traditions. With this line of thinking we can understand that the life-giving presence of God in Jesus and the community that bears his presence onwards in history need not, indeed must not, rule out other people experiencing God's intentional activity and orienting themselves to the mystery through different means generated by the same Spirit. Rather than canceling out this presence, the advent of the Word of God in the flesh in Jesus Christ points to divine mystery everywhere present, and explicitly so in the religions.

One Multifaceted Plan

In light of these reflections, theology in dialogue returns to the third great question about the meaning of the religions. Dupuis sharpens the point by framing the issue in technical terms. Does religious pluralism exist *de facto*, meaning is it just a fact of the world today, even a regrettable one meant to be overcome by the eventual conversion of all to Christ in the church? Or does religious pluralism exist *de jure*, meaning is it a good intended by God in principle? In other words, in terms of God's intent, is the plurality of religions only permitted or positively willed? The reverence experienced in interreligious dialogue leads a number of theologians to suggest *de jure* as a more adequate interpretation. Virtually every church pronouncement since

Vatican II, including *Dominus Iesus*, has acknowledged the presence and activity of the Spirit in the religions themselves. Is this just haphazard behavior on the Spirit's part, a casual engagement with people's spiritual quest willy-nilly? Such superficiality is unthinkable. If the Spirit of God is active, God is acting "in principle." The religions, then, are part of "God's own plan for humankind." Religious pluralism can be seen as part of God's single, rich, intricate design for the salvation of the human race, one divine love working itself out through a multifaceted plan.

This positive assessment of pluralism is profoundly theological. It rests not on the value of diversity in general as seen in biology and culture, but on a glimpse of God's overflowing plenitude. Dupuis' words capture the realization of those who have dialogic experience: "The expansiveness of God's inner life overflowing outside the Godhead is the root cause for the existence in history of divergent paths leading to a unique common goal, the absolute mystery of God." As different paths to salvation, the religions belong to the overflowing communication of the triune God, who speaks "in many and diverse ways" to peoples and nations, as the letter to the Hebrews attests (1:1). Like everything in our fractured world, including Christianity, religions exist under the sign of ambiguity, good and evil, grace and sin mixed. But their positive wisdom and grace, brought about by the Spirit of God, allows the judgment that religious pluralism is a divine gift. In principle it rests on the magnificent, superabundant generosity of God who is Love.

THE DIGNITY OF DIFFERENCE

Interreligious encounter leads to the praxis of sincere respect, careful dialogue, mutual learning, appreciation, and cooperation on a local and global scale to further the coming of God's reign. Rabbi Jonathan Sacks proposes some arresting analogies to show the enrichment this praxis can bring. What would faith be like if we acknowledged the image of God in another, whose truth is not our truth? It is like feeling secure in one's own home, yet moved by the beauty of foreign places, knowing they are someone else's home, not mine, but still part of the glory of the world that is ours. It is like being fluent in English, yet thrilled by the rhythms of an Italian sonnet. It is like realizing that your life is a sentence written in the story of your own faith, yet pleased to know that there are other stories of faith written in other lives, all part of the great narrative of God's call and humanity's response. Those who are confident in their faith are not threatened but enlarged by the different ways of others. As we discover deeper truth than what we thought we possessed as a monopoly, the dignity of difference becomes a source of blessing.

FOR FURTHER READING

An excellent overview of this whole field and its various models of thinking is laid out in Paul Knitter, *Theologies of Religions* (Maryknoll, N.Y.: Orbis, 2002). A helpful way into the issue is Diana Eck, *Encountering God: A Spiritual Journey from Bozeman to Banares* (Boston: Beacon, 1993/2003), which combines scholarly insight with personal experience. Terrence Tilley, *Religious Diversity and the American Experience: A Theological Approach* (New York: Continuum, 2007) analyzes theological positions on the religions from the perspective of the pluralist society in the United States, shedding much light on the debate. Women's experience across many traditions is detailed in Leona Anderson and Pamela Dickey Young, *Women and Religious Traditions* (New York: Oxford University Press, 2004).

The Asian nerve center of the practice of dialogue is examined by Peter Phan, *Being Religious Interreligiously: Asian Perspectives on Interfaith Dialogue* (Orbis, 2004). The actual practice of interreligious dialogue is illustrated in John Hick and Edmund S. Meltzer, eds., *Three Faiths, One God: A Jewish, Christian, Muslim Encounter* (Albany: State University of New York Press, 1989); and John B. Cobb and Christopher Ives, eds., *The Emptying God: A Buddhist–Jewish–Christian Conversation* (Orbis, 1990), which carries the Abe–Tracy dialogue. Archbishop Michael Fitzgerald offers wise insights born of his experience as head of the Pontifical Council on Interreligious Dialogue in *Interfaith Dialogue: A Catholic View* (with John Borelli; Orbis, 2006).

A focus specifically on God glimpsed through dialogue comes to the fore in the major work by Jacques Dupuis, *Toward a Christian Theology of Religious Pluralism* (Orbis, 1997). The God-question also runs through Mary Boys, *Has God Only One Blessing: Judaism as a Source of Christian Self-*

Understanding (New York: Paulist, 2000); Jeannine Hill Fletcher, *Monopoly on Salvation? A Feminist Approach to Religious Pluralism* (New York: Continuum, 2005); and Werner Jeanrond and Aasulv Lande, eds., *The Concept of God in Global Dialogue* (Orbis, 2005).

The practice of comparative theology is demonstrated by Francis X. Clooney, *Hindu God, Christian God: How Reason Helps Break Down the Boundaries between Religions* (New York: Oxford, 2001); James Fredericks, *Faith among Faiths: Christian Theology and Non-Christian Religions* (New York: Paulist, 1999); and Leo Lefebure, *The Buddha and the Christ: Explorations in Buddhist and Christian Dialogue* (Orbis, 1993). Personal essays add light, warmth, and distinctive insights in the collections by Gavin D'Costa, ed., *Christian Uniqueness Reconsidered* (Orbis, 1990); and Catherine Cornille, ed., *Many Mansions? Multiple Religious Belonging and Christian Identity* (Orbis, 2002), which includes Clooney's essay on Antal.

The text of *Dominus Iesus* is printed in *Origins* 30 (Sept. 14, 2000) 209-19. It appears also in a volume that discusses it from all sides: Stephen Pope and Charles Hefling, eds., *Sic et Non: Encountering Dominus Iesus* (Orbis, 2002). Jonathan Sacks's analogies are presented in his *The Dignity of Difference: How to Avoid the Clash of Civilizations* (New York: Continuum, 2002).

9

CREATOR SPIRIT
IN THE EVOLVING WORLD

THE VIVIFIER

Consider the idea of God emerging from human engagement
with the natural world in our day. In photographs taken from
space, our home planet looks like a bright blue marble swirled
around with white clouds. Floating against a background of endless
black space, it is a precious little spot that alone among all the planets, moons, and asteroids we have explored to date is covered with a
membrane of life. Astronauts who have seen this view with their
own eyes speak of its power to change their deepest feelings. Saudi
Arabian astronaut Sultan bin Salman al-Saud, part of an international crew, recollected: "The first day we all pointed to our own
countries. The third day we were pointing to our continents. By the
fifth day, we were all aware of only one Earth." Astronaut Rusty
Schweigert, who walked on the moon, noted from that vantage
point that Earth is so small you can block it out with your thumb.
"Then you realize," he mused, "that on this beautiful warm blue and
white circle, is everything that means anything to you," all of nature
and history, birth and love. And then you are changed forever.

Since the 1960s this picture has become the common heritage
of all Earth's people. It symbolizes a new awareness of planet Earth

growing among people around the globe, an understanding shaped by a unique dialectic. On the one hand, we stand in wonder at the intricate workings of this world as uncovered and popularized by contemporary science. On the other hand, we lament in distress at how human predation is rapidly spoiling this natural world. In this dual ecological context of wonder and wasting, people of faith are rediscovering an ancient theme, namely, the presence and action of the creative Spirit of God throughout the natural world.

In seeking understanding here, we are not well served by the theology of recent centuries. For one thing, unlike Orthodox theology of the Greek and Russian churches, modern theology in the West has shortchanged pneumatology, the study of the Spirit. It has treated the Spirit, in Walter Kasper's words, like the Cinderella of theology, the one who stays home doing the drudge work while the other two get to go to the ball. Modern theology has also neglected the natural world as a subject of religious interest. This began to happen at the time of the Reformation. Prior to that, God, the human race, and the natural world formed three pillars of theology, a three-legged stool that together comprised Christian as well as Jewish and Islamic philosophical and theological reflection. But the fierce conflict over how we are saved from sin, with Protestants insisting on Christ's redemptive work being effective by faith alone and Catholics holding out for faith and good works, caused a focus on the human dilemma that blinkered eyes to the rest of creation. As happens in any fight, people lost sight of the wider reality. In the centuries that followed, Catholic theology tied the Spirit very tightly to church office and the teaching of the magisterium, while Protestant theology fastened onto the Spirit's work of justification and sanctification in the individual person. This focus on humanity led both sides to forget biblical, patristic, and medieval theology's witness to the cosmic presence and activity of the Spirit from the beginning, throughout history, unto the end.

In revisiting this ancient theme for our day, then, ecological theology needs to work on two fronts at once, the Spirit and the natural world. The Nicene Creed offers a subtle clue by identifying the Spirit as "the Lord and Giver of life," in Latin *Dominus et vivificantem*, the one who vivifies, the Vivifier. This clue to the Spirit's work in the world receives further precision from a trio of metaphors crafted by the third-century North African theologian Tertullian. First, if God the Father can be likened to the sun, then Christ is a sunbeam, that is, of the same substance as the sun and coming forth to earth. And the Spirit? The Spirit is the suntan, the spot of warmth and light where the sun arrives and actually has an effect. This pattern repeats in the example of water: there is an upwelling spring in the hills, the same water in the river flowing through the valley, and the irrigation ditch (the Spirit) where the water reaches plants and actually enables them to grow. Similarly, this thinker compared the trinitarian God to the root, the shoot, and the fruit of a tree, that is, the tree's deep unreachable foundation, its visible sprouting forth into the world, and its flowers, fragrance, fruits, and seeds (the Spirit), which beautify and nourish the world. These are all metaphors for the one God who exists as incomprehensible mystery beyond the world, comes forth incarnate in history, and—here is the point—pervades the material world with graceful vigor.

It is crucial to remember at the outset that the Spirit is never *less* than God. The Creator Spirit is always *God,* who actually arrives in every moment, drawing near and passing by with life-giving power. The stunning world opened up by Big Bang cosmology and evolutionary biology on the one hand, and the vulnerability of life on Earth needing protection on the other, is leading ecological theology to glimpse the Spirit's presence and activity with new contours, as the living God who is the source, sustainer, and goal of the whole shebang.

THE NATURAL WORLD

Wonder

Keeping in mind the image of Earth from space, consider four aspects of this planet and its place in the universe.

₵ First: it is all very old. In billions of years, the key numbers are 14, 5, and 4. The universe originated in a primordial flaring forth, rather inelegantly named the Big Bang, about fourteen billion years ago (more precisely 13.7 billion years ago, according to current scientific consensus). From that explosive instant onward to this day, the universe has continued to expand, as galaxies and their stars come into being and pass away. Our own sun and its planets emerged about five billion years ago, coalescing from the dust and gas left by previous generations of stars that exploded in their death throes. On planet Earth about four billion years ago, a new eruption occurred, *life*, emerging in communities of single-celled creatures deep in the primeval seas and evolving into the more than one million species present today.

In his book *The Dragons of Eden*, Carl Sagan uses the timetable of a year to dramatize the sequence. If the Big Bang occurred on January 1st, then our sun and its planets came into existence September 9th. Life on Earth originated on September 25th; and the first humans emerged onto the scene on December 31st at 10:30 P.M. Placing this timetable onto a graphic physical structure, the American Museum of Natural History in New York built a spiraling cosmic walk that traces the history of the universe. Starting at rooftop level with the Big Bang, each normal-sized step down the walkway covers millions of years. At the bottom, one steps over all of human history in a line as thin as a human hair. We human beings are newborns in the universe, only recently arrived.

❧ Second, the universe is incomprehensibly large. There are over one hundred billion galaxies, each comprising of billions of stars, and no one knows how many moons and planets, all of this visible and audible matter being only a fraction of the matter in the universe, which, being not well understood, is called "dark." Earth is a small planet orbiting a medium-sized star toward the edge of one spiral galaxy. We are but a speck.

❧ Third, the universe is complexly interconnected, everything being related to everything else to some degree. Speaking of the redness of human blood, for example, British scientist/theologian Arthur Peacocke wrote, "Every atom of iron in our blood's hemoglobin would not be there had it not been produced in some galactic explosion billions of years ago and eventually condensed to form the iron in the crust of the earth from which we have emerged." Quite literally, human beings and all creatures on this planet are made of stardust. The story of biological evolution, moreover, makes evident that we humans share with all other living creatures a common genetic ancestry tracing back to the original single-celled creatures in the ancient seas. Bacteria, pine trees, blueberries, horses, the great gray whales—we are all kin in the great community of life. In Abraham Heschel's beautiful metaphor, this makes human beings the cantors of the universe, able to sing praise and thanks in the name of the whole cosmic community of which we are a part.

℃ Fourth, the universe is profoundly dynamic. Even as you read these words, new space is coming into being as the universe continues to expand outward. Galaxies whirl around their central black hole; our planet revolves yearly around our star and rotates on its axis every day; whole species emerge, thrive, and go extinct, as do individuals whose time span arches from birth to death. No longer, then, can theology contrast nature's static regularity with human history, or oppose the fixed pagan gods of nature with the mobile God of the Israelites on the move in history. Nature itself is historical.

This dynamism accounts for the emergence of the human species itself. From the evolutionary life and death of single-celled creatures flowed an advancing tide of life: creatures that live in shells, fish, amphibians, reptiles, insects, flowers, birds, and mammals, among whom emerged human beings, we primates whose brains are so richly textured that we experience self-reflective consciousness and freedom, or in classical terms, mind and will. Matter, zesty with energy, evolves to life, then to consciousness, then to spirit (from the pebble to the peach to the poodle to the person). Human thought and love are not something injected into the universe from without, but are the flowering in us of deeply cosmic energies, arising out of the very physical dynamism of the cosmos, which is already self-organizing and creative. In this telling, human persons are not aliens set down in a strange physical world but an intrinsic part of the evolving story. In Sallie McFague's inspired appellation, we are "earthlings," creatures who belong here. Our personal yearnings and cultural creativity encapsulate the energetic vitality of the cosmos itself; our little nugget of historical time concentrates the wild and exciting undertaking going on in nature itself. This makes us distinctive but not separate, a unique strand in the cosmos, yet still a strand *of* the cosmos.

On the one hand, wonder. But on the other hand, distress, for this story has entered a new and threatening chapter on our home planet.

Wasting

We humans are inflicting deadly damage on our planet at an accelerating pace, compromising its identity as a dwelling place for life. Overconsumption, unbridled reproduction, exploitative use of resources, and efflorescing pollution are rapidly depleting life-supporting systems on land, in the sea, and in the air. Every year, for example, 20 percent of Earth's people in the rich nations use 75 percent of the world's resources and produce 80 percent of the world's waste. An example: Chicago with three million people consumes as much raw produce in a year as Bangladesh with ninety-seven million people. Such overconsumption is driven by an economy that must constantly grow in order to be viable. Its greatest goal is a bottom line in the black without counting the ecological cost. Another example: in 1950 the world numbered two billion people. At the turn of the millennium we numbered six billion. If predictions hold, by the year 2030 there will be ten billion persons on the planet. If someone born in 1950 lives to be eighty years old, Earth's human population will have multiplied five times during his or her lifetime. To translate these statistics into a vivid image: another Mexico City is added every sixty days; another Brazil joins the planet every year.

The carrying capacity of Earth is being exhausted by this human use; our species consumes resources faster than Earth's power to replenish itself. This assault on the planet, intended or not, wreaks ecological harm of great magnitude. The unholy litany is well known: global warming, holes in the ozone layer, clear-cut forests, drained wetlands, denuded soils, polluted air, poisoned rivers, overfished oceans, and, over all, the threat of nuclear conflagration. Appallingly, widespread destruction of ecosystems has as its flip side the extinction of the plant and animal lives that thrive in these habitats. Ours is a time of a great dying off. By a conservative estimate, in the last quarter of the twentieth century 10 percent of all living species went extinct. When these living beings, these magnificent animals or little plants go extinct, they never come back again. We are killing birth itself, wiping out the future of our fellow creatures who took millions of years to evolve. Their perishing sends an early-warning signal of the death of the planet itself as a dwelling place for life. In the blunt language of the World Council of Churches, "The stark sign of our times is a planet in peril at our hands."

The picture darkens as we attend to the deep-seated connection between social injustice and ecological devastation. Poor people suffer disproportionately from environmental impoverishment; ravaging of people and ravaging of the land on which they depend go hand in hand. In the Amazon basin, for example, lack of land reform pushes dispossessed rural peoples to the edges of the rain forest, where in order to stay alive they practice slash-and-burn agriculture, in the process destroying pristine habitat, killing rare animals, and displacing indigenous peoples. In wealthy nations, the economically well-off can choose to live amid acres of green while poor people are housed near factories, refineries, or waste-processing plants that heavily pollute the environment. Birth defects, general ill health and disease result. The bitterness of this situation is exacerbated by racial prejudice, as environmental racism pressures people of color to dwell in these neighborhoods.

Feminist analysis clarifies further how the plight of the poor becomes exemplified in poor women whose own biological abilities to give birth are compromised by toxic environments, and whose nurturing of children is hampered at every turn by lack of clean water, food, and fuel. Women-initiated projects such as the Chipko movement in India, whereby village women literally hug the forest trees to prevent lumber interests from cutting them down, thus ensuring clean water, fuel, and fruits; and the Green Belt movement started by Nobel Peace Prize winner Wangari Maathai in Kenya, whereby women plant millions of trees and receive a small income for nurturing them, show how protecting and restoring the Earth interweaves intrinsically with the flourishing of poor women and their communities. Poverty and its remedy have an ecological face.

When people begin to think about God in relation to *this* world, the stunning natural world opened up to our wonder but being destroyed by our wasting leads to a whole new approach. In former times, the basic conception of the world was that it was created in the beginning and remained a static entity; God's activity consisted primarily in maintaining what had already been established. Now that we realize that the world is becoming, that genuinely new things come into being by evolution and other processes, fresh ideas of divine presence and agency are needed. To date these have centered on the Spirit of God, called the Creator Spirit in the great medieval hymn *Veni, Creator Spiritus*. As it integrates the revelatory experience of a personal God into an expansive cosmological setting, ecological theology, replete in its fullest measure with social justice and eco-feminist insights, is mapping yet another new frontier.

DIVINE PRESENCE

Attending to the idea of the Creator Spirit brings to the fore the belief that the presence and activity of God pervade the world and that therefore the natural world is the dwelling place of God. This divine presence can be explored under three rubrics: it is continuous; it is cruciform; and it abides in the mode of promise.

Continuous Presence

At the end of his popular book *A Brief History of Time*, physicist Stephen Hawking asks a famous question: "What is it that breathes fire into the equations and makes a universe for them to describe?" In the integrity of his adherence to atheism, he leaves the question open. Biblical faith offers a different option, daring to believe that it is God's own Spirit who breathes life into the equations, thereby bringing forth this exuberant universe. The mystery of the living God, utterly transcendent, is also the creative power who dwells at the heart of the world sustaining every moment of its evolution.

The mental model that allows for the most intelligible interpretation of this presence is panentheism (all-in-God). In recent centuries theology worked mainly with the model of theism. This construal infers God to be the highest member of the order of being. It insists on God's difference and distance from the world while paying little attention to divine nearness. Its opposite model is pantheism (all is God), which erases the difference between created and uncreated, thereby collapsing God and the world into each other. Unlike either of these patterns, panentheism envisions a relationship whereby everything abides *in* God, who in turn encompasses everything, being "*above all and through all and in all*" (Eph 4:6). What results is a mutual abiding for which the pregnant female body provides a good metaphor.

Martin Luther, who had a rich and sophisticated understanding of divine presence, used a homely example of a grain of wheat to illuminate the point:

> How can reason tolerate that the divine majesty is so small that it can be substantially present in a grain, on a grain, over a grain, through a grain, within and without . . . entirely in each grain, no matter how numerous these grains may be? And how can reason tolerate that the same majesty is so large that neither this world nor a thousand worlds can encompass it and say 'behold, there it is'? . . . Yet, though it can be encompassed nowhere and by no one, God's divine essence encompasses all things and dwells in all. (*WA* [*Weimar Ausgabe*] 23.134.34–23.136.36)

Seen in the light of this continuous divine presence, the natural world, instead of being divorced from what is sacred, takes on a sacramental character. Sacramental theology has always taught that simple material things—water, oil, bread, and wine—can be bearers of divine grace. This is so, it now becomes clear, only because to begin with the whole physical world itself is the matrix of God's gracious indwelling. Matter bears the mark of the sacred and has itself a spiritual radiance. In turn, divine presence is sacramentally mediated in and through the world's embodiment, not necessarily nor absolutely, but graciously and really.

The indwelling Spirit of God moves over the void, breathes into the chaos, quickens, warms, sets free, blesses, and continuously creates the world, empowering its evolutionary advance. Bringing the Spirit back into the picture this way leads ecological theology to envision God not at or beyond the apex of the pyramid of being as in modern theism, but within and around the emerging, struggling, living, dying, and renewing circle of life and the whole universe itself.

The Cruciform Pattern

There is yet more to be said. For the natural world is not only beautiful in its harmonies; it also presents us with an unrelentingly harsh and bloody picture, filled with suffering and death. The bodily existence of every living creature requires eating other creatures, be they animals or plants. Predation and death are an inescapable part of the pattern of biological life. On a grand scale, the history of life itself is dependent on death; without it, there would be no evolutionary development from generation to generation. Where is God amid this suffering and death over millions of millennia? The temptation is to deny the violence and escape into a romantic view of the natural world. But there is another option, namely, to face the pain and interpret it in the light of the gospel.

Those who believe that Jesus is the Wisdom of God made flesh see his life and destiny as the most important lens through which to interpret the character of the living God, not comprehensively, for the mystery remains, but truly. What do we glimpse through this lens? In terms of divine relationship to human beings, we glimpse a merciful love that knows no bounds. Jesus' ministry, replete with scenes of healing, exorcising, feeding, forgiving, and preaching the reign of God, made the love of God experientially available to all, the marginalized most of all. His unjust execution on the cross linked divine compassion deeply with the sinful condition of this world, with its painful suffering and terrifying death. His resurrection reveals that by so entering these depths, the Spirit of God opens the promise of new life through and beyond death. Together as one paschal mystery, the cross and resurrection of this Jewish prophet who ministered in a graciously inclusive way become the revelation of divine solidarity with human beings in our sin and pain, awakening resistance and grounding hope.

Seeing the living God as Creator not just of human beings but of the whole world in which we humans are embedded, ecological theology finds warrant to cross the species line and extend this divine solidarity to all creatures. It proposes that the Creator Spirit dwells in compassionate solidarity with every living being that suffers, from the dinosaurs wiped out by an asteroid to the baby impala eaten by a lioness. Not a sparrow falls to the ground without eliciting a knowing suffering in the heart of God. Such an idea is not meant to glorify suffering, a trap that must be carefully avoided. But it works out an implication of the Creator Spirit's relation to an evolutionary, suffering world with an eye to divine compassion. Nature's crying out is met by the Spirit, who groans with the labor pains of all creation to bring the new to birth (Rom 8:22). Thus is the pattern of cross and resurrection rediscovered on a cosmic scale.

Abiding in the Mode of Promise

The scientific account of the expanding cosmos and of the evolution of life on this planet makes it clear that the universe, rather than being a settled phenomenon, can be described today only in terms of an open-ended adventure. In the beginning was a homogenous sea of radiation. Rather than remain at a granular level of existence, the universe has unfolded extravagantly over time, emerging in increasingly elaborate array into forms ever more complex and beautiful. Biologists such as Stephen Jay Gould warn against interpreting this story as a necessary directional, linear march from the Big Bang to the human race. The story of life is more like a branching bush, with humanity itself one recent twig on one branch of the bush. While granting this point, Peacocke and others argue that since the universe as a whole has in fact moved in a certain direction from its cosmic origins, it obviously has propensities toward ever more complexity, beauty, and ordered novelty. Taking the long view, we can see that from the beginning the universe is seeded with promise, pregnant with surprise. "More" regularly comes from "less." The cosmic story has been one of restless advance rich in fecundity that produces the genuinely new.

This unfinished openness of natural phenomena places the world squarely within the parameters of biblical faith. For this faith forever encounters a God of promise who approaches from the future with a call to "come ahead." From the call to Abraham to travel to a new land, capped off by the surprising gift of a child to him and Sarah in their old age and sterility; to the summons to the enslaved Hebrew people to cross out of Egypt into freedom; to the commission to the women disciples at the empty tomb of Jesus to go and tell the news of his resurrection: divine presence in human history is rife with surprise.

Reflecting on the world's evolutionary history in tandem with these stories of faith, theology proposes that we understand the Creator Spirit to be the generous wellspring of novelty not only for human beings but for the whole natural world. Indwelling the world with creative power, the Spirit sets it off on a grand adventure, saying at the Big Bang, in effect, "Go, become, explore, bring forth the new, because more is still possible. And I will be with you." Nature, it appears, bears a raw openness to the future. More than a sacrament of continuous divine presence, more than a locus of divine compassion, it is also the bearer of a divine promise. The living, ever-dawning God abides in the world most intimately in the mode of promise: *"Behold, I make all things new"* (Rev 21:5).

To sum up: ecological theology proposes that the Creator Spirit dwells at the heart of the natural world, graciously energizing its evolution from within, compassionately holding all creatures in their finitude and death, and drawing the world forward toward an unimaginable future. Throughout the vast sweep of cosmic and biological evolution, the Spirit embraces the material root of life and its endless new potential, empowering the cosmic process from within. The universe, in turn, is self-organizing and self-transcending, energized from the spiraling galaxies to the double helix of the DNA molecule by the dance of divine vivifying power.

DIVINE AGENCY

The creative, suffering, promising presence of the Spirit in the natural world raises in direct fashion the question of divine agency. How does God act in an evolutionary, emergent universe? Modern forms of theism assume that God intervenes in the world at will to accomplish divine purpose apart from natural processes. But the scientific picture of the universe indicates that this is not necessary. Nature is actively organizing itself into new forms at all levels. Even the emergence of life and then mind can be accounted for without special supernatural intervention. The bitterness of contemporary debates between some scientists and religious adherents of "intelligent design" flows precisely from these contrasting assumptions, with the former finding no trace of divine activity in the physical world while the latter posit some sort of direct divine action and overall plan. The fundamental view of divine agency that both parties hold, however, is no longer adequate.

Disputes within theology over divine agency can be just as fierce as those between science and religion. At least six positions claim a seat at the table. Single-action theory understands God to have acted once, in the beginning; since then, God sustains the world while the details of cosmic history are just how it all happens to work out (Gordon Kaufman, Maurice Wiles). Positing much more divine involvement, process thought holds that God provides initial aims to every concrescing event, and acts by the power of persuasion to lure the world in a desired direction (Alfred North Whitehead and friends, including John B. Cobb, David Griffin). Making an analogy with the agency of embodied human persons, a third position envisions the world as the body of God, with God acting in the world the way the soul acts in the body (Sallie McFague). Using information theory, the top-down causality position understands that God acts in the world by way of the influence of the whole upon the parts (Arthur Peacocke). The "causal-joint" theory uses the innate openness of physical processes to predicate that God acts as one of the initial conditions of an event, inputting the pattern that influences the overall outcome (John Polkinghorne, Nancey Murphy, Robert Russell).

A more classical position holds to the distinction between primary and secondary causality, seeing God as the primary cause of the world, the unfathomable Source of the world's existence, while natural forces and individual creatures are secondary causes that receive from God their power to act with their own independence. These two causes are not two species of the same genus, not two different types of causes united on a common ground of generating effects. They operate on completely different levels (itself an inadequate analogy), one being the Cause of all causes, the other participating in this power to act as things that are burning participate in the power of fire. In this view of divine agency it is incoherent to think of God working in the world apart from secondary causes, or beside them, or in addition to them, or complementary to them, or even in competition with them. God's act does not supply something that is missing from a creature's act or rob it of its power so that it is only a sham cause. Rather, the mystery of the living God acts in and through the creative acts of finite agents which have genuine causal efficacy in their own right.

Aquinas, who endorsed this view, held that God's governance of the world would in fact be less than perfectly good if creatures were not endowed with their own independent agency. Hence, events both ordinary and extraordinary take place according to the rhythms and dynamisms of nature's own capacities. At every moment divine agency will be physically undetectable. It is not a quantifiable property like mass or energy, not an additional factor in the equations, not an element that can be discovered among the forces of the universe at all. But in and through the creativity of nature, the boundless love of the Creator Spirit is bringing the world to birth. As Australian theologian Denis Edwards who, along with other contemporary Thomists adheres to this position, observes, "Aquinas never knew Darwin's theory of evolution, but he would have had no difficulty in understanding it as the way that God creates."

I recall one conference at Berkeley where tension among these various positions ran so high that scholars actually accused each other of blasphemy. These positions, however, all have much in common. They shun an explicitly interventionist model of divine activity. They seek to make intelligible the idea that the Creator Spirit, as ground, sustaining power, and goal of the evolving world, acts by *empowering* the process from within. They see divine creativity active *in, with, and under* cosmic processes. God makes the world, in other words, by empowering the world to make itself.

Chance

Even granting this, what makes the conversation so dicey for theology with its belief in a provident God is the element of chance. Unlike the science of the Enlightenment period, which envisioned the universe operating in a determined, mechanistic way, today's science has revealed the existence of extensive zones of openness in nature. In these areas what happens next is *intrinsically* unpredictable. This is not because we have not yet developed instruments capable of measuring such systems and thus predicting outcomes. Rather, there is something in the nature of the beast that defies total measurement.

℧ The microscopic realm studied by quantum physics is one such zone. Our inability to plot simultaneously both the position and speed of a single particle has even given rise to the aptly named "uncertainty principle." Rather than simply referring to the limits of measurement and thus to our knowledge, philosophers of science now surmise that this refers to the nature of the phenomenon itself. The uncertainty principle is not just epistemological, in other words, but also ontological.

℧ Large, nonlinear, dynamic systems studied by the physics of chaos are another such zone. The striking feature here is that the new, self-organizing patterns that emerge are extremely responsive to initial conditions. A favored illustration is the butterfly effect on weather. One day a butterfly flutters its wings in Beijing; the small current of air it sets in motion cascades upward in ever-amplifying intersection with other air currents; one week later, as a result, there is a major storm in New York. There is no simple cause and effect, but an open, dynamic system that can be tipped this way or that way with the most minute changes. Over time, a certain pattern will emerge as the system works over and over again. But in any given instance no sure prediction is possible.

℧ The biological development of species by natural selection is a third such zone. A gene mutates as a result of bombardment by solar rays, or a hurricane blows a few birds off course to a new island, or the Earth is struck by an asteroid. As the environment changes, those who adapt best in procreating and caring for their young, finding food, and warding off predators will make it into the next generation, but there is no way to foretell this in advance.

In these and other instances, contemporary science has laid bare the existence of emergent, adaptive, self-organizing systems in nonhuman nature, systems whose functioning over time has led to genuine novelty in the universe. The regular lawlike pattern rolls along; it gets interrupted by chance; but rather than everything falling apart, new, richer, more intricate and beautiful forms of order arise at the edge of disorder. The future keeps opening up. Technically speaking, the shape of the world that we inhabit today has been crafted by random events occurring within lawful regularities over eons of time. If there were only law in the universe, the situation would stagnate in a repetitive and uncreative order. If there were only chance, things would become so chaotic that no orderly structures could take shape. But chance occurring within law disrupts the usual pattern while being held in check, and over millions of millennia the interplay of the two advances the world to a richer state than would otherwise be possible. Peacocke suggests that this chance-within-law pattern over deep time is precisely what one would expect if the evolving universe were not predetermined but were left free to be able to explore its potential by experimenting with the fullest range of possibilities inherent in matter.

This means that as far as science can fathom, the universe's unfolding has not happened according to a predetermined blueprint. Because genuine randomness cannot be predicted, there is an open-endedness to the process by which the universe generates new modes of being that can be narrated only in retrospect. A startling moment occurred at an annual meeting of the Catholic Theological Society of America when William Stoeger, Jesuit astrophysicist from the Vatican Observatory Research Group at the University of Arizona, asked: Rewind the clock of the world back to the first moment and let it start ticking again—would things turn out the same way? The scientific consensus is an emphatic no. There was stunned silence and then an eruption of argument as a roomful of theologians tried to wrap their minds around this idea and relate it to our basic assumptions.

Relating this insight to the indwelling Spirit of God, ecological theology proposes that as boundless love at work in the ongoing evolution of the universe, divine creativity is the source not just of cosmic order but also of the chance that allows novelty to appear. Empowering the world from within, the Spirit not only grounds lawful regularities but also embraces the chanciness of random mutations and the chaotic conditions of open systems, being much more closely allied to disorder than our older natural theology ever imagined. Unpredictable upheavals might be destructive, but they have the potential to lead to richer forms of order. In the emergent evolutionary universe, we should not be surprised to find divine creativity hovering very close to turbulence.

Theology has sought further explication of divine agency in a world of chance by analogies with divine action glimpsed in Christian teaching about grace and the cross.

Grace

When the Spirit offers the very life of God to human beings, they are not forced to accept. Their own freedom is respected, to the point where they may even opt for hell. It is not that the Spirit is standing by, idling in neutral; theology teaches that all kinds of promptings lure the human heart to turn toward the face of God. But coercion is not in the picture. The covenant relationship of grace requires a free human response. As with human beings, so too with the universe: the ever-faithful God is graciously courteous toward the freedom of the natural order. Rather than intervening from outside, the Creator Spirit enables ongoing creation from within (these spatial metaphors are inadequate) by endowing the universe with the capacity to transcend itself toward ever new forms. Self-organizing, complex systems keep on introducing surprises as the world of chance occurring within lawlike structures evolves over eons of deep time. In, with, and under these processes, the generous Spirit of God energizes the ongoing creation of the world.

Cross

Rather than acting like Caesar writ large, Jesus did not cling to godly dignity but "emptied himself," foolishly, thereby opening up new life for others (Phil 2:5–11). This enacts a *kenotic* form of divine power. It is not the power of force, imposing one's will. Neither is it, as some fear, impotence. Rather, as lived out historically in Jesus Christ, it is the power of giving oneself freely in love with the effect that others are empowered; they are loved in such a beautiful way that they become capable of their own action. As on the cross, so too in the universe: ecological theology proposes that divine *kenōsis* did not happen only once at Jesus' death but instead is typical of God's gracious action in the world from the beginning. Allowing the christic pattern of self-giving to interpret the Spirit's creative action within the evolving universe means that divine agency does not have the character of determining, even dictating, all occurrences. Rather, divine *kenōsis* opens up space for the genuine integrity of finite systems, allowing chance its truly random appearance.

In view of the openness of the natural world, John Haught suggests, happily in my view, that we should no longer think of God as having a *plan* for the evolving universe, but rather a *vision*. This vision aims at bringing into being a community of love. The Creator Spirit is at the heart of the process, guiding the world in that direction, all the while inviting the world to participate in its own creation through the free working of its systems. At the quantum level, in nonlinear dynamic systems, through natural selection, and by human agency—the new emerges! Grounded and vivified by such freeing power, the universe evolves in the integrity of its own adventure.

TO LOVE THE EARTH

Clearly, this theology of the Creator Spirit who creates, indwells, compassionately loves, and empowers the world on its great adventure has implications for all of theology. It especially undergirds an ethic of responsible, assertive care for the Earth. A moral universe limited to human persons is no longer adequate. If the Earth is indeed a sacrament of divine presence, a locus of divine compassion, and a bearer of divine promise, then its ongoing destruction through ecocide, biocide, geocide is a deeply sinful desecration. In the tradition of biblical prophecy and the spirit of Jesus, the response of people of faith needs to become prophetic and challenging, promoting care, protection, and healing of the natural world even if these go counter to powerful economic and political interests—and they do. We need to use all the techniques of active nonviolent resistance to halt aggression against the vulnerable, be it ever so humble a species or ever so vast a system as the ozone layer. One stringent criterion must now measure the morality of our actions: whether or not these contribute to a sustainable life community on Earth.

Grounding this praxis is a stunning principle first articulated by Pope John Paul II in 1990: "respect for life and for the dignity of the human person extends also to the rest of creation." Pragmatically, humans shall survive together with other creatures on this planet or not at all. The issue is more than practical, however, for respect for life cannot be divided. Not only human life but the whole living Earth is God's beloved creation, deserving of care.

This in turn requires us to shift ethical attention away from human persons alone and to recenter vigorous moral consideration on the whole community of life. In an ecological ethic, Jesus' great command to love your neighbor as yourself extends to include all members of the life community. "Who is my neighbor?" asks Brian Patrick, "the Samaritan? The outcast? The enemy? Yes, yes, of course. But it is also the whale, the dolphin, and the rain forest. Our neighbor is the entire community of life, the entire universe. We must love it all as our very self." If nature is the new poor, as Sallie McFague argues, then our passion to establish justice for the poor and oppressed now extends to include the natural world, life systems, and other species under threat. "Save the rain forest" becomes a concrete moral application of the commandment "Thou shalt not kill." The moral goal becomes ensuring vibrant life in community for all.

In our day we discover that the great, incomprehensible mystery of God, utterly transcendent and beyond the world, is also the dynamic power at the heart of the natural world and its evolution. Groaning with the world, delighting in its advance, keeping faith with its failures, energizing it graciously from within, the Creator Spirit is with all creatures in their finitude and death, holding them in redemptive love and drawing them into an unforeseeable future in the divine life of communion. Rather than simply being stages on the way to *homo sapiens*, the whole rich tapestry of the created order has its own intrinsic value, being the place where God creatively dwells. Augustine imagined this vividly:

> I set before the sight of my spirit the whole creation, whatsoever we can see therein (as sea, earth, air, stars, trees, mortal creatures); yea and whatever in it we do not see.... And Thee, O Lord, I imagined on every part environing and pervading it, though in every way infinite: as if there were a sea, everywhere and on every side, through unmeasured space, one only boundless sea, and it contained within it some sponge, huge, but bounded; that sponge must needs, in all its parts, be filled with that immeasurable sea: so conceived I Thy creation, itself finite, yet full of Thee, the infinite; and I said, behold God and behold what God hath created. (*Confessions* 7.7)

And behold how we are encompassed! As Paul preached at Athens, "*we live and move and have our being*" in the Creator Spirit envisioned just this way (Acts 17:28).

FOR FURTHER READING

A clear, persuasively argued introduction aimed at a general reading public is Denis Edwards, *Ecology at the Heart of Faith* (Maryknoll, N.Y.: Orbis, 2007). Sallie McFague, *Super, Natural Christians: How we Should Love Nature* (Minneapolis: Fortress, 1997) mounts a spirited argument of why Christians should be great lovers of the earth. Brian Swimme and Thomas Berry, *The Universe Story: From the Primordial Flaring Forth to the Ecozoic Era—A Celebration of the Unfolding of the Cosmos* (San Francisco: Harper-SanFrancisco, 1992) present the background science in readable and religiously evocative prose.

An excellent resource is Dieter Hessel and Rosemary Radford Ruether, eds., *Christianity and Ecology: Seeking the Well-being of Earth and Humans* (Cambridge, Mass.: Harvard University Press, 2000), the fruit of an international conference on the subject. Nine companion volumes in this Harvard series deal with ecology in major world religions such as Hinduism, Islam, and Buddhism. For more compressed treatment of the religions and ecology, see Mary Evelyn Tucker and John Grim, eds., *Worldviews and Ecology: Religion, Philosophy, and the Environment* (Orbis, 1994).

Some works deal in a comprehensive way with the God-question in ecological theology. Arthur Peacocke, *Theology for a Scientific Age* (Fortress, 1993), is a *tour de force* that presents an entire systematic theology from the perspective of the evolving world; his *Paths from Science Towards God* (Oxford: Oneworld, 2002) aims to explain these new ideas to the general reader. Gloria Schaab, *The Creative Suffering of the Triune God: An Evolutionary Theology* (New York: Oxford University Press, 2007), explicates and expands Peacocke's insights. John Haught's excellent *God after Darwin: A Theology of Evolution* (Boulder, Colo.: Westview, 2000) deals directly with the presence and agency of God in light of scientific challenge. Sallie McFague, *The Body of God: An Ecological Theology* (Minneapolis: Fortress, 1993) builds powerfully toward a holistic vision. Rosemary Radford Ruether, *Gaia and God: An Ecofeminist Theology of Earth Healing* (San Francisco: HarperSanFrancisco, 1992) explores the prophetic and sacramental resources of the Christian tradition. Denis Edwards's books *The God of Evolution* (New York: Paulist, 1999), and *Breath of Life: A Theology of the Creator Spirit* (Orbis, 2004) connect theology with an earth-oriented spirituality in an accessible and enlightening manner. Resources in the Bible are highlighted in Carol Dempsey and Mary Margaret Pazdan, eds., *Earth, Wind, and Fire: Biblical and Theological Perspectives on Creation* (Collegeville, Minn.: Liturgical Press, 2004).

Other works zero in on one particularly rich aspect. The kenotic view of divine power and divine suffering in the universe is examined in John Polkinghorne, ed., *The Work of Love: Creation as Kenosis* (Grand Rapids: Eerdmans, 2001); see especially Arthur Peacocke, "The Cost of New Life," pp. 21–42. Panentheism as a model of God's relation to the world is explored in Philip Clayton and Arthur Peacocke, eds., *In Whom We Live and Move and Have Our Being: Panentheistic Reflections on God's Presence in a Scientific World* (Grand Rapids: Eerdmans, 2004). John Haught's work *The Cosmic Adventure: Science, Religion, and the Quest for Purpose* (New York: Paulist, 1984), presents this metaphor of openness to the future in accessible prose; his essay "Chaos, Complexity, and Theology," pp. 181–94 in Arthur Fabel and Donald St. John, eds., *Teilhard in the 21st Century: The Emerging Spirit of Earth* (Orbis, 2003), explains the religious implications of nature's ability to self-organize and bring forth the new.

The intertwining of ecology and social justice comes to the fore in David Hallman, ed., *Ecotheology: Voices from South and North* (Orbis, 1994); and Leonardo Boff and Virgilio Elizondo, eds., *Ecology and Poverty: Cry of the Earth, Cry of the Poor* (Orbis, 1995). Ivone Gebara, *Longing for Running Water: Ecofeminism and Liberation* (Fortress, 1999) gives voice to poor women in the developing world, as do Mary Judith Ress, *Ecofeminism in Latin America* (Orbis, 2006) and Rosemary Radford Ruether, ed., *Women Healing Earth: Third World Women on Ecology, Feminism, and Religion* (Orbis, 1996). Multiple connections between earth, women, and the sacred are discussed in Carol Adams, ed., *Ecofeminism and the Sacred* (Continuum, 1993); and Elizabeth Johnson, *Women, Earth, and Creator Spirit* (New York: Paulist Press, 1993).

Ecological ethics are explored in excellent discussions by James Nash, *Loving Nature: Ecological Integrity and Christian Responsibility* (Nashville: Abingdon, 1991), written with a view to public policy; and Larry Rasmussen, *Earth Community, Earth Ethics* (Orbis, 1997), which taps into church traditions to promote responsibility. Harold Coward and Daniel Maguire, eds., *Visions of a New Earth: Religious Perspectives on Population, Consumption, and Ecology* (Albany: State University of New York Press, 2000) bring religious perspectives to bear on troubling consumption and population issues; while John B. Cobb, *Sustainability: Economics, Ecology, and Justice* (Orbis, 1992) lays out the clear link between ecology and economics.

The Web site of the National Religious Partnership for the Environment (nrpe.org) carries official Catholic, Protestant, and Evangelical, and Jewish teachings as well as practical programs.

10

TRINITY: THE LIVING GOD OF LOVE

THE POINT

"The grace of our Lord Jesus Christ, the love of God, and the fellowship of the Holy Spirit be with you all" (2 Cor 13:13). With this blessing, originally spoken in the first century and still recited at liturgical gatherings in the twenty-first, Christians signal a particular understanding of the living God. If one took this blessing literally, its triadic structure might lead to the idea that Christian faith departs from monotheism. Such, however, would be a mistaken impression. Christians do not believe in three Gods but in one. What is particular to this faith is the belief that this one God has graciously reached out to the world in love in the person of Jesus Christ in order to heal, redeem, and liberate—in a word, to save. The experience of salvation coming from God through Jesus in the power of the Spirit sets up such a powerful encounter with the Holy that it requires a new language. This language is trinitarian. Far from being a definition or a description, trinitarian language is an interpretation of who God is in the light of the glad tidings of salvation. It lifts up God's gracious ways active in the world through Jesus Christ and the Spirit, and finds there the fundamental revelation about God's own being as a self-giving communion of love.

At the outset and all through this chapter it is crucial to keep this point in mind: the point of trinitarian language is to acclaim the living God as the mystery of salvation. Whether found in scripture, creed, liturgy, doctrine, or theology, it is Christian code tapping out the belief that the living God made known through Jesus and the Spirit is dynamic Love encompassing the universe who acts to save. At its most basic it is saying, very simply, *"God is love"* (1 John 4:16).

Realistically, of course, the triune symbol has not functioned this way for centuries in the West. It has been neglected, treated like a curiosity, or analyzed with conceptual acrobatics entirely inappropriate to its meaning. Consequently, the doctrine has become unintelligible and religiously irrelevant on a wide scale. One can see this happening already in the eighteenth century, when Friedrich Schleiermacher relegated the Trinity to the last few pages of his magisterial work *The Christian Faith*, convinced that the doctrine had little practical value or connection with the essence of the faith. In his own book on the subject, *The Trinity*, Karl Rahner lamented that so weakly does this belief function in the spirituality, theology, and actual faith life of the church that if officials announced that a fourth person of the Trinity had been discovered, it would probably cause little stir. Nowadays peoples' eyes glaze over when they hear mention of the Trinity. At best they prepare themselves with a sigh for discussion of an esoteric matter. This is terribly unfortunate because, to repeat, here we are dealing with the very heart of the Christian idea of God, born of experience. As Walter Kasper bluntly puts it, "Trinity is the Christian form of monotheism."

As I see it, the various theologies traced in the chapters of this book have been rediscovering the triune God in a practical manner out of their struggle for life, healing, and understanding in different contexts. In more direct fashion, the field of trinitarian theology itself has also been undergoing rebirth in contemporary systematic theology fertilized by biblical and historical studies. By tracing the story of the disconnect between the Trinity and Christian life, and examining three tasks necessary to weave the two back together again, this chapter maps a renaissance of insight into the critical, hopeful, practical meaning of the Trinity in our contemporary world.

HISTORY OF A BREACH

Trinitarian speech arose in the first century in the context of peoples' encounter with God's saving graciousness through Jesus Christ in the power of the Spirit. As Leonardo Boff has written and most would agree, "An encounter with divine Mystery lies at the root of all religious doctrine." This is no less true of the Trinity than of any other doctrine. What specific encounter triggered this development? It was an encounter with Jesus Christ, whose life, death, and risen presence in the Spirit made tangible God's gracious mercy poured out in the midst of sin and suffering. Speaking about God in a threefold way arose historically to express this experience, to codify it and pass it on. Salvation is the experience without which there would be no talk of Trinity at all.

The first believers in Jesus were monotheists, members of the Jewish community who worshiped the one God who bore the sacred, unpronounced name YHWH. This was the God of their ancestors, who led them out of slavery in Egypt, covenanted with them, spoke through the prophets, brought them back from captivity in Babylon, and promised a blessed future. Jesus' disciples, as indeed Jesus himself, grew up with this story of the God of heaven and earth who had a saving history of involvement with the world. The Jewish women and men who followed Jesus and formed the nucleus of the early church encountered this living God of their tradition with new intensity through Jesus' ministry and person. As their company grew by the inclusion of Gentiles from the wider Hellenistic culture, these early Christians saw that what was happening in their lives and their community with each other resulted from a new gift. The utterly transcendent God of Israel, Creator and Redeemer, had drawn utterly near in Jesus, indeed had become (amazingly) enfleshed and was with them still in the Spirit who inspired the gifts in their community: charity, joy, peace, patience, speaking with boldness, healing, prophecy, administration, and all the other charisms named in the New Testament.

In shorthand, we might say that they experienced the saving God in a threefold way as beyond them, with them, and within them, that is, as utterly transcendent, as present historically in the person of Jesus, and as present in the Spirit within their community. These were all encounters with only one God. Accordingly, they began to talk about God in this threefold pattern: "the grace of our Lord Jesus Christ, the love of God, and the fellowship of the Holy Spirit be with you all." Early Christian letters and gospels are filled with this threefold cadence that appears in hymns, pithy greetings, confessions of faith, liturgical formulas, doxologies, and short rules of faith. This cadence carried the glad tidings of salvation. In the process, the monotheistic view of God flexed to incorporate Jesus and the Spirit.

The New Testament, the literary precipitate of the life of faith of these early Christian generations, contains no full-blown doctrine of the Trinity. The threefoldness of God is not the subject of direct systematic reflection, nor does the word "Trinity" even appear. The New Testament writers and the churches for which they wrote understood themselves to be monotheists in tune with the great *Shema* of Israel: "*Hear O Israel: the Lord our God, the Lord is one*" (Deut 6:4; Mark 12:29). But they knew and experienced this God in the continuing work of the Spirit, whose activity was intimately tied with the ministry, death, and resurrection of Jesus. Their language expanded creatively to accommodate this threefold religious experience, always in the context of prayer, praise, and preaching.

A shift to more formal considerations took place in the fourth century as a result of a controversy over the divinity of Jesus Christ. The Egyptian priest Arius had made the seemingly sensible claim that the one high God cannot be divided; divine being could not be shared with another. Therefore, the divine *Logos* or Word was actually a creature. True, he was a superior creature, created before time and the one through whom all else was made—but all the same, a creature. Thus, when the Word was made flesh and dwelt among us, it wasn't God's true being we encountered in Jesus Christ, but the created being of the *Logos*. While this might sound reasonable, it flew in the face of the church's faith that Jesus is God's self-revelation, the true Wisdom of God sent to save and set free. The church had been initiating people into the community of salvation by baptizing them "In the name of the Father, and of the Son, and of the Holy Spirit." Since only God can save, the baptismal words implied that Jesus Christ, human like us in every way yet without sinning, was also divine. Arius's claim to the contrary made baptism look like an empty foolish gesture.

To protect the church's implicit faith that Christ is truly God-who-saves, the bishops gathered in council at Nicaea in the year A.D. 325 and drew up the rudiments of the Nicene Creed, which is still in use today. This confession of faith declares explicitly that Jesus Christ is "not made" but is "one in being" with the Father; therefore he is not a creature but "God from God, light from light, true God from true God." Some fifty years later a second council at Constantinople in 381 expanded this creed to include a similar confession about the divinity of the Holy Spirit.

The Nicene Creed and other creeds that developed in the early Christian centuries transposed the short threefold formulas of the New Testament into more formal statements of belief. Structured in a tripartite manner, these creeds give a running review of what is known of the one God who creates, becomes incarnate to redeem, and sanctifies the world while pledging a blessed future. They do not explain *how* the one God can be at the same time triune. On the basis of the faith experience of the church, they just confess that this is so. In essence, they are interpretations of New Testament faith in God using the idiom of a later era. Some were composed under duress in response to error, but, as is the case with creeds composed even today, all had the primary purpose of facilitating engagement with God in liturgical and catechetical settings.

Explicit reflection that led to the more detailed doctrine of the Trinity arose in the years that followed. Even today there is much profit in reading the treatises of the trio of leading Eastern theologians Basil, Gregory of Nazianzen, and Gregory of Nyssa, known as the Cappadocians, and Western thinkers with Augustine at the head of the list. Eastern or Greek theology of the Trinity begins with the monarchy of the Father, from whom issue both the Son and the Spirit as if, poetically, they are the two hands of the Father reaching into the world. Western or Latin theology starts with the one divine nature in which the three divine persons share equally, similar to the way memory, understanding and will exist in the same human being. The monarchy of the Eastern pattern differs greatly from the nature-person structure of the Western, but both theological ideas seek to illuminate the faith that the creed confesses.

Soon a problem began to rear its head, one that the theology of later centuries exacerbated. Theologians started to make a real distinction between God revealed in the history of salvation, otherwise known as the economy of salvation, and God who exists apart from the world in an eternal, divine realm. This breach between Trinity *pro nobis,* or God for us, and Trinity *in se,* or God in Godself, continued to widen through the speculation of medieval times. Aquinas separated discussion of the one God (*De Deo Uno*) from that of the triune God (*De Deo Trino*), and parsed the relations of Father, Son, and Spirit in the inner Trinity before discussing the missions of the Son and Spirit to the world. Increasingly separated from prayer and sacramental life, the doctrine lost its footing in the religious experience of salvation and began to become something complicated and elite.

The coup de grâce was dealt by theology done in the spirit of the Enlightenment. As seen in chapter 1, modernity's project in that era was characterized by the attempt to come up with clear and distinct ideas as part of rationally defensible philosophical systems. When theology adopted this method and applied it to God, the result was the idea of a solitary deity viewed alone in "himself," possessing infinite attributes in contrast to the created world yet still an entity in the overall scheme of things. It was not immediately apparent that this one God is triune. Discussion of the Trinity was introduced as an afterthought, almost as an appendage to the basic doctrine of God. The analysis that was done, furthermore, described the Trinity prior to and apart from the revelatory events narrated in scripture. The treatise became philosophically abstract, saying little if anything about salvation.

While it gave lip service to divine incomprehensibility, Catholic neo-scholastic theology done according to this method engaged in luxuriant technical description of God's inner self-differentiation through relationships of origin, employing specialized terms: the two processions of generation and spiration give rise to four relations, namely, paternity, sonship, spiration, and procession, which in turn constitute the three persons of Father, Son, and Holy Spirit, who are persons in the sense of subsistent relations, which comprise the one divine nature. This form of theology delineated in some detail how the three are persons in relation to one another by these processions and by love for one another, in much the same way that human persons relate to each other by generation-birth and attendant love. The account is presented as a fairly straightforward analysis of three actors engaged in various personal processes and influences within the being of God. Artists transposed this theology into the popular imagination with depictions of the Trinity as a white-haired older Caucasian man, a younger brown-haired man often with a cross, and a dove.

Today this school of thought's laborious explanation of various fine points in the trinitarian construct elicits a host of criticisms. The fundamental problem lies in the fact that reflection lost touch with the historical story of redemption, where all trinitarian meaning has its roots, ending up with a description of God that had little or no contact with Christian life. It presented its thinking in highly obtuse prose; scholars today take issue with its "abstruse analysis," "irrelevant abstractions," "philosophical mazes," "elaborate theological maneuverings," "complex celestial mathematics," and "obscure language," along with its "sheer long-windedness." For all its abstraction, furthermore, this theology presented its findings as if they were a literal description of a self-contained Trinity of three divine persons knowing and loving each other. This, of course, is not the case, no such literal description being possible. As this type of theology translated itself into the popular imagination, the resulting lack of understanding fully deserves Sandra Schneiders's half-exasperated, half-humorous, totally accurate criticism: "God is not two men and a bird."

Yet another criticism today is raised by feminist thinkers who point out how the symbol of God the Father became hopelessly entangled with a patriarchal understanding of fatherhood. The doctrine of the Trinity emerged within a patriarchal and imperialist culture. Men were assumed to be the active principle in the biological creation of new life; they owned property including women, slaves, and children; masculine nature functioned as superior and at the center of reality. This political reality melded with the name of God the Father to produce the view that divine authority rules over the world in the same way that men rightly rule the household and the state. The subversive trinitarian notion that God is not an absolute monad but one whose very nature is communion, relation-to-another-who-is-equal, became submerged in waves of theory that justified the domination of some over others. This had disastrous consequences for the symbol of God, which took on the contours of a self-sufficient masculine Father-God. It also had pernicious effects on Christian self-understanding, both politically and in the family, and especially on women. But according to the reign of God preached by Jesus, patriarchy is not the *archē*, or rule of God. Catherine LaCugna makes the point cogently:

> In God's new household the male does not rule; God rules together with us, in solidarity with the poor, the slave, the sinner. Male and female are equal partners in God's household. Jew and Greek, slave and free, circumcised and uncircumcised, belong equally to God's rule. *The substitution of the rule of any one of these for the rule of God is idolatry.*

The redemptive reign of God excludes every kind of subordination among persons. Either trinitarian theology sets up love and communion among persons equally, or its interpretation has gone off the tracks.

Given the vitality of trinitarian awareness in the New Testament and the early centuries of the church, Catherine LaCugna has put into play the metaphor of "defeat" regarding its downfall. In the course of time the biblical story of encounter with God—the story of the personal God of Israel encountered in the concrete life and destiny of Jesus of Nazareth and present through the Spirit in the life of the church and the world—was transposed into an abstract, complex, literal, and oppressive trinitarian theology. No wonder it has not inspired Christian life and piety with any great dynamism. Today theology reminds us how little we know positively of God's inner being, nature, and processes: we must think with humility. In addition, the meaning of salvation through Jesus Christ requires a view of God that leaves no one subordinate, silenced, or derivative: we must think of the Trinity with liberating power. The breach between the founding experience of salvation and its expression in theologies of the Trinity needs to be healed.

THE POINT, AGAIN

Christians do not believe in just any God, a generic God so to speak, but the God revealed in Jesus Christ. Ignoring the Trinity, as John Calvin wrote, leaves "only the bare and empty name of God flitting about in our brains." Talk of the one God as triune, by contrast, points to an unfathomable divine plenitude who has a history with the world, one that includes knowledge of suffering and death. The intent of this trinitarian symbol is not to give literal information but to acclaim the God who saves and to lead us into this mystery. In so doing, it bespeaks a divine life structured in love. And this life is "ecstatic," directed outward toward the world to redeem and heal and bring about a future. Nourished at the table of this love, people of faith are called to the praxis of justice and peace so that all people and all creation may share in this communion.

Today a great ferment is brewing in trinitarian theology. Efforts at retrieving its vital meaning are proceeding on many fronts. At least three distinct but related tasks are involved.

ROOTED IN THE EXPERIENCE OF SALVATION

The first task entails bridging the gap between experience and thought to reclaim the ground of the triune symbol in the religious experience of salvation. One of the most influential bridges flung over the gap is an axiom coined by Karl Rahner. It reads: "the economic Trinity is the immanent Trinity, and vice-versa." Economic here refers to the work of salvation; immanent refers to God's own being imagined apart from any connection to the world. The axiom is shorthand for the realization that we know God from the way God has acted in history, through incarnate Word and renewing Spirit. It affirms that God really exists as these revelatory events have disclosed. We are not duped. There is not another cruel or indifferent deity hiding behind the one whose story is told in scripture. The God whom Israel knows as creator and liberator, whom Christians know and experience through the Messiah, Jesus, who spoke with authority, healed the sick, died on a Roman cross as King of the Jews, and was raised by Spirit on the third day, the same Spirit who is present now in the world—this is who God really is even when no one is looking. As Catherine LaCugna explains succinctly, "In Jesus Christ and the Spirit, we do not know a shadow image of God but the real living God. The real living God who saves—this is God!"

To draw this out using Rahner's example: in revelation we experience that God is creator, the *unoriginate origin* who is source of all, and in this light Christian tradition calls God Father. But that is not all there is. God is God a second way, as *self-uttering* into time and space, becoming enfleshed in Jesus Christ to save, and now we call God the Word, Wisdom, or Son. But that is still not all. God is God a third time, continually *gifting* the world with gracious divine presence, sparking love, drawing all things toward the future, and now we call God Holy Spirit. It is all the one God, but we use a triple mode of address to signal the threefold way God has self-communicated in history. The crucial understanding basic to all trinitarian theology holds that the living God exists eternally in a threefold distinction which corresponds to this history.

Theology today is healing the breach by speaking of God only through the lens of saving history. Although this first task is well under way in theological circles, it is far from finished in terms of the church's preaching, religious education, and piety. If the Trinity is not grounded in the experience of salvation, the triune symbol will remain in the dust, defeated.

SPOKEN ALLUSIVELY

The second necessary task is to remember that the incomprehensible mystery of God is always ever greater than our thought, and thus the Trinity is a doctrinal symbol whose interpretation is governed by all the rules of engagement that pertain to God-talk. It presents its meaning indirectly, analogically, through "is" and "is not," rather than through literal description. Forgetting this is what has led to so much highly technical trinitarian language, almost as if we had a telescope of some sort to peer into the ineffable and see what those three were up to. We need to deconstruct our naive imaginations on this score and rediscover the power of the doctrine to suggest that God is the mystery of saving love. The key notion of "person" and the numbers "one" and "three" illustrate how this can be done.

Person
The concept of person as used in the doctrine of the Trinity is not perfectly clear and obvious. Early trinitarian discussions used the Greek word *hypostasis* to designate the divine three. This was translated into Latin as *persona* and thence into English as "person." The problem we face is that *hypostasis* did not connote a person as we mean it today. Originally it meant something akin to "the firm ground from out of which a thing stands forth and exists," or more technically, "a distinct manner of subsistence." Over the centuries the word "person" has undergone a great semantic shift from the philosophical to the psychological sense. Today we think of person more along the lines of an individual with a distinct center of consciousness and freedom in relationship to others. Applying the word in its contemporary usage to the triune God almost inevitably leads to the danger of tritheism, to imagining three distinct somebodies and then expending energy trying to explain how the three can be one. The agony of the Trinity Sunday homily results.

Consider, however, Augustine in his influential work *On the Trinity*. Laboring to find appropriate language, he realizes we really have none:

> When it is asked, therefore, what the three are or who the three are, we
> seek to find a generic name which may include the three together. But we
> come across none, because the excellence of divinity transcends all the
> limits of our customary manner of speaking. For God is thought more
> truly than can be uttered, and exists more truly than can be thought.
> (7.7)

The existence of God, our thought about God, and our language about God
exist in descending order of capability, so that no word really makes sense.
Nevertheless, theology seeks a word that would characterize all three. It cannot be the names Father, Son, and Holy Spirit, he figures, because these
point to what is distinct. Nor will "essence" do, for if tripled this would indicate more than one God. "Person" recommends itself because, although
scripture does not use it, it does not contradict it either. Moreover, it is used
in tradition. But mainly we use "person" because we have to say *something*
when the question arises:

> But still you ask "three what?" Now the poverty from which our language
> suffers becomes apparent. But the formula "three persons" was coined
> not in order to give a complete explanation by means of it, but in order
> that we might not be obliged to remain silent. (5.10)

In other words, "person" is the best of an inadequate lot.

In explaining this point, Edmund Hill, the South African theologian
who translated *On the Trinity,* suggests that we would catch Augustine's
meaning if we referred to the persons as three *x*'s in God, or again as A, B, C,
so unknown is the content of the word "person." The early medieval theologian Anselm of Canterbury speaks similarly in his *Monologion* of "three
something-or-other," or again of "three I-know-not-what," *tres nescio quid.*
These and other great minds of classical theology were aware of the poetic,
allusive, and ultimately inadequate nature of the term "person" when we
speak of the Trinity. They never at all intended that it should be taken literally in either an ancient or modern sense. Rather, they used it to signify the
mystery of threefold distinctiveness that abides in communion in the heart
of God.

A more recent debate illuminates the difficulty once again. Karl Rahner
suggested that theology retire the word "person" for a time and use instead
"manner of subsistence," a phrase that gets closer to the original meaning of

hypostasis. The one God subsists in three distinct manners of self-subsistence. One of his critics objected that if this were preached from the pulpit, people would not understand it. Rahner responded that this was undoubtedly true, but at least people would not be getting the wrong idea, which they inevitably do when "three persons" are talked about without nuance.

Numbers One and Three

These terms inevitably seem to stand for mathematical quantities, but such is not the intent of the doctrinal language. Once more, Augustine provides an excellent illustration of the difficulty with his example of three gold statues:

> In equal size statues, three together amount to more of gold than each singly. And one amounts to less of gold than two. But in God it is not so. For the Father, the Son and the Holy Spirit together is not a greater essence than the Father alone, or the Son alone. But these three persons—if such they must be called—together are equal to each singly, which the natural human mind does not understand, for we cannot think except under conditions of bulk and space, phantasms or as it were images of bodies flitting about in our mind. (*On the Trinity* 7.11)

In the triune symbol, one and three do not refer to numbers in the usual sense. As soon as they connote quantity so that three is greater than one, we get the idea that God, like Gaul, is divided into three parts. But the intent is much more subtle. To say that God is *one* is to negate division, thus affirming the unity of divine being: there is only one God. To say that the "persons" are *three* is to negate solitariness, thus affirming that divine being dwells in living communion. The holy mystery of God is not a single monolith with a rigid nature, an undifferentiated whole, but a living fecundity of relational life that overflows to the world. Most basically the numbers point to the livingness of God. In Augustine's inimitable phrasing:

> In that highest trinity, one is as much as the three together, nor are two anything more than one. And they are infinite in themselves. So each are in each, and all in each, and each in all, and all in all, and all are one. (6.12)

A fresh insight into the lively character of this divine relationality comes from Western theology's rediscovery of the idea of *perichoresis* (pronounced per-ee-kor-ee´-sis) to describe the inner life of God. Coined in Eastern theology, the Greek term describes a revolving around or a cyclic movement like the revolution of a wheel. When applied to the life of the Trinity, this metaphor indicates that each of the "persons" dynamically moves around the others, interacts with the others, interweaves with the others in a circling of divine life. While remaining distinct, the three coin- here in each other in a communion of love.

Seeing an analogy between *perichoresis* and the cognate word for chore- ography, some theologians muse that trinitarian *perichoresis* conjures up the lovely picture of God's inner life as a divine round dance. To Edmund Hill, it puts us in mind of a country folk dance with the partners circling each other, each pair cycling around other pairs, and the whole floor whirling. The metaphor can be extended further. If God is dancing, why not step out to the contagious rhythms of salsa, merengue, calypso, swing, or reggae, or to the intricate a-rhythmic patterns of modern dance? The point is, with the three circling around in a mutual, dynamic movement of love, God is not a static being but a plenitude of self-giving love, a saving mystery that over- flows into the world of sin and death to heal, redeem, and liberate. The whole point of this history of God with the world is to bring the world back into the life of God's own communion, back into the divine dance of life.

Today theologians are working to keep trinitarian language mindful of its allusive, indirect nature. Whether interpreted as analogy, metaphor, or symbol, it is talk that points to God's being as a communion of love, while the dissimilarity to anything we know is always ever greater, for the unfath- omable living God cannot be caught in language.

EXPRESSED IN CONCEPTS OF OUR DAY

Re-rooting the Trinity in the experience of salvation and rediscovering how it refers to the living God in nonliteral fashion clears the deck for theology's third task, namely, to voice the mystery anew in contemporary idiom. Whether tapping into rich veins of tradition or drawing on ideas typical of our age, theology today is crafting fresh vibrant approaches. Two character- istics mark this work. First, it focuses primarily on the trinitarian God in engagement with the world, the One who is "God for us." Second, when it does venture into reflection on the Trinity apart from the world, it thinks through the salvific lens and proceeds with reticence, making any metaphysical claims about God's inner life function directly with respect to the economy of salvation.

Irish thinker James Mackey suggests that trinitarian theology should be satisfied with a brief formula. It is important to affirm that the one God exists in three manners of subsistence, distinct and mutually related. Once that truth is safeguarded, however, we should dispense with any further investigations into the relations between "the three" and get on with preaching about Christian life in light of God present and active throughout the world from its origin to its end through incarnate Word and gifting Spirit.

In her groundbreaking work *God for Us,* Catherine LaCugna agrees. She actually draws a parabola that starts at the top of the page with the hidden God in heaven, comes down the page, forth into time, and loops around to go up the page again, drawing all things back into divine communion. This outlines a true diagram of the Trinity, for the revelation of "God for us" gives us grounds to think that there is no God simply existing who is not at the same time relational. For God "to be" means "to be in relation." Consequently, further analysis of the inner life of the Trinity apart from saving concern for the world is a distraction. Metaphysical claims about God's inner life, if such need to be made, must function directly with respect to God's redemptive work. Otherwise the glad truth carried by trinitarian monotheism is betrayed.

Compared with theology prior to the twentieth century, we are currently witnessing a renaissance in trinitarian theology. Books have proliferated, putting forth the reflections of both those who agree with this reticent approach and those who venture to speak more explicitly about the inner life of God. As with any burgeoning field, disputes proliferate. How to get a handle on all of this?

R. Kendall Soulen has rendered a valuable service with an idea that allows us to map the field while at the same time providing a capacious framework supporting many different theological approaches. His suggestion is that language about the Trinity should itself be trinitarian, that is, carried out in a threefold manner. The thesis runs thus: the name of the holy Trinity is one name in three inflections. According to the dictionary, an inflection is a modulation of the voice in speaking or singing, a change in the pitch or tone of the voice. It can also mean a modification of a word to indicate a change in its grammatical function, for example, from the adjective "slow" to the adverb "slowly." To say that the Trinity is one name in three inflections is to identify three different tones that sing of this truth, three different grammars by which it is spoken. One tone corresponds to the first "person," one to the second, and one to the third. Each inflection refers to the triune God as a whole but does so in a distinctive way, in a modulation of voice characteristic of one trinitarian person and the relations in which that person stands. Exploring this thesis will allow the richness of contemporary work to stand forth.

1. The Theological Inflection

At the heart of this inflection is the holy name revealed to Moses at the burning bush at the start of the exodus story: "God said to Moses: YHWH", variously translated as "I am who I am," or "I will be with you" (Exod 3:14). Known technically as the Tetragrammaton, this four-letter name YHWH is the personal name of the God of Israel, God's "self-given name," as LaCugna describes it. Far from just a superficial label, the name stands for the incomparable uniqueness of the One made known in the history of the people of the covenant by works of steadfast love and faithfulness. It is the most sacred name for God in Judaism and the most common name for God in Israel's scriptures. Out of reverence the Jews gradually held back from pronouncing this name, using instead circumlocutions such as *adonai* in Hebrew or *kyrios* in Greek, both translated into English as "Lord." But the name YHWH shines through the circumlocutions. In prayer to this day the Jewish community magnifies and sanctifies the Name, looking forward to the day when it will be honored in all the Earth.

The Tetragrammaton entered the New Testament as a name saturated, drenched, with God's covenant history with Israel. In this new setting, it directed the logic of Christian identification of God the way magnetic north directs the needle of a compass. When the New Testament speaks of God, it is referring to the Holy One of Israel known by this name.

As an observant Jew, Jesus prayed to this God and taught his disciples to do likewise. Note how in the Lord's Prayer the first petition prays: "hallowed be thy name." The use of the passive voice, "hallowed be," is typical of Jewish reverence for God's name. Far from implying any ambiguity regarding *who* is being called upon, "in the context of Israel's piety for the Name, Jesus' reverential use of the passive voice actually serves to specify—indirectly but unmistakably—the exact identity of this petition's logical agent: the God whose name is the Tetragrammaton" (Soulen). The first petition is a plea that YHWH act now to display the divine glory in works of fidelity to Israel and mercy toward the nations. "Hallowed be thy name" means "make thy name great in all the earth."

Once we learn to recognize Jesus' use of the passive voice to refer to God, we see that it runs through his speech like a golden thread. "Blessed are they who mourn, for they will *be comforted*" (Matt 5:4); "Only believe and she will *be saved*" (Luke 8:50); "your sins *are forgiven*" (Matt 9:2); "knock, and the door will *be opened* for you" (Matt 7:7). This pattern links every aspect of his teaching and ministry to the God whose name is YHWH, never named directly but referred to by the grammar of the "divine passive."

The New Testament takes this indirect form of speech, so characteristic of Jesus' preaching and prayer, and uses a wide array of idioms to enfold Jesus and the Spirit into the identity of the one Lord. The great hymn in Philippians 2:5–11, for example, makes the startling point that the "*name above every name*" is now given to the crucified and exalted Jesus. The Spirit too is identified as the "Spirit of Lord," that is, the Spirit of YHWH (Acts 5:9).

This is the *theological* inflection of the trinitarian name. Focused on the first "person," it modulates speech about the Trinity into the key of the covenant with Israel. Far from a supersessionist position that would see the God of the Old Testament nullified or replaced by the God of the New Testament, as if progress were being made, this inflection requires that the whole history of God with Israel flow into Christian understanding of the triune God.

2. The Christological Inflection

This second inflection comes to expression in the familiar formula "the Father and the Son and the Holy Spirit." Here the name of God springs from the distinctive experience of the life, death, and resurrection of Jesus Christ as received and witnessed by the early church. This name gives centrality to the Word made flesh: Christ is the filter through whom God is made known. Unlike the name YHWH, which is mysterious and generative of

wide-ranging circumlocutions which express it, the second inflection identifies God in a simple, fixed, and pronounceable form that became central to
Christian mission. In the New Testament the disciples are commissioned to
baptize in this name, which continues to this day. As befits a formula
intended for liturgical use, it stabilizes the referent of prayer in a single, coor-
dinated phrase.

This inflection, while unique in its christological grammar, is inseparably intertwined with the theological inflection that identifies the same three
persons in a different idiom centered on the Tetragrammaton. In the prayer
Jesus taught his disciples, the opening phrase "Our Father who art in heaven,
hallowed be thy name" is not a redundant expression, as though Father were
now the name of God all by itself. Rather, the words "Father" and "name"
point to two dimensions of Jesus' identification of God, both indispensable
and mutually interpreting of each other. As a Jew, Jesus believed in the God
of Israel, identified by the unpronounced name YHWH; as a unique Jew, he
called God *Abba*. The one who taught this prayer practiced a hallowing of
God's name precisely by addressing God as Father rather than using the
sacred, unspoken Name.

Both the theological and the christological inflections identify the
same divine reality but from different perspectives. The theological inflection, centered in the Tetragrammaton, serves to identify Jesus and the Spirit
with respect to the God of Israel. The christological inflection, centered in
the Word made flesh, serves to identify the God of Israel and the Spirit with
reference to Jesus Christ. In their difference and mutual relation, the two
grammars or musical keys point to the same triune God of self-communicating love.

3. The Pneumatological Inflection

This inflection operates differently from the other two in always naming all
three persons, "if such they must be called," in an explicit way. Being the
presence and action of God actually arriving and affecting the world (think
of the suntan, the irrigation ditch, the fruit of the tree), the Spirit continuously draws attention to the unreachable source (the sun, the spring of water
in the hills, the tree's roots) and to the source's coming forth (the sunbeam,
the river, the tree trunk). While it might conceivably be possible to think of

one high God who never speaks, or of God's self-uttered word that is not heard, the presence of the Spirit testifies that the Source of all does in truth self-communicate and that this word is actually effective. Apart from the dynamic pattern of God's coming forth in love, the Spirit is not thinkable at all. The tone of this inflection, therefore, is inclusive of all three persons.

Bespeaking a constancy of the gift of life coming from the living God, this inflection has no fixed vocabulary of its own but through the centuries enlists forms of speech characteristic of the discourse of peoples, tribes, and nations and gives them a new imprint in the service of the gospel. It improvises, like jazz. The early church's technical vocabulary of person, nature, substance, subsistence, and its gathering of these into a trinitarian theology provides one good example of this inflection, being an expression of belief in a nonbiblical philosophy characteristic of Hellenistic culture.

Multiple rich images of the Trinity in our day are being voiced eloquently in the tone of this pneumatological inflection. They sing in triple notes of the one God in many different ways. Some use nonpersonal imagery, some personal, some a combination of both. The examples set out here for savoring are all seeking to express some little understanding of the ineffable mystery of love glimpsed in the experience of salvation. The first set uses nonpersonal metaphors to speak of the Trinity in the pneumatological inflection.

    ☜ In existential-ontological terms, John Macquarrie works out the notion that divine being is the energy that lets-be and self-spends; letting-be here means letting others be, giving life to others. Trinitarian talk of three "persons" points to "movements" of this energy of divine being, namely, Primordial Being, the deep, overflowing source of all; Expressive Being, which mediates this letting-be and self-spending outward in the world; and Unitive Being, closing the circle to accomplish a rich unity in love.

    ☜ Interpreting the Trinity in the language of modality, Karl Barth writes of God's threefold mode of being. This is made known in God's threefold repetition in the event of revelation, which allows us to know God as the Revealer, the Revelation, and the Revealedness.

    ☜ Constructing the concept of God, Gordon Kaufman imagines divine absoluteness, divine humaneness, and divine presence as three dimensions of the one living God, a concept that relativizes all idols and judges all human inhumaneness.

❧ Correlating the blessing of God to the dilemma of the human world, Paul Tillich posits God as creative power vis-à-vis our finiteness, saving love vis-à-vis our estrangement, and ecstatic transformation in the face of the ambiguity of human existence; or more philosophically, the element of abyss, the element of form, and the unity of the two.

❧ Langdon Gilkey speaks of God as divine being, divine logos, and divine love; or source, principle of possibility and order, and recreative power.

❧ Emphasizing that our images reveal God to be precisely imageless, Nicholas Lash develops the idea of the Holy One as eclipse, word, and presence.

❧ Conscious of the threefold experience at the heart of Hindu as well as Christian faith, Raimundo Panikkar interprets holy mystery as source, being, and return to being, which is analogous to the biblical affirmation that God is "*above all, through all, and in all*" (Eph 4:6).

❧ In the context of creation, Keith Ward envisions the Trinity as the primordial depth and pattern and power of love throughout the universe.

❧ Drawing on the most fruitfully life-giving shape in the natural world, I have suggested that we might think of a triple helix, combining and recombining to bring forth, heal and repair, and create ever-new forms at the heart of the universe.

These are all attempts to speak of the trinitarian God as the mystery of salvation in a way that avoids personal imagery with its accompanying misunderstandings. Other attempts do engage personal imagery with creative twists.

❧ Walter Kasper envisions three modes in which divine love subsists as a giver, a receiver and giver, and a receiver, or a source, a mediation, and a term of love.

❧ Building on Bernard Lonergan's transcendental analysis of the mature person's condition of being in love, Anthony Kelly proposes the analogy of the triune God as Being-in-love. This entails a giver, a gift, and a giving, all signifying a love that burns with such intensity it veers into incomprehensible mystery.

❧ Peter Hodgson limns the triune figuration as the one (Father) who loves (Son) in freedom (Spirit) in the midst of the world's fractured history.

❧ Heribert Mühlen uses communications theory to illuminate divine reality as the I, Thou, and We of love.

❧ Using a social model, both Jürgen Moltmann and Leonardo Boff speak of a motherly Father or fatherly Mother, a Jesus who is in solidarity with the poor and marginalized, and a Spirit akin to the feminine symbols of Wisdom and Shekinah. These form a community of mutual and equal relations which models the goal for human and cosmic community.

❧ Working more picturesquely in a "thought experiment," Sallie McFague interprets the one God as Mother, Lover, and Friend of the world which is God's body. These trinitarian "persons" are linked with the three forms of love described in classical Greek thought. The first person expresses *agapē*, the self-giving form of love that looks for no return but empowers others to come alive and thrive; the second acts according to *eros*, passionate love for the other shot through with desire that can lead to suffering; the third acts with *philia*, the love of friendship that crosses boundaries even of nature to create nourishing bonds of unity.

❧ Letty Russell conceives of the Trinity in a functional way as Creator, Liberator, and Advocate who calls human beings into partnership with divine care for the world.

❧ A number of biblical texts depict the work of God using the female imagery of Wisdom-Sophia who creates, redeems, and makes holy the world. Drawing on these texts I have suggested the language of Spirit Sophia, Jesus Sophia, and Mother Sophia, the one God who is Holy Wisdom herself: unoriginate source of all, Wisdom incarnate amid the suffering of history, and mobile, gracious presence throughout the world.

The threes keep circling around. Whatever the categories used, the terms seek to express a livingness in God who is beyond, with, and within the world and its history; a sense of the Holy One from whom, by whom, and in whom all things exist, thrive, struggle toward freedom, and are gathered in. To use one more model, this time from the twelfth-century theologian Hildegard of Bingen, there is a brightness, a flashing forth, and a fire, and these three are one, pervading all creation with compassion. At the end of the day the pneumatological inflection cannot be fixed in a single form of speech nor in a fixed name. Its specific task is to express the inexhaustible fullness of the mystery of the living God, a fullness for which no one expression is ever totally adequate.

The name of the holy Trinity is one name in three inflections. Taken together, the theological inflection that speaks in the tone of the Sacred Tetragrammaton YHWH, the christological inflection that uses the grammar of the Father and the Son and the Holy Spirit, and the pneumatological inflection that voices the idiom of different peoples and eras, unfold the church's trinitarian faith in a valuable way. On the generous scaffolding of this thesis the height and breadth of contemporary creative thought seeking understanding about the triune God can make its contribution.

THE POINT, YET AGAIN

Lest this foray into the work of many theologians make us forget, it is good to remember why this understanding is so important. In its own singular way religious belief in the triune God sums up the experience that far from being an isolated monad, the unfathomable mystery of God is a communion of overflowing love enfolding the world with gracious compassion. "*God is love*" penned an early Christian letter writer (1 John 4:8), summing up in this brief phrase the experience of salvation coming from God through Jesus in the Spirit. Anyone who talks of Trinity talks of God as Love in an idiom particular to the Christian story. Conversely, the symbol of the Trinity safeguards this Christian experience of God.

A MOST PRACTICAL DOCTRINE

A rationalistic trinitarian theology, dysfunctional and divorced from Christian life and ethics, has little practical effect. A revitalized trinitarian theology, however, has strong down-to-earth ramifications. The opening sentence of Catherine LaCugna's influential study *God for Us* articulates this surprising claim with vigor: "The doctrine of the Trinity is ultimately a practical doctrine with radical consequences for Christian life." The logic of this assertion is clear. God lives as the mystery of love. Human beings are created in the image of this God. Therefore, a life of integrity is impossible unless we also enter into the dynamic of love and communion with others.

What practical pattern of life best enables us to do so? La Cugna proposes that the key resides in the reign of God, which Jesus preached and enacted. As glimpsed in his parables and practices, the reign of God is a gracious rule of saving love and communion. As a place where God's will is done on earth as it is in heaven, it sets up a new kind of community where "the least of these" brothers and sisters are included, a gathering where the Samaritan woman, the tax collector, and the leper are equally at home. In this community tyranny is countermanded in the light of God's self-giving ways; male and female are equal partners, as are Jew and Greek. Justice, peace, and the well-being of all creatures are the goal. If we are not living out the types of relationships that serve this pattern of the truth of the reign of God, then we haven't got a clue about who God is. Knowing God is impossible unless we enter into a life of love and communion with others.

To say that the Trinity is inherently practical is not to imply that this belief gives immediate solutions to war and violence, blueprints to eliminate hunger, or concrete remedies for inequality. Rather, it functions as a source of vision to shape our actions in the world, a criterion to measure the fidelity of our lives, and a basis for resisting every form of oppression that diminishes community.

Deeply harmful attitudes and practices have arisen in church and society because one group imagines itself superior to another. The resulting stratification of power, with some dominant, some subordinate, shapes institutions of racism, sexism, ecclesiastical clericalism, and ruination of the earth, among other pernicious sins. The revitalized idea of the Trinity makes clear that, far from existing as a monarch ruling from isolated splendor and lording it over others, the living God is an overflowing communion of self-giving love. The practical importance of this notion lies in the way it exposes the perversion of patriarchy, racism, and other sinful patterns.

Because such breaks in community totally oppose God's very own way of relating, people of faith have compelling reason to behave otherwise.

The church's identity and mission pivot on this point. Called to be a sacrament of the world's salvation, the church is to be a living symbol of divine communion turned toward the world in inclusive and compassionate love. Only a community of equal persons related in profound mutuality, pouring out praise of God and care for the world in need, only such a church corresponds to the triune God it purports to serve.

Revitalized trinitarian theology makes it clear that a God conceived of as an individualized monarch or as a self-enclosed, exclusively inner-related triad of persons, a God who watches from a distance as an uninvolved, impartial observer, a God who needs to be persuaded to care for creatures— such a God does not exist. This is a false God, a fantasy detached from the Christian experience of salvation. Rather, "God is Love," related to the world in a threefold pattern of communion. Assimilating this truth we gain fresh energies to imagine the world in a loving way and to act to counter the self-destruction of violence.

YHWH's covenant with Israel, the ministry and life of Jesus Christ, and the nourishing bonds of community on earth created by the Spirit are all icons that reveal the one God's unfathomable, triune, relational nature oriented in compassion toward the world. In light of the trinitarian God we can tweak Irenaeus's axiom once again to declare: the glory of God is the communion of all things fully alive. Wherever the human heart is healed, justice gains a foothold, peace holds sway, an ecological habitat is protected, wherever liberation, hope and healing break through, wherever an act of simple kindness is done, a cup of cool water given, a book offered to a child thirsty for learning, there the human and earth community already reflect, in fragments, the visage of the trinitarian God. Borne by "the grace of our Lord Jesus Christ, the love of God, and the fellowship of the Holy Spirit," we become committed to a fruitful future inclusive of all peoples, tribes, and nations, all creatures of the earth. The reign of God gains another foothold in history.

FOR FURTHER READING

Catherine Mowry LaCugna's work cited in this chapter, *God for Us: The Trinity and Christian Life* (San Francisco: HarperSanFrancisco, 1991), has become a modern classic; the last chapter on the Trinity as a practical doctrine is especially important. Anne Hunt, *Trinity: Nexus of the Mysteries of Christian Faith* (Maryknoll, N.Y.: Orbis, 2005) is a highly readable presentation of contemporary theology that shows the links between the Trinity and other key areas of faith; a more popular treatment is her *What Are They Saying about the Trinity?* (New York: Paulist, 1998).

Karl Rahner, *The Trinity* (New York: Seabury, 1974) sounded the bugle for new advance. Both Walter Kasper, *The God of Jesus Christ* (New York: Crossroad, 1989), and Gerald O'Collins, *The Tripersonal God:*

Understanding and Interpreting the Trinity (New York: Paulist, 1999) offer strong systematic presentations of doctrine. For historical background, see Thomas Marsh, *The Triune God: A Biblical, Historical, and Theological Study* (Mystic, Conn.: Twenty-Third, 1994). Sallie McFague, *Models of God: Theology for an Ecological, Nuclear Age* (Philadelphia: Fortress, 1987) conducts a thought experiment that reinterprets the trinitarian God for an ecological, nuclear age. For careful interpretation in the light of postmodern ideas, see William Placher, *The Triune God: An Essay in Postliberal Theology* (Louisville: Westminster John Knox, 2007).

R. Kendall Soulen's proposal about the threefold inflection of the name of the Trinity is put forward in "The Name of the Holy Trinity: A Triune Name," *Theology Today* 59, no. 2 (July 2002): 244–61; and "Hallowed be Thy Name! The Tetragrammaton and the Name of the Trinity" in *Jews and Christians: People of God*, ed. Robert W. Jenson and Carl Braaten (Grand Rapids: Eerdmans, 2003): 14–41.

The practical nature of belief in the triune God is worked out in liberation theology by Leonardo Boff, *Trinity and Society* (Orbis, 1988), and in European theology by Jürgen Moltmann, *The Trinity and the Kingdom: The Doctrine of God* (New York: Harper & Row, 1981). The essays collected in Miroslav Volf and Michael Welker, eds., *God's Life in Trinity* (Minneapolis: Fortress, 2006) show how ripe this doctrine is for yet further interpretations, especially M. Douglas Meeks, "The Social Trinity and Property," and Daniel L. Migliore, "The Trinity and the Theology of Religions."

Today's realization that the Trinity cannot be separated from the spiritual life leads to beautiful insights in Yves Congar, *I Believe in the Holy Spirit* (Crossroad, 1997), and Michael Downey, *Altogether Gift: A Trinitarian Spirituality* (Orbis, 2000).

Epilogue

Every era has its insights. This book has been mapping frontiers where insights into the living God are flaring forth in our day as a result of faith's encounter with changing, life-or-death circumstances. The growth of atheism, the experience of unspeakable suffering, struggles for justice for poor people, women, and racial and ethnic minorities, the global encounter of religions, and new ecological awareness of our physical universe—each of these contexts calls for new understanding and contributes clues as to how thought can proceed. In response, different theologies have been glimpsing God again, not in the sense of deducing all there is to know or uncovering the divine in all clarity—the Holy is not available to us in this way—but in the sense of illuminating and unlocking the unsuspected presence of the gracious divine mystery amid the ambiguity, suffering, justice-making, and vast discoveries of our times.

In each case we have been offered a set of images or catchwords, substantiated by biblical exegesis, historical tradition, or church teaching and buttressed by cogent lines of reasoning, under which the totality of the experience of God is summed up and comes toward us anew. Rather than discussing simply one aspect of the divine, each particular approach intends and amplifies the meaning of the whole, like different gateways opening into the one garden. Together these gateways offer us glimpses of the living God at once ineffable, vulnerable, liberating, relational, justice-loving, beautiful, generous, cherishing, dynamic, and adventurous; at once creative, redemptive, and embracing; in a word, Love.

The symbol of God functions. It has powerful consequences for the communal identity and personal lives of those who believe. Consequently, this book has also aimed to show consequences for ethics and spirituality that flow from these new insights. None of the theologies detailed here is politically disinterested, that is, unconcerned with power and powerlessness and how these play out in the world. All grasp that a doctrine of the living God that is not opposed to evil in the concrete is unorthodox, is, in fact, a fantasy, not consistent with divine glory. For given the destructive power of sin, both God's glory and the flourishing of the whole creation, human and cosmic together, are terrifyingly at risk in history. In the face of this risk, the active presence of the living God in the world, *regardless*, is one of the oldest and most enduring of biblical promises. By listening with people to where the Spirit is moving in their lives today, by attending to what this signifies, by interpreting it creatively in terms of the treasure of biblical faith, and by calling for the praxis of universal solidarity in suffering and hope, these theologies shed light on ways in which that ancient promise does not disappoint. Buoyed by hope, we can begin to imagine the world anew and commit our energies in responsible, healing, and liberating action.

Indirectly these chapters have illustrated one other phenomenon. The fact that voices from around the world, including many from the periphery of established centers of power, are contributing to the idea of God indicates the end of the Constantinian era and the dawning of a truly global Christianity. No longer simply concentrated in Europe, which for centuries has been the mother continent of Christianity, theology now emerges from multiple geographic and existential centers of life and thought. The universality of the church is served precisely by these centers' fidelity to the quest for the living God in their own particular circumstances. Reading the signs of the times and calling the whole church to discipleship, they each discover something of the breadth and length and height and depth of the love of God which surpasses all knowledge, including that of theological systems.

The quest continues. It will do so as long as the unfathomable mystery of the living God calls human beings into the future, promised but unknown, which is to say, as long as people exist. Toward the end of the play *A Sleep of Prisoners,* a soldier declaims a beautiful soliloquy, every word of which became truer and truer in my own mind as this book took shape.

With thanks to the artist, I offer it as a stirring conclusion that keeps the subject open.

> The human heart can go to the lengths of God.
> Dark and cold we may be, but this
>   Is no winter now. The frozen misery
>   Of centuries breaks, cracks, begins to move,
> The thunder is the thunder of the floes,
>   The thaw, the flood, the upstart Spring.
> Thank God our time is now when wrong
>   Comes up to face us everywhere,
> Never to leave us till we take
>   The longest stride of soul men [and women] ever took.
> Affairs are now soul size.
>   The enterprise
>   Is exploration into God.*

*Christopher Fry, *A Sleep of Prisoners* (Oxford: Oxford University Press, 1951), 47–48; insert mine.

INDEX

Abe, Masao, 166–67, 179
African Americans
    slavery and, 113–31
    spirituals of, 117–22
    theology of, 113–31; liberation, 122–26;
        womanist, 94, 126–28
agnosticism, 27
Amaladoss, Michael, 163
analogy: and language for God, 18–19
Anderson, Leona, 179
androcentrism: and feminist theology, 95
Aquinas, Thomas
    on God, 31; governance of world of,
        193; incomprehensibility of, 37
    on incarnation, 40
    on many names for God, 21–22
    on Trinity, 206–7
    on women, 92
Aquino, María Pilar, 89, 151
    on God as mystery, 81
    on liberating women, 96
    on popular religion, 137, 139
Arellano, Luz Beatriz, 79
Ashley, Matthew, 69
Asia: religious pluralism and, 158–61
atheism, 27, 30
Augustine, 1, 12, 17, 106
    on creation, 198
    and incomprehensibility of God, 13
    on Trinity, 211–12, 213
    view of women of, 92

Baggini, Julian, 47
Barth, Karl, 28, 158, 219
base human communities, 165
Boff, Clodovis, 88
Boff, Leonardo, 89, 204, 221, 225
Bonhoeffer, Dietrich, 56, 83–84
Boys, Mary, 179–80

Buber, Martin: on violence and religion, 9–10
Buckley, Michael, 24

Cardenal, Ernesto, 88
Carr, Anne, 33
Catholic Church
    Dominus Iesus, 160–61
    and religious pluralism, 155–61
    See also Second Vatican Council
Chávez, César, 141
Christ. *See* Jesus Christ
Christian faith
    and cross of Christ, 58–60
    personal decision and, 28–29
Christianity: as little church in big world, 27
christology
    and inflection of Trinity, 217-18
    and symbol of black God, 125
    See also Jesus Christ
Clifford, Anne, 110
Clooney, Francis, 168–69, 180
Cobb, John B., 192, 201
Cone, James, 117, 131
    on black liberation theology, 123
    on God as black, 124–26
consumer society
    injustice in, 84–88
    and suffering, 55
Copeland, Shawn, 111

Daly, Mary, 111; on gender and God, 99
Dawkins, Richard, 14
death: poverty as instrument of, 71–72
dialogue
    of religious experience, 170–74
    of theological exchange, 166–70
Díaz, Miguel, 141, 150, 151
Díaz-Stevens, Ana María, 152
Dickson, D. Bruce, 23

229